ICONS OF
ROCK

ICONS OF ROCK

IN THEIR OWN WORDS

JENNY BOYD

jb

First published in the UK by John Blake Publishing
an imprint of the Zaffre Publishing Group
A Bonnier Books UK company
4th Floor, Victoria House
Bloomsbury Square,
London, WC1B 4DA
England

Owned by Bonnier Books
Sveavägen 56, Stockholm, Sweden

www.facebook.com/johnblakebooks
twitter.com/jblakebooks

First published in hardback in 2023

Hardback ISBN: 978-1-78946-671-3
Trade paperback ISBN: 978-1-78946-711-6
Ebook ISBN: 978-1-78946-679-9
Audiobook ISBN: 978-1-78946-678-2

British Library Cataloguing-in-Publication Data:

A catalogue record for this book is available from the British Library.

Design by www.envydesign.co.uk

Printed and bound in Great Britain by Clays Ltd, Elcograf S.p.A.

3 5 7 9 10 8 6 4 2

Every reasonable effort has been made to trace copyright-holders of material reproduced in this book, but if any have been inadvertently overlooked the publishers would be glad to hear from them.

John Blake Publishing is an imprint of Bonnier Books UK
www.bonnierbooks.co.uk

'The goal in life is to make your heartbeat match the beat of the universe.'

Joseph Campbell

CONTENTS

IN LOVING MEMORY OF
CHRISTINE McVIE
12 July 1943 – 30 November 2022

'What most astounded me when I read Jenny's book again (it's been many years since the first time!) is what an interesting read it is, and as relevant today as it was twenty years ago.

It seems I had a very naive and joyful approach to writing and performing, a feeling I believe is still there in me somewhere. Over the years, after I retired, I gradually wrote less and less – whether that was lack of belief, motivation, or simply that I had nothing more in me to offer, I don't know.

I'm seeking help to restore that childlike pleasure I found in creating music. Someone dear to me told me recently that the gift never goes away, it only needs to be woken up – to get those juices active again.

So, this I am doing, and rediscovering the joys of song writing, because there's no doubt that when I write something good, it's with some kind of stunned disbelief that it came from me. I would love to feel that again.'

CHRISTINE McVIE, 2014

INTRODUCTION

THE YEAR WAS 1987 AND I HAD JUST SIGNED UP TO start my PhD dissertation. Having spent most of my life in the itinerant world of rock 'n' roll – my sister was married to Beatle George Harrison and later to Eric Clapton; I was married to Mick Fleetwood (twice) and, at that point, I was married to drummer Ian Wallace – it had not been easy to commit to anything throughout these years. I never knew when I'd be asked to accompany my husband on tour. I had recently moved back to L.A. with my children, having lived in the English countryside near my sister Pattie, and Eric, for the previous five years. I had started off by enrolling into the BA programme at a college near Santa Monica (on a three-month trial as the principal wasn't sure, after I'd told her about my background, if I was suitable!). I felt very wobbly once I began the programme, not sure if I'd made the right decision, not being used to studying, and my brain ached with every paper I wrote. I then went on to get my Master's in Counselling Psychology, before embarking on a

PhD. I wanted to write about something I was interested in, and spent days trying to think of possibilities, my mind scrabbling in the dark. And then it hit me. Somewhere, out of nowhere, came the expression 'Write about what you know'.

I had spent the last twenty-something years surrounded by talented musicians and had watched them playing their instruments and creating songs. I was immersed in their world, and had witnessed their creative process first hand. Whether it was watching Paul, George and John sitting on the roof of our bungalow in India creating songs that were later to appear on *The White Album,* or Fleetwood Mac searching for lyrics in the communal house we shared in Hampshire, or sitting in the studio a few years later in Sausalito making their mega-hit album *Rumours,* it always left me wondering what it must feel like to be so creative.

It seemed to be an obvious opportunity to finally research what exactly goes on during the creative process, and who better to choose as my subjects than the musicians I knew through the life I'd led in their midst. From there I would spread my net wider and look for other artists from different genres.

I realised, as I sat pondering this subject, that what lay deeper than writing about musicians and their imagination, and what had plagued me for most of my life, was the belief I was not creative. I felt too locked inside. Even though I discovered my love of writing at an early age, I didn't think of it as 'creative'. Being a deeply introverted child, it was the most natural means I had of expressing myself, trying to make sense of buried thoughts and feelings. As I got older, in my teens, I wrote poems about vivid dreams, about life, complicated thoughts and existential questions, but I still didn't think of it as 'creative' – even though my writing world had always felt like a glimpse into the real me.

INTRODUCTION

I needed to write this dissertation for people like me; people who didn't believe they had the ability to be inventive, not necessarily in music, but maybe in a less obvious way.

With great excitement, I began making a list of questions to ask these musicians, questions about their childhood: was their imagination encouraged? What gave them the drive to create? Did drugs and alcohol help or hinder? Did they ever ask, 'Why me?' One of the books on creativity at that time was by a psychologist called Abraham Maslow who wrote extensively about the Peak Experience. He described this as a transcendence, moments of euphoria, when everything comes together and there is a loss of self or ego. I was very keen to know how many of these musicians experienced this feeling when they were at their peak, whether it was composing, writing songs or playing onstage. And did they believe everyone had this ability?

I started by interviewing Don Henley. The results were inspiring and it spurred me on to keep going. Next, I interviewed George Harrison, Eric Clapton, Mick Fleetwood and all of Fleetwood Mac. I interviewed Ian Wallace and, because he was playing with musicians such as Bonnie Raitt and Crosby, Stills and Nash, I was able to interview them all. And so it grew.

The synchronicity was extraordinary. I found after a while I only needed to think of someone whom I'd like to interview for them to miraculously appear. Once I'd interviewed forty musicians and read countless books on creativity, I wrote my dissertation. I thought this might make a fascinating book and I sent some of the transcribed interviews to a literary agent. She was very encouraging but told me I had to interview thirty-five more musicians! And so, I did. Not long after, and with the help of a writer/editor my agent recommended, I met Holly George Warren. We worked together on the transcribed interviews I

3

had completed. It was at this point, after a lot of writing and interviewing, that I began to feel more confident and to trust my own creative ability. Words for the book were spilling out of me, just waiting to be found and added to the script.

Most of the interviews were conducted between 1988 and 1990. The book was published by Simon & Schuster in 1992 in America and Japan.

I moved to England shortly afterwards and in 2014 the book finally came out in the UK under a different heading, with a different publisher and a different cover.

For many years once the original book came out, I carried all seventy-five of the precious cassette tapes of these interviews with me wherever I went – tucked away in cupboards or kept in vaults. I was determined to keep them safe. Each musician had trusted me with their innermost thoughts and feelings on a subject that was very important and personal to them. As years went by and cassettes became redundant, I began to worry about transferring them to USB sticks. With ever-increasing digital theft, I was acutely aware of the desirability of the content.

I had protected these tapes fiercely, fearful they could get stolen, until some twenty-five years later when I decided to destroy them. But in my mad frenzy, I saved – and I'm still not sure if there was any logic to it – eight of the interviews: Joni Mitchell, George Harrison, Eric Clapton, Ringo Starr, Graham Nash, Ravi Shankar, Tony Williams and Don Henley. And these are the ones that have been transcribed for this book in their entirety for the first time, no longer trapped in a cupboard or a drawer. I have released their voices from that time, and at the end of each interview is a description of what they're doing now – or if, sadly, they are no longer with us.

The remaining musicians still have a voice but, instead of small quotes being designated to specific chapter headings, all the pieces have been put together under their own names.

Bonnier Books is now publishing this new edition. As well as the original interviews, I have added four current musicians to show the difference in the music world today compared to the late eighties: Eg White, Jacob Collier, Atticus Ross and Sarah Warwick. The 'drive' is still a major part of their creativity, and they speak about the Peak Experience, or being 'in the zone' and how that feels.

Musicians and their creative process is still a magical component to me, even after all these years. It is timeless. Listening to them speak and reading what they've said, reminds me that we all have the ability to do something creative, something that will give us the buzz, that will light our fire and allow us to become more of who we are. I realise now that there are times when something as simple as finding what brings you joy can turn into inspiration.

As I worked on the interviews, I couldn't help but feel enormously privileged to have had the opportunity to hear these musicians describe what it's like to play onstage in front of thousands, or to write a song and not know where the words came from, to hear about the magic of the muse or describe a transcendence of self. For most it appears to be the greatest feeling of integration they experience in life, where they feel more at peace with themselves, more complete.

It wasn't long, though, before I realised that all artists experience this creative peak in one way or another. Although they admitted it was very difficult to describe, most were happy to talk about it, the majority saying they'd never discussed it before. Many explained that it was not something they could consciously make happen. There was no formula.

There is a wonderful line when jazz drummer Tony Williams points out the difference between creativity and talent, and that other thing that's beyond creativity – the spirit that touches people. I felt that every one of these musicians had the spirit that touches people.

PART ONE

*'Songs just keep us company, that's all;
they help us feel less alone, and they make
us feel like there's somebody else out
there who feels the way we do'* –

DON HENLEY

DON HENLEY

Singer, songwriter, drummer and solo artist and founding member of The Eagles.

I FIRST SAW THE EAGLES PLAYING IN 1974, OUR SECOND night in Los Angeles. John, Christine McVie, our friend Sandra, my then-husband Mick Fleetwood, me and our two small children had just given up our communal home in the English countryside and swapped it for the land of plenty, the land of sun and music. Everyone's excitement at the thought of living in this other world was mixed with feelings of trepidation. Would the band survive the outcome of this huge decision? The Eagles were playing in Santa Monica, and Fleetwood Mac were fresh off the boat, limping along, full of hope and dreams of making it big in America. They had recently put an injunction on their manager in the UK and were not allowed to go out on the road until that was sorted. The thought of living in L.A. was thrilling, even if it was only for six months (or so we thought). And so here we were, about to see one of the growing number of bands that represented Southern California music.

I remember the feeling of elation mixed with jet lag as we sat in the Civic Auditorium and listened to The Eagles playing. Some of the songs were familiar to me such as 'Take it Easy' and 'Peaceful Easy Feeling'. John McVie was a big fan of their music and I would often hear their cool melodic voices as I passed his and Chris's kitchen in the big country house. I watched the drummer singing while he played his drums. As the months went by and we ended up staying in L.A., Fleetwood Mac re-emerged with Stevie Nicks and Lindsey Buckingham, and the band gained the success they had hoped for vying with The Eagles and other California bands for the top position in the charts.

I finally met Don in the mid-eighties when my then-husband Ian Wallace played drums for him in the studio, and on the road, for a couple of years. He had a great band and we all became like family; either we would all visit Don at his house on Mulholland or he would have dinner with us in Sherman Oaks. I would sometimes go on the road with Ian and the band and we'd spend a lot of time together. Although there was much laughter between them all and Don had a wicked sense of humour, I could tell he was a thoughtful person, a deep thinker. He was the first person I interviewed for the book. I had never spoken to him one-to-one before and remember feeling a little nervous as we sat opposite each other in his sitting room. I had recently bought a rather professional-looking cassette player for the interviews, with its own plug-in microphone, and while I was listening to him answering my first question, I couldn't stop my eyes from darting over to the cassette player, making sure the lights were blinking and the spool was moving. But it didn't take long, once Don had started talking, that my attention was fully taken up with what he was saying.

Tell me how and at what age you got into music, and who were your music heroes?

I grew up listening to many different kinds of music. My grandmother, who lived with us, would sit in her rocking chair and sing Protestant hymns and Stephen Foster songs. My parents liked 'big band' music. I grew up in Northeast Texas, near the Arkansas and Louisiana borders, so, as a youth, I heard hillbilly music, blues, country and western, country swing, gospel, a little bit of everything. Elvis Presley's rendition of 'Hound Dog' hit the airwaves about a week before my ninth birthday, and it was the first rock and roll record that I collected. I ended up getting several of those seminal rock records . . . Chuck Berry, Buddy Holly, the Everly Brothers, Little Richard, Fats Domino, Jerry Lee Lewis, all that early stuff, prior to the 'British invasion'. In my room, I had one of those brown Bakelite RCA Victor 45rpm record players with the red spindle top. I was into music, but I really didn't plan on making a career of it until The Beatles came along. They changed the course, for me. They became the major musical influence in my life, along with The Beach Boys, The Byrds and Buffalo Springfield. But, as far as singers go, Ray Charles was it, for me. He could sing the phone book.

My first instrument when I was a child, before my teens, was the ukulele. There was a kid who lived across the street who had one, and his father had taught him how to play, and so he taught me a few chords, and then my mother bought me a ukulele. After I got into junior high school, the thing to do, where I was brought up in Texas, was to play football – that was the heroic, natural thing for a male to do. I only weighed about ninety-eight pounds when I was fifteen, so let's just say that I didn't excel at playing football. I got pounded, royally, by the bigger boys, and the coaches, who were barely out of college, were sadistic and mean. Pre-season practice began in the blazing hot months of late summer, and we were made to run laps until we collapsed or threw up . . . or both.

After my foolhardy attempt at football, I joined the marching band – the high school band – at the behest of a friend of mine, who also had a little musical combo with his father and some other local folks. They were playing Dixieland jazz. My first instrument after I joined the high school marching band was trombone. That's what most of the guys were playing, and trombone was the instrument this friend of mine was playing. Having spent the fall of my freshman year warming the bench at football games, I missed 'beginner band', so I didn't get tutored in how to play trombone. So, for an entire school term, another football dropout and I had to practise by ourselves, in a back room in the dilapidated old band hall, with little to no instruction. Neither of us was progressing much, but we tried it for about six months. It was funny because this same kid and I used to go around beating on our textbooks with our fingers and with pencils. We used to do it in class and it annoyed the hell out of everybody.

Then, one day, somebody said, 'Why don't you both try playing the drums instead of the trombone? It looks like you have a natural aptitude for it and, besides, the marching band needs drummers.' So, we both switched immediately from trombone to drums. I taught myself how to read drum music and spent the next two and a half years in the high school marching band playing the snare drum. Also, during that time, I was invited to join my friend's jazz combo, which gradually morphed into a rock and roll band. We weren't singing at that time. We had a world-class trumpet player, and so we were doing pop and jazz instrumentals with a few classics thrown in. I had cobbled together a mismatched drum kit, using old, discarded drums from a storage room in the high school band hall.

One day in the summer of 1963, my mother said, 'Get in the car. We're going on a little road trip.' I did as I was told, and we headed west, on Interstate 30. I kept asking mom where we were going, but she was evasive. After about two hours, we arrived at McKay Music Company in Sulphur Springs, a small East Texas town about eleven miles northwest of where my dad was born and raised. Sitting on display in the music store was a set of Slingerland drums with a red sparkle finish. I stared in disbelief as that drum kit was boxed up and loaded into the trunk of my mother's Pontiac. Then, we headed back towards home, stopping, along the way, to show the kit to my dad, who had apparently not been informed of my mother's plan. But, he was cool.

Sometime, in late 1964 or early 1965, after The Beatles completely changed the musical landscape, we decided we were going to have to sing. We couldn't just continue to play instrumentals. That's when I started singing. I'd already been playing the drums. We all auditioned one night in my friend Richard's living room for his father, who was our mentor. He was the one who had started the Dixieland band. After the audition, it was decided that we would all sing, but I would be the primary singer. But, it was tricky because I was the drummer, so I had to learn how to sing and play drums at the same time. After about nine months, I had figured it out, well enough, I guess, but I continue, to this day, to try to improve. People always say that it must've been very difficult, especially in the beginning. But, I like to say that I just didn't know any better.

So, I got the drum set, Richard and his dad made an electric bass, from scratch, in their shop; our guitarist somehow scored a Fender Jazzmaster, our trumpeter switched to keyboards, and away we went. One of our first gigs was at the local Chevrolet dealership. We were hired as part of a promotion for the debut of the 1964 Chevys. It turned into a dance party. Those were wonderful days.

Did you ever get into the zone while you were creating? What was it like?

I've experienced that in different ways. Getting into the zone while playing and getting into it while writing are two different things. But, in either instance it can be very euphoric. Drumming is, obviously, more physical, so there's an athletic, aerobic component there. There are those memorable nights – depending on the mood you're in, and whether enough of the other people in the band feel the same way – that you can have one of those 'Peak Experiences'. If you're part of a band, and you've been together for a number of years, then you're very in tune with what the other band members are feeling, and you're very aware of whether they're playing at their highest level, or not.

In my personal experience, it takes a majority of the band members performing at optimum level to achieve lift-off. It doesn't necessarily require everybody onstage to be on top of their game. But, if two or three of the other band members are playing well, and you're having a good night yourself, and the audience is having a good time, then you can get those transcendent experiences. Being able to do that, almost every night, is what it means to be professional. It's what the fans deserve, and when you and your bandmates deliver that, you get a great feeling of satisfaction; a sense that you're good at what you do, and that you're going to be able to continue; it's not going to be all over. Back in the early days, after a sub-par show, we used to feel like 'Well, I guess we'll never work in this town again'. But, those episodes just motivate you to work harder, to be better next time. We practised a lot.

The best feeling for me is the euphoria that happens during the writing – or co-writing – process. There have been a few times in my life when I've had those experiences that people talk about – those moments where you feel like something is being given to you, and it's coming from somewhere else . . . or it's coming through you . . . and you get this happy result, this *gift*. But, that elation tends to be short-lived, because then you begin to worry about whether you can get back to that place, that 'zone' again. There is the nagging fear that 'it', whatever it is, may have made its last appearance. But it always comes back, and every time it returns, it's like birds coming back for the summer. I'm always amazed, and I'm so grateful that my faculties are still intact. The last time it happened was during the creation of 'The Boys of Summer' – and it was fantastic. The imagery, the lyrics, the melody, were not in my conscious mind – it all seemed to be coming from my subconscious, or it was coming through me. These things can feel as though they're coming out of thin air sometimes. And when you get into an inspired, receptive frame of mind like that, the more things come to you; the more is given to you.

That particular song materialised just as we were about to finish the album. I thought I was done, but I had so much momentum going at that point that, everywhere I looked, there were things that I could see, images that I could put into that song. It seemed that, in every direction I turned, things were being given to me, or I could apprehend them. Maybe those elements – the ideas, the images, the notes – were there all the time, I don't know. But it was joyous. I was in the car, driving up the coast highway, and I had the music, blasting through the speakers. The instrumental track that Mike Campbell had sent to me was inspirational – the guitar sounds, the keyboard part, the chord progression, the rhythm, the textures and the ambience – all these elements came together in a way that was very evocative. It spoke to me. When a piece of music inspires me, it sparks visions; I see colours, I feel emotions, I hear melodies, and I hear words. I have a reservoir, somewhere in my head, that contains themes and melodies. If a particular strain of music moves me, then it dictates to me which subject matter, which theme, belongs with that particular piece of music. It's a kind of fusion, a merger, that I make in my head. A moving piece of music will unlock a certain set of words, images and melodies, and the assignment is to marry those various elements with that music.

Sometimes, I write the chord progressions and the arrangements myself. But, in this case I hadn't. Mike Campbell created that great track, and it struck a chord in me. Mike and my co-producers, Danny Kortchmar and Greg Ladanyi, helped bring it to fruition.

In instances where there's a pre-recorded piece of music, you sit down, usually with a legal pad, and play the tape, over and over, and just scribble – write down a lot of dreck, a lot of inane, clichéd crap, but then you edit, you narrow it all down. A line, here and there, might be pretty good, and then you'll combine a couple of lines and it eventually becomes clerical work. It becomes laborious, just sitting there, being a scrivener, and it requires a great deal of patience and focus. There's that initial burst of inspiration and insight, but then you often have to sweat out the rest of it. Bringing a song to completion can involve hours, maybe days or weeks, of tedium.

But, in the case of 'The Boys of Summer', it was coming right off the top of my head; the words and the melody were arriving at the same time – and then, on the second or third day, the verse about the Cadillac. I had been stuck for that musical bridge section, unable to figure out where to take the narrative. I was in L.A., driving down the 405 freeway, looked to my left, and suddenly it was like somebody said: 'Okay, here's this particular type of car, and here's this Deadhead sticker on it, and you can have this paradoxical metaphor for your song, if you want.' It was like someone – or some*thing* – just shoved it in front of me. I have since read that the notorious Interstate 405 is considered to be the busiest road in the US, with approximately 400,000 vehicles travelling it, daily. So, what are the odds?

It's an interesting phenomenon – the best songs seem to almost write themselves. This was true for parts of 'Hotel California' and even more so for 'Lyin' Eyes'. But, 'The Boys of Summer' was the biggest rush that I can ever remember getting.

So that's very different from when you're playing?

It is different from when you're playing because playing usually involves recreating something that's already been created, the exceptions being jazz or just 'jamming'. But playing – especially playing live – involves interaction with several other people, at least in my case, and you depend on feedback from those other players; you can read their thoughts. When you're in a band for many years, you know the others so well that you can always sense what kind of mood they're in. You can tell if they're playing as well as they can play, or if they're just 'phoning it in'.

It must be difficult to be that sensitive to everybody.

Yeah, it is awful! Horrible [laughs], it's just horrible. With writing, there isn't always the necessity to depend on proximity, or direct interaction with another person. That's why I like writing to pre-recorded music, or 'demos'. I used to write sitting in a room with one or two other people, and that's fine, except that it sometimes creates a lot of tension, because there has to be some candid back-and-forth. But if it's just you, alone, and a piece of pre-recorded music, a basic track, you feel less burdened, less vulnerable. Still, no matter how the thing gets accomplished, my best songs are all co-writes. I learned a lot from my collaborators.

Did you ever reflect why me?

Yes. A lot. The questioning began when the band started to become successful. In this business – and there's a reason they call it the 'music business' – you can become very wealthy and very famous at a young age, long before you're mature enough to know how to handle it. In most other professions you work until you're sixty or sixty-five, and, along the way, you get the spouse, the house, the garden, the 'stuff', and maybe the kudos, if you're lucky. But in this profession, you can get too much, too soon, and it messes with your head. We all tried not to take things too seriously, but the abnormal nature of the situation, the public dimension of it, and the pressure, was overwhelming. So, for several years, there was a great deal of struggle and confusion, on my part, as well as the other members of the band. The thing that bothered me then, and still bothers me now, is the sense of randomness.

There are great people out there, who have talent, who have good hearts, good intentions, and they really deserve a break of some kind. Some of them have been trying and trying for years, but they somehow don't get the recognition. And then there are people who are schmucks and don't have much talent at all, but they have this drive. I think a lot of it is simply wanting it really badly, and just making it happen some way or other. Perseverance is a big part of it. There are people who just won't take no for an answer. And, clearly, success doesn't necessarily have anything to do with talent, or whether you're a good person or not. There's a dispassionate dimension to it, like nature. I've often wondered, 'Why me?' But a lot of it is the drive, the desire. You've got to want it more than anything else in the world, and be able to do whatever it takes, and believe that you can – that's a very, very big part of it. You have to believe that you can, so that when opportunity knocks, you are ready.

There have been times in my life where it felt like I was being guided. Every time I came to a crossroads, or a fork, I've usually taken the right path, as if I'd been nudged in one direction or another. It sometimes felt uncanny, and I've never known whether to chalk it up to will, to instinct, or just blind luck. Maybe it's a little of all that. But, I also owe a great debt of gratitude to my parents and my mentors . . . the people who have encouraged me and helped me along.

There's a lot of power in that. I feel there's an order. The only time I doubted, for a little while, was when John Lennon died. That really affected me.

Me, too. It still affects me.

Do you see your creative abilities as a power?

I suppose I became aware of it, at some point, and it makes me uncomfortable. There are so many people out there who are not quite balanced, shall we say? And they misconstrue things that I have written, or co-written. I suppose I can't be blamed if people misinterpret what I've written or sung. But, I do feel a certain responsibility, a measure of sympathy, even if they're crazy. Back in the early 1970s, there was some poor truck driver who was distraught, because his girlfriend had left him, or he'd lost his job . . . I can't remember, exactly. But, whatever it was, it upset him so much that he went into the Asylum Records offices, in New York City, and took one of the employees as hostage. He demanded that they call a local radio station and have the DJ play 'Desperado' for him, and then he would let this person go, and he would leave the premises. So, the call was placed, and the song was played, and he left. He didn't hurt anybody, but it was a scary situation. You never know.

I used to get fan letters from people who'd obviously taken a lot of acid, or were just completely bonkers, and I've had people coming up here to my house, camping out by the driveway. I've had death threats, as have many of my colleagues. I've had women calling the management office, swearing that we're married and writing wacky letters saying, 'You're my husband, why don't you come and get me?' So, there's that kind of thing . . . the negative side of being a public figure, and then there's the positive side, where fame can be leveraged, and good things can be accomplished. I don't like to think of it as *power*, exactly . . . that word scares me a little bit. Basically, success, in any field, brings with it some measure of influence; it provides an entrance into certain arenas, such as politics, the environmental movement, social justice, and you can raise funds for good causes. You can sometimes influence your friends, your colleagues; you can do charitable works, and that part is good.

But it's a very fine line, and it can be very dangerous. I think some people are looking, a little too hard, for heroes and icons and demigods, and they don't think for themselves. I see common sense disappearing. Religion is one of the culprits, as is politics . . . and, of course, modern media have played an enormous role in creating several monsters. There's that great line, in the William Stafford poem, about 'following the wrong god home', I never wanted to be set up as some sort of icon. These media terms . . . 'star' and, now, 'superstar,' make me nauseous. I like to make people happy, to have a positive influence on people's lives; to help create community, to defeat loneliness. Songs just keep us company, that's all; they help us feel less alone, they make us feel like there's somebody else out there who feels the way we do. That's what good songs do . . . enable us to feel like we're a part of the world, a part of the human community.

Do you feel that everyone has the potential to be creative?

I think every human being has the potential to be creative in some way. Whether it's being able to lay bricks in a very neat, straight line, or do beautiful sewing, or cooking, or just doing any kind of a menial task very well, I think, is a form of creativity. I suppose you could say that there are different levels of creativity . . . from composing symphonies to knitting sweaters. But, there is an element of creativity in almost everything we do. Recognising, it and nurturing it . . . that's the trick.

Is emotional turmoil essential to your identity as a creative or performing artist?

[Groans] There was a time, not too long ago when I bought into that. But, I think I've gotten past it. Some actors do the same thing; they throw themselves into the part and live it. But that's really contrary to what the word *'actor'* means. If you're a good actor, you should be able to act the part, to call it up without actually living it, and the same goes for song writing. I'm learning how to draw on past experiences, although sometimes you do need to get out into the middle of the mess of life; things, both good and bad, need to happen to you. After a while, though, too much drama has a backfiring effect. If there are too many broken romances, too many disappointments, too much pain, something in you shuts down; walls go up. We need to remain open and hopeful, in spite of all the turmoil in the world.

What gives you the drive to create?

I believe that the basic drive to create is fed by the desire to communicate. I think we all have a need for community and connection. We all have a need to leave a mark, to somehow say, 'I was here.' And there are as many ways to do that as there are people on earth.

Is there a connection, when you feel more or less creative, to what's going on in your life?

Oh, absolutely. But, first of all, you have to have a life. I don't want to be totally caught up in the music business, I don't want to constantly think about, or talk about, gear – drums and guitars, amps and recording equipment, recording, touring. For some of my musician friends – my peer group – music is their whole life; it consumes them: the playing, the recording, the equipment. That's fine – I like to talk about music, too, and all the elements associated with it. But, in order to write lyrics, it's necessary to live a more diverse life, to have a broad range of things to think about and care about. As somebody once said, 'Life is short, but it's very wide.' So, I try to be involved in a lot of things besides music. But the problem then becomes one of balance. Spending time and energy on political or environmental matters, which are often intertwined, is important to me, and can sometimes provide material to write about.

On the other hand, too much social or civic engagement – too much activism – can easily crowd out the time needed for reflection, for reading novels and poetry, for spending time out in nature – things that feed the creative spirit. In order for inspiration to come to you – or *through* you – you must be open to it – you must clear the mental clutter; tame what the Buddhists call 'monkey mind,' and get yourself into a state where you're an antenna, a blank slate, and you're ready to receive. Sometimes, I'm afraid to try to get into that state, because I'm afraid nothing will come. But, in spite of all the distractions and my own procrastination, I'm thankful to say that 'it' – whatever 'it' is, still shows up.

I have found that driving is great for me, in terms of creativity. I've written a great many of my songs in the car with the cassette player blasting. That's how 'The Boys of Summer' and 'The End of the Innocence' were written. I think that creativity, as an adult, has a link to childhood. I was fortunate to have spent my childhood in a beautiful rural area, a safe area, where I could roam the woods with my dog and stay outside after dark. I think that that kind of freedom, that space to dream and imagine, nurtures creativity – creativity that carries over into adult life. There is a growing body of scientific research to support that.

Do you have a choice to create or does it just happen?

I have a choice as to whether to turn the phones off or not. I have a choice about whether I focus on writing or whether I turn my attention to environmental concerns, and related political matters, rather than going off somewhere and isolating myself. It's a constant tug-of-war, trying to strike a balance between creative time and social time. The further one moves into this thing we call 'adulthood', the more involved in the community and civic activities, the more difficult it becomes to turn all that off and pivot into a quiet creative space. Especially after you've gained some popularity, some clout, and people are calling you and urging you to join their crusades, many of them being very worthy. On the other hand, if I don't find the time – or 'make' the time – to write songs and record albums, I won't have all these opportunities to be of service. So, again, it's a constant balancing act. I'm still struggling with it.

Are you in touch with the child in you? To what extent?

I think so, yes. But, I definitely don't get into the outdoors as much as I did when I was a kid. Sometimes I don't go out in the yard for weeks. I'll just look out of the window and say, 'Yeah, that's nice out there; I should go out there sometime.' [L:aughs]. I'm working on it, but there are so many more distractions and responsibilities, here in adulthood, here in the 'world of work'. I have a ritual that I follow at Christmastime. I go back to the town where I was born and I visit my mother, who is a widow and lives alone now. I go out and walk around on the farm. I get back in touch with the child that way, through nature, by visiting the fields and forests where I roamed as a kid. Fortunately, that area is so remote that it hasn't changed much at all – hasn't been paved over or suburbanised. It's good if you can get in touch with the child – the beauty and innocence of being a child, without being childish. Adults are really just kids in grown-up clothing. For proof of that, all one need do is look at our governing bodies. There aren't any adults in the room.

How did drinking or drug taking affect your creativity? Did it enhance it or block it?

I've been creative on alcohol, and marijuana, and cocaine. I have also had my creativity totally blocked by all three of those things. It depends on how they're used, and how much of them you use. I think ultimately, all the creativity resides inside us, but manifesting it is a little scary sometimes – a strange combination of elation and trepidation. The only reason that I ever used drugs was to overcome shyness, or self-doubt, because writing often requires spilling some of your innermost thoughts and feelings to somebody else, sometimes to somebody you don't even know very well. And I think that alcohol and other substances were merely used as a form of, as we used to say, 'instant courage', to help us overcome those feelings of doubt that I mentioned before, like 'Who am I to be doing this?' 'Why do I deserve to get my thoughts, my opinions, on this black piece of vinyl that a million people are going to hear?' I think a lot of the drug taking was to overcome that feeling of unworthiness. A very odd thing, fame is. It messes with your head.

When you do coke, it makes you feel like everything you're thinking or saying is worthwhile and important, but that is mostly a delusion. I didn't use that stuff to actually create; it was simply used to buffer feelings of inadequacy, those feelings of 'I don't deserve this'. Or, sometimes we used coke simply to meet deadlines, to stay awake and to get the job done, both in the writing process and in the recording studio. Because the hours were long and gruelling, and the pressure was enormous. But, in hindsight, I don't recommend taking drugs to try to enhance or catalyse creativity. I think that all the creativity, the artistry, lives in our hearts and minds. We have to find ways to get it out, naturally. We have to trust our natural instincts. But, a healthy sense of self-criticism is also a necessity – the ability to be objective about the work – the ability to be resilient enough to accept criticism from your co-writers. I think that there is too much 'cultural relativism', these days, and that it's lowering the bar for music, film – all forms of art.

Did you ever feel a spiritual connection to the group as a whole?

I think Glenn and I were a great match, the way we were able to work, to compose, together. It's a bit like the attraction of opposites. Two people who are different from one another in many ways – maybe an introvert and an extrovert – can complete one another. I sometimes could feel a spiritual connection with the band when we were onstage and everything was clicking. Sometimes, in the middle of a concert, I would suddenly think about how long we'd been together and what we'd been through, what we'd survived, and I would feel lucky, and grateful.

It's also quite possible to have a spiritual experience with audiences, if it's a really good night. An audience can elevate a performer and, by their participation, take the performance to a whole different level – a higher level. It's a symbiotic relationship. They give us energy and we give it back to them, and round it goes. There is no better feeling, no better high than that.

Do you ever feel that the music today represents the unconscious feelings of the masses? That you're giving form to the unspoken word that's already lying just underneath the surface?

I wouldn't say that about every piece of music. I believe in the collective unconscious. I believe that writing – song-writing, poetry, literature, film – is tapping into that. I believe it's in the air. And the listener, or the viewer, picks up on it, if it's well done. In all these types of art, the writer is expressing thoughts and feelings for people in a way that they can't necessarily do for themselves. It's a communal experience. People crave connection, community. Fans create communities and clubs around our music, and I think that's wonderful. Anything that brings people together in times like these is a good thing.

Have you any idea where that creative force comes from?

I've never been quite sure, but I have the usual theories. The creative force comes from more than one source, I think: from the collective unconscious, from 'The Deity', or from what Emerson called 'The Oversoul', or from our own subconsciousness. I don't know, maybe from all of those places; from the culmination of all our experiences; from genetic memory, if you believe in that.

How do you feel on the verge of creating something?

There is a feeling of elation, certainly, but it has to be tempered, because the piece you're working on might not be quite completed, yet. But you can see that you're on to something good. So, you try to remain confident and calm, so that you can finish up the work, and finish it well. It's a strange mixture of excitement and serenity. But, there is a sense of being 'in tune', – of being, for lack of a better term, 'at one' with everything around you. Some days, I feel 'this is a good day to write'. I feel like everything's in balance, everything is in harmony, all is right with the world. 'I can do this.' And then you do it, and there's a sense of euphoria that is better than any drug . . . that is, until you remember that, now, you have to send your little creation, your baby, out into the big bad world, where it will be judged; loved by some, bullied by others. But, that just comes with the territory.

Don continues to tour with The Eagles to the present day. Their Hotel California *tour features the album performed live in its entirety, accompanied by an orchestra and choir and followed by a full set of their latest hits. Don's most recent album is* Cass County, *in 2015, named after the Texas county where he grew up.*

MICK FLEETWOOD

Drummer and founding member of
Fleetwood Mac.

WHEN I WAS FIRST INTRODUCED TO MICK FLEET-
wood, we were both sixteen, and though I was still a
schoolgirl, he had already left his home in Salisbury, in south-
west England, to make his way all alone to London. As a child
he had discovered the drums, and it was an intense revelation for
him: he knew without a doubt that he wanted to be a drummer.
This was much, much more than a childhood whim. From that
moment on, he lived and breathed the drums, much to the
dismay of his schoolteachers, whose classes he failed, and his
parents, who worried what would become of their wayward
son. They needn't have worried: Mick had more motivation
and drive – to become a professional drummer – in his little
finger than most studious schoolboys have in their entire being.
Mick knew deep inside that his destiny awaited him 'out there'
and that he was only biding his time until the day came when he
could begin his journey into musicianship.

'I was obsessed with wanting to be a drummer; I didn't drool over a musician and think, 'I've got to be like that player.' It simply happened. That was it: I wanted to be a drummer, and I can't remember why. It had to be from my dad. He would play the bottles or even play rhythms with the change in his pocket.

'I rely completely on instinct as a player. Often, while I'm playing, there are certain moments when I disappear. Peter was absolutely oozing with feel, and I've never played with anyone who was that profound and so involved with that conviction. I think he saw that in me: there was an affiliation with this funny guy who was not such a great drummer but someone who was able to express himself without worrying how clever he was, and that really applied to what Peter represented as a player.

'I remember one time when my family was driving through Europe, we stopped in a small German village. There were cows underneath the inn we stayed in and these old yogurt-eating guys who live to be 120, sitting around downstairs in the inn. They were all sitting around a 12-volt battery with a wire attached, getting a buzz out of it. That was the setting. Before going to bed that night, I crept downstairs and saw Dad in the bar with all these elderly guys, playing the bottles, having a great time. At boarding school I became obsessed with playing drums. I never had a kit, never played, it just started to happen. I had this dream: I wanted to be playing in London at a club. I had it all planned out. All I did at school was to send away for drum catalogues. The only other thing I enjoyed was the little bit of acting I did. I had a drum catalogue that was literally eight inches thick; I had taped them all together. I used to drool over these drums; it was my dream to have a Premier drum kit.

'I remember going out on my own and sitting underneath a tree. I had my catalogues with me, and I just made a secret pact then and there with myself that I was going to play drums. I remember tears pouring down my face – and that was it. That was the moment I knew I wanted to do this. I ran away from school because I had this vision. I knew what I wanted to do, so that was the commitment I made to myself. I made a private pledge, and I prayed to God, and then that was it.

'I didn't practise or work at being a drummer – I just did it. There were a few [drum styles] I mimicked, but that stopped after I started playing with other people. Apart from learning the songs, my practice was my playing. My dad was wondering what the hell I was going to do; he wanted to take me to an unemployment counsellor. But not long after that I started playing drums in London at the Mandrake Club.

'You have to work at it in some way, preserving that precious childlike part of you. There is some part in me that turns my back on bringing in too much information. I think it can be a little detrimental. It's more important to preserve that innocence that you have, the open book. As long as the whole book doesn't go yellow when you get older – if it's just the edges – then it means you're doing all right. And that's like a child: You come in and all you are is an open book, just waiting to absorb.

'Music is definitely a barometer of social malady or wellness. Music causes something that either excites or calms down or instigates, without even a word being said. A verbal onslaught is part of music, but what music should represent ultimately is harmony. That's my real sense of what sound is, to bring harmony. That would be the whole point that people can express themselves through. And there is nothing without rhythm, no order, seasons – nothing.

'In terms of real high points, without any question it would be when I was playing drums with Peter Green. I'd be completely crying, weeping. It still happens, but it used to happen all the time. I was so devoted to that; it was very, very vivid, and I was sort of addicted to it. There were times I would be pulled into his situation, and it was the highest quotient of that happening. A lot of it was because of literally being there with him. The ride was just as good as driving.

'A few drinks is a helper to me. When I go onstage, I like to have a few drinks; it's not any fear of getting up and playing in public, which could very well be a reason for people drinking. When I first started playing professionally, we always had a few beers. It was part of the situation. You don't play blind drunk, but there have been moments when you're totally uninhibited about what you're doing and are completely unleashing your abilities into the lap of the gods. For better or worse, there's been a lot of liberated moments under the influence of the bottle, and there's certainly been those moments straight.

'If I'm good at pulling feelings out of people who I play with and, hopefully, people that I'm with, I'm glad about that. It's a major thing to me. I want to be around people who really show themselves musically, don't let themselves be inhibited at all. I love to bring that out in fellow players; I need it.

Mick has lived on Maui, one of the Hawaiian Islands, for many years. He is now recording and collaborating with other musicians in his own home studio, and in Los Angeles. On 8 August 2023 his club and restaurant, Fleetwood's, where he would often play with his Island band, was destroyed in the horrific fire which engulfed all of the historic town, Lahaina. Mick performed at the 65th Grammys to honour his lifelong friend and bandmate Christine McVie. His Don't Stop Living the Dream Foundation is a mission to support children who have a passion for music.

CHRISTINE McVIE

Singer, songwriter, keyboardist, solo artist and member of Fleetwood Mac.

I MET CHRISTINE IN 1968 WHEN MICK AND I WERE together. She arrived at the flat in Notting Hill Gate which we shared with bass player Andy Silvester. Chris would often pop round to talk to Andy as they both played in Chicken Shack. She left Chicken Shack in 1969 and recorded her solo album. In 1970 Fleetwood Mac, plus families, and minus Peter Green, moved into an oast house in Hampshire, where we all lived together for a few months while the band rehearsed for their upcoming tour. At the last minute, Chris was asked to join Fleetwood Mac. With Peter missing, they were in need of new songs, so Chris and I wrote the lyrics for 'Jewel Eyed Judy', which ended up on their *Kiln House* album. On their return from the States we all moved into a large house in Hampshire for three years before moving to L.A. Chris was a dear friend, and as years went by, and living away from England, we became like one big family.

'There was always a piano in the house and I started playing it when I was about five years old. My dad wanted both my brother, John, and me to play. His father had played the organ in Westminster Abbey, but when he died, Dad had to become chief breadwinner. He had wanted to go to college to pursue his musical studies, but he couldn't. Instead, he had to get a job playing in the orchestra pits during pantomimes and things like that. Later on he . . . finished his studies and became a music teacher. I learned to play the cello at school when I was eleven, and my dad also used to give me lessons. Our family had a string quartet playing in the house at Christmastime: my dad and John on violin, my mum on viola, and me on cello. It was fun.

'Some songs I write I'm convinced don't come from just me. I'm not sure what it is. Many times, it feels like it comes from some other source. It's amazing because half an hour ago you had nothing, then you've created something from nothing. Sometimes it flows so freely and it seems so effortless that there has to be something else charging your energy to do it, especially when you feel whatever you've written is good and "how on earth could it possibly have come from me?" It was a powerful feeling because I wrote it just like that. I wrote the chords and the words and the melody almost as if it was coming from someone else and not me.

'Today the music is so diverse and quackish in a sense. There's a lot of wonderful music happening, a lot of really good creative stuff. There's also such a lot of trash. It's duping the public to go into the studio and use a bunch of electronics, which some people feel is equally valid. I couldn't argue with them, because they would say, "Well, that's my way of creating." To me, it takes all the spiritual out of it. To be going in with a bunch of gadgetry and creating a song on the computer is valid, but in a sense, it takes the human soul out of it.

'(When I'm in the zone) it's like magic, like a true elation that you can't really describe. You feel inspired; there's no other word for it. You just feel that you are electrically charged, something you have no real control over. When onstage, I feel a sense of great unity, like my father would say when he was playing his one violin in a team of first violin, second violin, violas, horns, oboes and flutes. And then out of all those different mouths and arms and hands comes this amazing *one thing* – all these people doing the same thing together, which is so beautiful. That's what it's like when you're really tight onstage: you know everyone's thinking the same chord at the same time. You're playing as one thing. To all be playing that one thing is a tremendous feeling.

'My experience is that alcohol doesn't block creativity; if it's there, it tends to make it come out easier. I used to do drugs, and I still drink wine when I'm writing, sometimes too much and then it really gets blown completely. There was a point when I stopped doing cocaine and I didn't know if I would be able to write without it. It was frightening, because you're lulled into a false sense of grandeur, a state of grace, when you do cocaine. You think you're invincible and everything you write is genius. I did write a lot of good songs on cocaine and a lot of bad ones too. Then there was the period of coming to terms with not doing cocaine any more. I didn't actually write for a long time. I was scared to. It's like looking at a virgin canvas and not knowing where to put the first stroke, without the aid of this drug.

'Then I got in tune with myself, with my head and my heart, so now I can write without even thinking about that naughty stuff any more. It's a very destructive drug. I'm not saying I didn't have a lot of fun, and I would not change it, but I would not go back. I wouldn't do it again. So now all those fears are completely unfounded, because of course, if you can write, you certainly don't need any artificial stimulus to bring out what's in there anyway.

'If I'm a brilliant songwriter but I'd rather be a gardener, and I'm out slogging away trying to grow orchards, I'm never going to grow orchards very well. I should really be acknowledging my true gift. A lot of people aren't even aware what their true gift is until they've reached middle age. It's all a question of interpreting our gift and knowing how to use it.'

Chris died in hospital on 30 November 2022. An album, Songbird (A Solo Collection), *had been released a few months earlier of some of her songs that had not been included on Fleetwood Mac albums.*

HANK MARVIN

Lead guitarist for The Shadows and Cliff Richard.
He is also a songwriter and solo artist. England's
first guitar hero still strumming at eighty and set to
star at the West Australian Guitar Festival.

I CAN'T REMEMBER HOW I MANAGED TO SPEAK TO
Hank Marvin. I think he must have been one of the first
interviews I did in England.

'I started to develop an interest in traditional jazz when I was
about thirteen, fourteen, which led to me wanting to play an
instrument somewhere within that framework. The first desire
was to play clarinet; it was such a fluid instrument. This didn't
materialise; what in fact happened was I found out our French
teacher in school had a banjo, which I bought from him for two
pounds and ten shillings. I learned a lot of chords.

'By fifteen, I started to play banjo with a couple of local trad
[traditional] jazz bands, and I was singing terrible jazz vocals. I
also started a skiffle group, trying to play what I thought was
more purist skiffle, not the commercial Lonnie Donegan-type

36

skiffle. We started to have this weird skiffle group, playing all these ethnic, real down-home, New Orleans folky things.

'When I was sixteen, my father bought me a guitar; by this time, I was beginning to lean more towards the guitar than the banjo. From somewhere I acquired an amplifier; it was about the size of a large cornflakes box, and it sounded very similar. That really gave me such a thrill to hear this guitar and amplifier. I then was asked to join another skiffle group by a guy at school called Bruce Welch, who later became a colleague of mine in The Shadows. I was singing harmonies with Bruce and playing lead guitar.

'At one point we started to put on our own dances in small villages. One night the band didn't show up, so we all decided we'd play some rock 'n' roll. I didn't know any rock 'n' roll, but Bruce knew a few Elvis Presley songs and a couple of things like that, so we had a quick half-hour rehearsal and went on and played these rock 'n' roll songs, and I really enjoyed it. This was late 1957; I heard a few rock 'n' roll things after that, like Buddy Holly and The Crickets and a couple by Elvis Presley. I was very inspired by the feel, and the sound was so different from anything I'd ever heard before.

'The guitar sound on the English records at that time was very bland, rather boring, and the reason was that the guitarists here were on to a different style of music; they were all jazz-influenced players. They all wanted to be jazz guitarists. A lot of them were session musicians; then along comes rock 'n' roll – they can't stand rock 'n' roll. It's got this very heavy off beat, which most of them don't like. It's based on a simple twelve-bar blues; it's repetitive. They don't like it and here they are having to play it. The American rock 'n' roll guitarists were from places where country music was very strong, but there was also an exposure to black blues music. The difference was incredible. I was so inspired by that, and I wanted to try and copy it.

'We recorded a piece of music called "Cavatina". It was released under the title of "The Theme from *The Deer Hunter*" and we had a big hit from that at the end of the seventies. When we went to record it, we just set up the gear and laid everything down. I went to put my guitar work on and just played it. It was almost perfect; everyone went, "Ooh, that's it!" and, in fact, it was it – virtually a one-take performance. It had such a lovely feel to it that it was just right. I knew it felt good when I played it.

'During a Peak Experience, playing has a magic; it just feels absolutely right, and you think, I couldn't have done it any other way. That's the way it should be. When it feels right, it creates an atmosphere: That's it; you've hit that lovely thing again. It doesn't happen as often as I'd like!

'Some nights the feeling between the different musicians onstage is just incredible. We've got an amazing drummer, Brian Bennett, who's been with the band since 1961. He's very creative and just loves music in all its facets. Also, you can get a fantastic audience that creates a wonderful environment, but that doesn't necessarily mean you're going to play as well as you did the night before or the next night. But when all those factors come together, then it is magic. You feel absolutely elated, a tremendous feeling of joy, because it's all working so well. You can almost get high on it, a very good feeling; you go to the stage and you know you're not going to do anything wrong that night, everything is up, the band is so tight, it's just wonderful – and we get paid for it as well!

'There's no way of knowing beforehand. We've had nights where we've felt terrific – a good sleep, a nice lunch, feeling very fit, very positive – and it's certainly not one of your better shows. And another night you've had two hours' sleep, a lot of travelling, you feel a bit under the weather, but you go onstage and it's wonderful. Now, why?

'People were popping pills, even in the late fifties; it was fairly subtle, not all over the place. I never used anything. I drink alcohol, but even with alcohol there is the danger that it can become addictive. Rather than enhancing creativity – from what I've heard of experiments with people under the influence of various drugs in creative situations – their performance is well below par. I suspect that would be the case. I think it's far better if your brain is clear and it can work properly. Creativity is all bound up with things working properly and coordination inside – not only the mechanical aspect of the brain but also the more abstract, creative side – all working together.

SINÉAD O'CONNOR

*Singer, songwriter, guitarist and solo artist.
Billboard named 'Nothing Compares 2 U' as the
number-one single of 1990 at its first Billboard
Music Awards. The video received heavy rotation
on MTV, directed by John Maybury.*

I WAS INTRODUCED TO SINEAD BY PHOTOGRAPHER
Neal Preston in L.A. She was in his studio having her
photograph taken when Neal happened to ask if she'd like to
be interviewed for my book. As soon as he'd told me Sinead
would like to be interviewed, I came to the studio and that's
where we met. When I was interviewing her, I had the feeling
she rarely felt listened to, and was keen to talk for longer once
she'd finished the interview. She came to our house for tea on a
couple of occasions, and brought her little son with her.

'Both of my parents were musical. They both came from
very old Dublin families, and Dublin people are very musical.
My mother used to sing opera when she was a teenager. I think
my father attempted to play the piano, but he wasn't very good.
When I was very small, my family used to sing songs all the

time. My father was always singing to us; each of us had our own special song that he would sing to us before we went to bed. Mine was "Scarlet Ribbons", which is a very upsetting, very disturbing song. So right from a young age I understood songs could get over very strong emotions. When I was about twelve, I started writing songs. I wrote in my head, but I didn't think of it as writing. I sort of sang to myself as I walked along to school.

'I felt very much different from the other kids and they contributed to making me feel different. I *still* feel different. I always got in trouble all my life for saying things, saying what I thought, expressing myself. It just never occurred to me to be any different; I wasn't trying to cause trouble. I'm not aggressive at all, but I'm very emotional. We're brought up to not be emotional. It's so hard, especially since I'm young. It's difficult because you're up against everyone, you're on your own, you're up against a wall of fucking trouble, because everyone's telling you that you're bad and you're awful and you're horrible, and you begin to ask yourself if you are. You begin to think it. It's so hard to actually retain what your purpose is – or to even realise what it is – and think it doesn't matter if they think you're a bastard.

'I have a specific function to perform, which is that I'm probably the only person around who communicates emotionally, who communicates very stark or turbulent emotions. My function is to get people to express themselves and get all the shit out. I express emotions about things that society doesn't want to hear about – like miscarriages, abortions, rape or child abuse. People never talk, for example, about whether they were abused when they were children. They're taught to squash it down, and as we're beginning to be aware, any emotion like that that's squashed down can make you sick. If somebody can come along into the world and encourage people to express very intense emotions about extremely deep issues that people have been taught never to talk about, it will help to heal people. So that's what I'm doing; I'm also healing myself because I've been through all of those things myself.'

Sinead passed away unexpectedly on 26 July 2023 at the age of fifty-seven

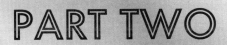

PART TWO

*'I'm sure music, poetry, painting –
all the arts – are languages, no more, and
some people are more adept at speaking
them, but no one is excluded'* –

PETER GABRIEL

EG WHITE

*Eg is a British musician, songwriter and producer.
Born into a musical family in 1966, both of his
parents being talented classical instrumentalists,
he formed his first band, Brother Beyond, with
his brother David in the late 1980s. He released
a pop album, 24 Years of Hunger, in 1991, in
collaboration with musician, singer and songwriter
Alice Temple.*

*In recent years, he has worked with many
well-known artists, such as Adele, Kylie Minogue,
Duffy, Will Young and Joss Stone, and many other
prominent names. He has won two Ivor Novello
Awards for his song writing, in 2004 and 2009,
and was twice nominated for a Grammy at the
51st Annual Awards with Adele's song 'Chasing
Pavements'.*

I MET EG THROUGH A FRIEND OF MINE. I SPOKE TO HIM
on the phone to ask if he would be interested in being interviewed
about creativity. 'I have a lot to say about creativity,' he told me.
The enthusiasm in his voice was all I needed to hear. I met him

at his house in London, and after a cup of tea we walked down the steps to his womb-like studio, filled with guitars, recording equipment and numerous instruments dotted around the room. It was an Aladdin's cave! The one question I asked him once we were sitting down ignited a stream of answers: everything I wanted to know about the difference between the music world today compared with the 1980s when I had interviewed the other musicians in this book.

'The biggest thing that's happened between the last generation and this one is that Spotify and the streaming agencies have now changed the way people use music. Lots of things have changed but the one that has had the biggest effect is what's coming from the streaming agencies in terms of what that does to the way music is listened to. Oh boy! It's different. If you go back to the mid-sixties, especially late sixties, early seventies, it wasn't just self-expression that people were aiming for. I think people were genuinely trying to touch something, if not divine, then at least something transformational in themselves that they could then bring into the world. I think the aim was very high at that point. That particular period – let's say '65 to '75. I think pre-'65 is closer to where it is now, where everyone's struggling just to get a pop record out that goes off and makes everybody wealthy. Obviously, in those days, in the very beginning, people didn't get so wealthy because they got so badly ripped off, and then suddenly everyone got phenomenally rich in the 1970s, ludicrously in the 1980s, and even in the mid-nineties, but then round about 2000 it wasn't quite so useful any more. But during that sixties to seventies golden period, I don't think the best people were trying to express themselves as much as trying to surprise themselves, trying to do something that went beyond what they knew they were capable of doing. I guess the 1980s became a much more realistic period. You then had this wonderful time around 1977 with punk when everything got smashed to pieces until 1979 when they started cautiously putting it back together again. And so, '79 to '83 felt to me as if that was a period where everyone believed they could rebuild with any ingredients, that white people can really enjoy listening to black music and incorporating black music into their music. It wasn't quite so much going the other way yet. In the 1970s, technique was really important, it really mattered that you could play well. But '77 comes along and smashes it all up. It's not about how well you can play any more, it's what are you trying to do? What are you trying to say here? What are you trying to break? And then, finally, of course, playing sneaked back in the room around '79 and that's when you've got all these fantastic records that happened, such as The Clash, where reggae is now being incorporated into rock music, Talking Heads. They're listening to West African music, like really listening to it and trying to incorporate it into rock.

'I think what's happening now is we're back in the fifties and there's also an optimism. The nice thing about it is no one's making money out of it in the same way as they did.

'That said, people are getting ripped off now, just like in the 1950s, so you can't expect to see measurable royalties from a moderate success. If you have a huge success, you can expect to see royalties from everywhere including unexpected places. But in terms of the money, you get paid by record companies for having made your record; the deals are not *technically* so different to how they were then, but the money coming in is a fraction of what it was.'

What is the music saying these days? When I lived in San Francisco in 1967, the songs were about love and peace, that was the message.

I think nowadays, in terms of professional music, people are scrabbling, trying to get something away, trying literally to put some food on the table. But also, there was this fundamental difference in what was and is available. In 1967 people weren't really buying albums. If music was being consumed in San Francisco in 1967, it was probably through radio and live shows. And those are both about a collective experience of music being experienced simultaneously. Someone plays some music on the radio and people around the city will hear it simultaneously. That same thing peaked for me in the 1980s with *Top of the Pops*.

I remember seeing Adam and the Ants on *Top of the Pops* in 1981 and going to school the next day and two thirds of the people in the playground had seen them playing and were, to some extent, unconsciously or consciously affected by the revelation of Adam and the Ants. There would be a simultaneous union that everybody had had the same experience. Everyone had received three minutes of transformation at the same moment. But nowadays people are listening to their music on headphones, and its consumption is so different.

I had to cross London recently so I took the Tube with a pair of headphones at seven o'clock in the evening. Everyone was coming home tired from work. I'm listening to my music and I suddenly realise rock music does not work on the Tube. I've got a downloaded playlist of stuff I'm listening to which is super-broad. I'm listening to stuff that I've been given by someone I'm working with the next day and, because I know I'm going to be on the Tube, I download it before I get on and then realised rock music just sucks. It fills up the room, it fills up my head. But R&B with great spaces, loud bass drums and snares, but huge amounts of space and echoes. I suddenly knew the modern music that people are making totally made sense.

Like Billie Eilish, it opened up a complete space in the Tube train and I'm looking at people's faces, the lighting's good and there's a space that opens up, a kind of poetic grandeur opened up in the Tube from the space opened up by this music. And it was just like, wow, that is a complete technological change affecting the way I consume music and what works and what doesn't work. I don't want energy in here. I want some space. I looked around the carriage at all the people with headphones on. Imagine they're all listening to the same kind of thing, music that opens up space in a complicated, crowded environment.

The other thing that's changed is you used to have enormous breakthrough successes in a given year. There might be four or five huge successes, who then had a chance at achieving some sort of longevity. That's still happening, but not so much. There are people who get away with one song and then they're not really able to come back. Loyalty's kind of gone. There's a huge oversupply.

Now I'm in total transition as I have no idea what I should be doing. It's so complicated. I have a choice. I have a real studio with drums, with nice fine microphones and piano and the whole works. And too many guitars. And good synths. I have a holy grail in here. Anything you might possibly need, 72, 85, 97, 2017 is all here. There is not a single tool that I could want, but I find when I make records, when I do songs for people and, instead of playing everything, if I steal all of the ingredients, legally or illegally online, people say to me, 'Wow! your stuff sounds really fresh and really contemporary.' And I get a, 'How amazing an old guy like you is still making contemporary sounding productions.' When I do it using real instruments, it sounds a lot more amateur. It takes a lot longer to do, harder to kind of integrate the new and the old. And yet there are some people who say, 'That's what I want.' Quite a few of them do. But I have to not slavishly recreate the early seventies recordings or the early sixties, but add something new. That's what I'm finding hard, it's how to integrate the two worlds, the stolen, processed, computer-generated modern world or the more authentic world. How to combine the two? How do you also make a living doing that?

And I think the reason I'm not quite succeeding at it is because I'm still writing songs. And here's where we get back to Spotify, the whole thing circles round. Throughout, Spotify enormously rewards stuff which sounds good in the first twenty seconds, but the classic pop song gets you in the door in the first twenty seconds, lays something out in the next thirty seconds and then surprises you by revealing a gloriously transfigured landscape for the chorus and makes you say, 'God, you didn't see that coming did you?' The best pop songs do that. They open up, you turn a corner and you think, I know where this is going and, 'Wow! It's all gold in there!' The really wonderful songs will have a transformation at one minute, but those songs don't translate well on Spotify because the listener tends to jump before they get there. Spotify intriguingly pays the artist if you play thirty-one seconds of a song, but doesn't pay them if you play twenty-nine seconds. You'd think that threshold would be enormously important but I don't think it is. I think listeners are inclined to jump much earlier than that.

Spotify serves up a classic thing called New Music Friday on a Friday. Every record that's been released, that they've then decided is good enough to go on this playlist, about seventy or eighty records, they choose for the English playlist, and probably more for America. They choose what goes on there and it will be from very mainstream or super-not-at-all and then the listener chooses whether they jump or not. Spotify knows if they jump or not, and if the listener jumps, then Spotify won't put it on other playlists. It'll just sort of quietly die on the vine.

It sounds very contrived?

Oh, well, it goes further than that. The whole form of making music has changed. I have someone coming in today. She's not that young and we will probably be writing with some kind of vague country elements. We will sit down. I'll probably sit at a piano or play the guitar, and we might start with a lyric and I might start by playing some chords or something like that, and then we'll write the song that way. That is how songs are classically written when they're songs. But the stuff that does well on Spotify isn't written that way at all.

Al Shuckburgh is a very, very good producer and writer, and actually a superb musician. And Al came over the other day and we were talking about his song-writing process, and what he does. He told me, 'I've got quite a few synthesisers and I sit there and I'll kind of start making music and something will kind of begin to coalesce. And I won't probably even put the drums down because you've really got to stay on top of drum sounds. So, I'll probably then send it off to these two people I know who are really good at the contemporary things that are going on. He lives in L.A., so he'll start with a musical thing at a particular tempo, but he won't put the drums on. He'll then send it to his drums guy who then puts the drums on, and then it'll go to a set of top liners. And these are people who just sort of go into a woozy state, then they start singing, and then they hopefully get something where they are feeling, 'Yeah, this is pretty good.' And the words begin to coalesce. And then if they've got something good, especially if it's got a good chorus, then they'll sing a demo of it, and pretty soon the conversation will be, 'Right, who are we going to send it to?' And they'll think of three or four celebrities or top singers and they'll send it to them and ask if they want it. Then the singer will add their own little bit, and then the thing will have got through an iterative process whereby, if it was going to be knocked out, it would have been knocked out by one of these four or five stages. If it gets as far as the top singer, then it is because it was probably good to listen to from its opening, from the first ten seconds, then aiming for a strong memorable chorus. They can ask themselves, 'Have we got a decent chorus here? Have we got that moment of transformation?'

But no, that's not the most important question, that question is: is this piece of music that Al did on his keyboards good enough to get people in the door on Spotify? Because if it's good enough to get the beats guy and good enough to get the top liners working on it, because the top liners get sent twenty things and they can say, 'Oh, fuck it, I'm not doing that one.' But then they'll hear something more appealing, and they'll say, 'Oh, I fancy that one.' And so it goes. This process of selection and attrition is what is shaping what gets to the stars and then the stars will then add their own thing and sing it, God willing, with vigour.

When you're working on a song, do you go around the houses like that?

No, I don't. The terrible thing is, you look at those songs in America, I look and I'm so jealous of 258 million plays in two weeks. Bloody hell! The thing is going and you know it's unstoppable. And then I look at the list of writers – there are twelve to fifteen writers, and of course that's because everyone has to have a chunk. If it got past them, they get a chunk.

The star is going to say, 'Well, look, I'm going to sing it, so I'm going to take thirty per cent,' or something like a proper chunk, and Al will say, 'I started the fucking thing.'

And they're thinking about Spotify and how well that's going to go?

They were until they all got taken out by TikTok.

TikTok came along and killed a lot of that model. So, TikTok is another thing. You know it's even more bonkers. I mean, way more bonkers. So, what happens is TikTok's MO is completely different. I know nothing about this. Everything I say has no authority. I'm just making this shit up. But I might be right too. Which is that TikTok's primary MO is for people to look attractive. The people who post, their fundamental reason, I believe, is that they are doing it is so that they will look attractive, in order to sleep with more attractive people, probably primarily in order eventually to start attracting money, because then people are going to say, 'This person has 800,000 people watching them so we can promote our trainers through there and tell them, "I'm going to give you fifteen pairs of trainers and maybe even a few thousand dollars if you just say, 'Oh, there they are.'"' That's the kind of thing that goes on. And I think a lot of this stuff is spoken voice only, but a lot of it is music. Very often the music people choose something whereby the lyric, in some way, enables their process of seeming attractive. So it could be that the lyrics are really funny and clever and just an arch little snide attack on dating. Or it might be a little thing about materialism and the positive side. It could be anything, just a tight little human phrase that works in about eight to eleven seconds.

This is unbelievable and it's so great hearing all this stuff. That's what it takes nowadays – so different from watching George, Paul and John sitting on the roof of a bungalow in India as they create songs that end up on *The White Album!*

These forces nowadays are shaping whether it's used or not, but they always were. The Beatles were a pop group and later on less so. But they had a huge captive audience. By '64, '65, they could do anything and, provided they satisfied themselves, they brought their audience with them. There's a huge difference between The Beatles and now: it's loyalty and control of the marketplace. Because record companies WERE inherently stupid, conservative, and because there were only a few studios, because they cost a fortune, because it was technologically really hard to make a record, though, that said, Abbey Road sounded really good. But because of all these reasons, The Beatles and the Stones had pretty much enormous control of the market place.

Whereas now, because anyone can do it on a laptop, no one has any control, no one can maintain the advantage for five minutes.

When you're writing a song with, say, Adele or other well-known singers, are you then thinking of Spotify? Are you both thinking of Spotify?

I am. Well, here's where I get to the fact that in some crucial way, I'm failing to evolve and I'm refusing to evolve. And I may even be right.

If I was truly evolving, I would say, 'Damn the pithy, careful working of the lyric and making sure that the whole thing is coherent. To hell with the middle eight! Increasingly, I work with American artists and they often say, 'Yeah, we don't need a middle eight. We don't need a bridge. Fuck it, we can stop it at two minutes twenty. Why write a bridge? Why? If we do something good enough, why make them wait another minute. Make them play it again. Keep it short, then we get paid twice and our numbers look better! No middle eights. That's one example of it, but basically, in order to properly evolve, a lot of song structure would go. You'd think, why are we writing a three-minute mini-symphony when ultimately what it all boils down to is, is there a pithy little line there that'll fit great in those seven, eight seconds? And while I say all of this, my own kids and pretty much everyone else I know, all of their kids too, they're all listening to Queen and the Stones and Bob Dylan, and they were listening to Joni Mitchell, *before* she ripped her stuff offline, which of course I think she should have done. So, I may be saying, this is how people consume stuff, but by the time they're about seventeen, they're kind of done with it.

Phoebe Bridgers is one of the very few people who is a huge surprise. Everyone's saying, 'How did that happen?' It's because her stuff is really good. She writes her own stuff or co-writes, presumably collaborates, with people like me or whomever. But her work is long form and her work is minutely observed and probably isn't being driven at all by TikTok. But she's good enough that it's going off and she's one of the very few success stories of people running old-style, long-form, carefully observed work and the equivalent, if you like, of a well-made film.

So where does creativity fit into all of this?

It does fit in. Whether or not you're acknowledging that you are led by the market or if you still maintain the semi-truth that you're doing it in order to surprise yourself – I no longer use terms like self-expression, I don't know why not, I suppose I think humans are too rich and complicated. To surprise myself, that's my kind of mantra. I really want to do something where, you know, suddenly something appears and you go, I haven't done that before. And it's inevitable. It's really good. Something I've never done before. That is the thing that seems to be making me and the people I work with happiest.

That's like an adventure.

Yeah. And so, the answer, of course, has to be play. You know, you're not going to get there consciously. You can say, 'Today we're going to write a masterpiece.' And that will do you no bloody good at all.

You have to say, 'Okay. I'm not going to write a piece of shit.' That you definitely have to do, but beyond that is vanity and probably misguided.

So, you have to try to stay true to yourself?

I wouldn't even say that. I don't think you do. If anything, I'd say it's the opposite; you have to be false to yourself. You have to do something that you didn't think was true. You have to in some way break a boundary that is unconsciously or consciously imposed upon yourself.

Does any of your creativity come from dreams?

Rarely. I used to get more dreams that turned into, 'Oh, that's a really good song.' I do sometimes, probably twice, three times a year, wake and go, 'Oh, that's good enough.' I keep a phone by the bed. Dreams can certainly consolidate a song that's gone wrong. Sometimes, you know it's a piece of crap but it's got two or three good elements in it and I can't bear to let those good things go just because we can't go any further, and sometimes a dream will unlock that. Not often, but sometimes.

Different people have completely different things. I remember meeting Tobias Jesso Jr, a very, very nice guy. He'd just written a huge hit song with Adele and I remember him coming in here and me saying, 'I run cold. Ideally, neither of us have got anything. I like that situation the best. If something does come to me, I might write a line on my phone, but that'll be as far as I'll go.' And he said, 'No, I plan. If I have a session with somebody, I'll have three or four good starts that I'll bring to them.' And, of course, it's a much better idea. I met Max Martin and somebody told me Max Martin really prepares, he'll come in with ideas. It's obviously a good idea if you've got something when someone famous is coming. You should make sure you've got two or three great song starts. But I just love it when it appears in the room. When you've got nothing and you go bang, bang, bang and you suddenly find yourself singing. 'That's great! That's great!'

I really love it when it's totally fresh. That's when I think, 'Oh, now we're really doing something.' Even if you think you've got a wrestling match to make all the bits fit together. It slows you down and you think you've killed it. But I happen to really like that. And other people plan like crazy. I think probably planning is a better idea. But again, the question is about the line between the conscious and unconscious, isn't it? Obviously, the unconscious should be the thing making it. And your question is how much do you control that? I heard a great story about Prince.

A friend of mine had to record him in the middle of the night. Four o'clock the phone goes: 'Hey, could get here in ten minutes?' He says, 'Yeah, yeah, okay.' And it's Prince in Wembley who just wanted to play his guitar on a track. So, my friend put the tape on and Prince is playing guitar and my friend said, unlike other people when they play something really bad, I see them wince. You just see their bodies tighten up but when they play something really good, I see them kind of rocking and they've got that groovy look on their face like the whole thing's going well, but he said, Prince didn't do that. He played something really shit and it's like nothing. And then he plays something amazing, I'm looking and he's not flinching and he's not getting bigger. He's not oscillating with it. And he said, 'You know, he played some really shockingly awful things and some absolutely amazing stuff, the whole range. And then about ten minutes later he'd say, 'Okay, kill that one, kill that one, keep that, kill, kill, kill, keep.' And he somehow managed this thing, which I think it would be the holy grail, and he managed to separate the executive function from the generative function. He could generate these ideas and not judge them in the present tense, but subsequently, a few minutes later. The real problem is how to generate something and not be knocked for six when it turns out to be a false lead and, at the same time, to have enough discretion that you don't chase something that is mediocre down the road for the rest of the day and find that, when you get there, it's just a piece of shit.

Song writing, I think, probably equates more closely to gambling than anything else. And I'm not just talking about with respect to success, I'm talking about with respect to the creative process, the outcome of the song. All the time you're playing a game of poker with the song. Trying to work out is the hand any good, are we going to win here? Where's the weakness? What cards do I dump? Sometimes you have to dump quite good-looking cards because they're just not part of the play. And it's agony. And sometimes you don't bounce back from it. And sometimes you get to four in the afternoon and you realise, having invested in the thing, that it's rubbish. And sometimes at that point, you write something great. Yeah. Freed from the tyranny of being yoked to a piece of crap.

And then you've got the other person.

Yeah, well both of you are judging and you're hoping that they're going to sing something that's fantastically brilliant. And sometimes there's the other thing whereby you're just going slowly through the lyric. And you're hoping the other person is going to make some breakthrough, and you're hoping you'll make a breakthrough, and you're lobbing stuff in and sometimes it's a good idea to lob in crap. I've been in lots of sessions whereby just lobbing something keeps it going. Tells the other person or people what it is they don't want.

It must be an amazing feeling when you're working with somebody, when you actually both agree on something and you both know it because it's just so lovely.

Yeah! Done! Move on! It's a lovely feeling. And the terrible thing is, it's amazing how many things you have to get right in a pop song and how few things you have to get wrong for it to be good. And in some ways, a simple song, for having fewer ingredients, is less of a miracle and it's not quite right. I tend to overwork it. I just keep putting stuff in until it has gained traction or the illusion of communality to try and give it more force. Oh, yes. It's a really good job. It's really fun and it can be really agonising.

It's amazing to still be doing it forty-three years in or whatever. I've been writing since I was fourteen. Forty-two years, and still to feel pathetic in the light of it and not so much to learn but rather so many stones unturned.

One thing I noticed in all the musicians I interviewed in 1989/1990, is the humility they all had, and it didn't matter how famous they were. It was a sense of openness to something greater than themselves.

I think play is at the centre of the whole thing, collaborative play. Without play, you get horrible outcomes; it's play, and how to manage the unconscious mind. In a way that's what Prince managed to do, to separate the conscious no-mind from the one generative unconscious mind.

I feel sad because it's a very physical thing. You know, I think of Prince sitting there and he's playing the guitar. You know, that's the kind of thing that's shaking and the noodling and everything and it's physical and a lot of that has gone. I'm very keen to try and find ways of getting the physicality into the computer-based process. I'm not really succeeding. There are a few people trying and I have my own dreams, but it's not happening. The computer-based process is not physical and I think you lose a lot. The only thing left is the singing. That's the only physical process left in contemporary pop music – the singing. Some people do play guitars and some people do play drums and then manipulate them heavily to make them not sound like a 1970s drum kit that you stole!'

LINDSEY BUCKINGHAM

Lead guitarist, singer, songwriter of
Fleetwood Mac.

I MET LINDSEY AND STEVIE AT THE SAME TIME, WHEN they walked into Mick's and my house in Laurel Canyon in 1974. Mick had recently heard them singing on their record, *Buckingham Nicks*, when he was looking for a studio for the band to record in. Both Lindsey and Stevie were a well-needed shot in the arm for the remaining members of Fleetwood Mac.

'In general, my parents were supportive of everything; they were supportive of me as a person. When I first started playing music at age six, I didn't take lessons; I just learned to play by ear and by listening to my brother's records. It was a hobby, something ingrained in me at a very young age, so the guitar has always been there. I never felt like I had to sit down and learn to play the guitar. It was something that excited me, that animated me; that charged me up. It meant a great deal to me. I would just play along to songs and learn chords, and my style just sort of evolved. I don't think my mother was of a mind that music would be something that I should pursue professionally. I think she knew the entertainment business was a rough one, and that there are a lot of pitfalls and a heavy lack of stability. So, she didn't encourage me to seek that out, but she certainly encouraged me to play.

'One of the reasons I enjoy working alone is because that's when things will quite often come out well. It's very akin to a religious experience. There is some tie between religion and art; I think there's a lot of cross-over. What I do is get really centred and get into a space that I assume has religious connotations to it. Someone else's anchor could be going to church; the anchor for me is when I work on my own and I really get very close to something.

'In music you get into things beyond technique; you start to move into things intangible. I don't know what makes people have the quality that touches, but they must have taken something in their life that rings back true on the way out. Once I asked someone I respected, "Should I take music classes?" And he said, "Knowledge is always going to help, but you might stomp out something that is original about you; you'll start second-guessing things you do that might not be by the book but which are you."

'Today, you've got such an influx of technology that you've got kids now who aren't musicians but computer programmers making music. But I think you're going to find that for every bit of high tech, people are going to need 'high touch' on the other side to balance it out.

'There's no real defining what a Peak Experience is. It becomes magical; it's very uplifting. It can happen while playing an instrument. The process of my writing is so tied in with working on a 24-track or two 24-track machines and overdubbing. It becomes a painter and his canvas. You go in with certain preconceptions in mind, but when you have that intimate one-to-one with the canvas, you may impose a certain thing on it, but at some point, it will start taking on a life of its own and speaking to you about what's needed. That kind of rapport on a one-to-one can provide very thrilling moments, euphoric moments. When you lock into a track you're playing, it's sort of a unidimensional thing. You may lock into a certain emotional tone, a sort of resonance of some kind. Two tangents meeting is usually one of the points that produces creativity; two things that don't necessarily relate begin co-relating and forming something else. That happens more tangibly in the studio, where you suddenly see that if you put this with that, you can visualise, almost see them as shapes, and that kind of thing can go on in multiples. It happens less on lyrics than it does with the form, the shape and the colour – the emotional tone of the music. The initial inspiration feels like it's coming through me. By the time I get it down, it sometimes goes, but as things evolve, it happens again. It has to happen more than once in the process.

'Cocaine is not part of my style: I certainly have done my share, but I don't buy it, I don't like it; it's not good for work. It might be good if you want to put yourself in the position of having to work twenty-four hours, but why do that? I work fourteen-hour days in my studio and I don't need cocaine to do that; I can just do it on natural energy.

'I do smoke pot. It's not great for things like memory, but within the relative security of the studio, in the womb-like atmosphere where I know what's going on in there, it's very helpful. It breaks down preconceptions you have about something; it allows you to hear it fresh. If you've been working on something for a few hours and you smoke a joint, it's like hearing it again for the first time. You walk away for ten minutes and come back, and it allows you to keep coming back in for more and enjoy it. It seems to open a lot of the right-brain stuff. It seems to fire off a lot of things. For me, it's tied into a certain ability to visualise. It puts you way inside it. I would imagine if you smoke a strong joint, it's mildly psychedelic and it puts you in touch with things. You journey inside.

'Things seem to come out of nowhere sometimes; it throws you a bit. You have to get unsure of yourself if you're going to break down preconceptions, if you're going to feel out of control. You're never going to do a good piece of work if you're just imposing your ego on something. But the other side of that, the alcohol, is something I've stopped doing. That and cocaine are not creative things.

'All children are creative; it's just that ninety-five per cent get it capped off. The instincts go away, and people are channelled into certain ways of being, of thinking. I think it can be redeveloped, but I think most people's sense of creativity has been stomped out of them. Everyone can come up with something creative, but maybe they just dismiss it. A lot of being creative is being committed enough to what you're doing to follow through on it. The seed is only the beginning; it's the work that you put into it, and putting yourself on the line to actually follow through.

'I had a problem with the success of *Rumours*. I thought it was good on some level, but I always thought there was a huge discrepancy between what the album was and how well it was selling. That's dangerous ground when you don't really think what's going on is all that great, that it's way out of proportion. Then you're caught in this machine, the great American axiom of, 'If it works, run it into the ground.' That's what my thing on the *Tusk* album was. The idea was to say there's no way I'm going to be involved in making a *Rumours II*. I've had mixed feelings about the whole Fleetwood Mac experience. If I was to do something that I really believed in, and it were to do that well, I would have a much stronger sense of having done something that I could get behind.'

After his 2018 split with Fleetwood Mac, and heart surgery in 2019, Lindsey released his seventh solo studio album, Lindsey Buckingham, *in September 2021. Unfortunately, health issues forced him to cancel the European tour to promote this album, and no tour dates are set at present. Lindsey is now reportedly working on a new solo album.*

PETER GABRIEL

Singer, songwriter and solo artist who was a founding member of Genesis.

BECAUSE I WAS LIVING IN LOS ANGELES AT THE TIME and Peter was living in England, I wasn't able to meet up with him, unfortunately, so we conducted our interview on the phone.

'I used to sing in the choir when I was very little and always loved music. My parents bought me a couple of records, and I started listening to the radio and taping things off the broadcast, and then dancing. I stopped piano classes when I was young because I hated all my lessons. Then I started relearning it when I was twelve or thirteen, picking out a note one finger at a time. At school there was a sense that I could cut through the repression, just letting my hair down and dancing and screaming. It was physical and emotional and intellectual all at once.

'I put a lot of myself into my music and so I think people find echoes of themselves in it.

'I think you plug into this electricity – it's like a river in a way. No question when the magic's there, everyone in the room feels it. You're a bit like a radio aerial and you quiver when you're on to something. One of the things we try and get a lot more conscious about now is to make sure we record those moments in whatever form possible at that moment. You don't take an hour trying to get sounds right, trying to get all the bits and pieces operational and then find you've lost it. Immediately you put the red light on and catch whatever is around. And then even if it's only on two tracks of the twenty-four, you can always pull them back up again, even if it's not usable in its own form. It will then speak in a language of magic to the musicians.

'Performers feed off the audience; sometimes you can tell how a gig's going to at the moment you walk onstage. You know what sort of electricity and energy is being put up towards the stage. I respond to that a lot. Sometimes you can generate that from nothing, but it is a lot harder.

'Music is spiritual and is a doorway into that world. Its power comes from the fact that it plugs directly into the soul, unlike a lot of visual art or text information that has to go through the more filtering processes of the brain.

'Mind-altering substances of one kind or another have been traditionally part of many cultures and have a place in shaping creativity. But I don't think it's something I would recommend to anyone, nor that it is necessary. I think it's possible to get to wherever you want to go without it. Perhaps sometimes it does short-circuit longer routes that maybe allow you to look through a window perhaps at a state that might be arrived at through spiritual work. I'm not sure you actually get there. It's a very dangerous road.

'I'm absolutely certain that everyone has the potential to be creative. The example I used to use, which isn't perfect, is that if I could convince someone in the street, anyone, that their survival was dependent on producing something very creative – whether it was music, painting, or whatever – if they took me seriously, then they would find they were creative. I'm sure music, poetry, painting, all of the arts, are languages – no more. Some people are more adept at speaking them, but no one is excluded or no one need be excluded. If a baby is dependent on drawing to get his milk, then he would become as talented as possible. I remember reading about some music students in Czechoslovakia who were hypnotised into thinking they were their favourite composers. They sat down at their instruments and didn't play new sonatas or whatever, but sat down with a self-assurance that they lacked left to their own devices, and that enabled them to really raise their standard. We put our own limitations on nine times out of ten.'

On the first full moon of 2023, Peter Gabriel released 'Panopticon', the first song from his new album, i/o. The subsequent singles from the album are all due to be released on full moons, reflecting Peter's strong connection with nature and fears for destruction of the planet.

TEDDY PENDERGRASS

R&B singer and songwriter, and formerly a member of Harold Melvin & the Blue Notes.

I INTERVIEWED TEDDY ON THE PHONE. UNFORTU-
nately, we weren't able to do the interview in person but it didn't seem to matter – it was just as good.

'In my performances I don't consciously perform. I find when I consciously do it, I make mistakes. When I don't think and I just go for it, it all works out and it's basically flawless. When I second-guess it and think, "Well, what am I going to do here?" or, "What note am I going to sing?" or, "Which place am I going to move to?" Ultimately I always mess up.

'Especially rap, but all kinds of music reflect what's going on, because it's what people write about. People write about what they experience, what they see. It reflects today's society. Rap music is one of those serious art forms. I must say I'm very glad that it's uniquely a black art form that also reflects what these kids are thinking. It's an expression, and I'm glad the expression exists, which gives me an opportunity to see what's going through these kids' minds.

'Being creative is part of me; I do it at every level of life. I do it with my home, I do it with clothes, I do it with singing, with writing, with decorating the home. That is just my thing.'

Teddy died on 13 January 2010. He was fifty-nine years old. A BBC film documentary on his life was released in 2019.

JOHN LEE HOOKER

Blues guitarist, songwriter and singer.

THIS IS PART OF AN INTERVIEW I HAD WITH JOHN LEE Hooker, one of the few interviews I had to conduct on the phone. It was a pleasure and an honour to speak with him, having been a huge blues fan in my teens.

'I was aware of my music when I was about twelve. My stepfather [Will Moore] was a musician and he taught me how to play guitar in the style he played in. He played stuff that I'm playing now. My stepfather was playing with people like Blind Blake, Charley Patton and Leroy Cobb. He would go out and play in these house parties that I couldn't go to; I heard the records. My stepfather had one of those old machines that you wind up. I heard their music and I really liked what they did. I knew I wanted to be a musician and I was determined not to be a farmer.

'Sometimes when I'm playing the blues, tears come into my eyes. There's no limit to what I feel. It goes so deep.'

71

John died in his sleep at home in Los Altos near San Francisco on 21 June 2001. He was either eighty-three or eighty-eight.

PART THREE

'I always resort back to music because it doesn't have words. It's just a voice that can be understood by anyone' –

ERIC CLAPTON

ERIC CLAPTON

Guitarist, songwriter and singer, who before becoming a solo artist played in such bands as the Yardbirds, Cream, Blind Faith and Derek and the Dominos.

I FIRST MET ERIC IN 1965 WHEN I WAS SEVENTEEN AND going out with a young Mick Fleetwood. I would often see him in one of the clubs, such as the Flamingo, where he would play with John Mayall in his Bluesbreakers band, or at the Marquee or Klooks Kleek, where Mick was playing in a band called The Peter B's, with a young blues guitarist, Peter Green. I seem to remember Eric asking me to dance! I had bumped into him over the years, and then in the early seventies he went out with and later married my sister, Pattie. I lived near them with my daughters during five of those years and would often see him and Pattie at their home in Surrey. We'd watch him play at the local gigs in Cranleigh and Guildford, and then go back to their house for a night of revelry. There were times when I found him to be no different than a rather annoying but funny older brother! I interviewed him many years later. By then he was no longer with my sister and he was no longer drinking.

I wondered what this new Eric would be like as I drove into the drive of this once familiar house, a place where I had spent many inebriated evenings with him, my sister plus his old school friends from Ripley.

Tell me what your upbringing was like and where you were born.

I was born in Ripley in Surrey in 1945, near the end of the war. I was brought up by my grandparents because my mother was too young to bring me up. She was fifteen when I was born. And my father had been transferred back to Canada, being a Canadian airman. And I don't really know whether she left me in terms of abandonment or whether she was told to go. It's not very clear. I was brought up in the Church of England. It was a fairly religious sort of society in the village, and at the age of nine my mother came back to see if I was alright. That was when I found out that things were not what they appeared to be. And from then on, I had a very confused childhood. Up until then it was pretty normal, except I think the other kids knew that there was something different about me because they must have known because my name was Clapton and the people that I presumed to be my parents, which were my grandparents, were known as Clapp. It was an extremely strange coincidence because my grandmother's first husband was named Clapton and her second husband was named Clapp. I suppose the other kids might have noticed that, or at least they had heard their parents talking about it. But I wasn't aware of it until I was nine.

Did you feel different from the other kids?

I felt different from most of the other kids, but there was a little gang of about four or five of us that all seemed to have something in common in terms of being maladjusted. And most of these kids were kids that had moved in from outside the area at the age of five or six. They'd been uprooted from where they were originally from and placed in this little village and weren't at all happy with their situation. So, we seemed to have something in common. They were the kids I hung out with, and we were the first ones to start smoking and [listening] to rock and roll.

How old were you when you knew you wanted to play the guitar or have anything to do with music?

I wanted to be a musician from the minute I was born. I wanted to play anything that my parents would get for me, or my grandparents would get me, and that included drums, violin or trumpet. I actually had a violin. They couldn't raise enough money for a trumpet; it was quite an expensive item and you can't just get one in a jumble sale. I went through the whole range of instruments trying to find my niche. And I think by the time I was thirteen, I'd probably lost a bit of interest in terms of what direction to go. But when I first heard Elvis and Buddy Holly, I wanted to imitate that. So, I honed in on the guitar.

Did you feel you were encouraged?

I remember being encouraged from a very early age to do a turn, which was a big thing. Everyone would have their own song and my gran used to sing a certain song if there was a bit of a piss-up or it was Christmas or if people came round to visit. I was inevitably put up in the bay window when it was my turn, the curtain would be pulled back and I would sing 'I Belong to Glasgow', that was my turn. I was a tiny tot and that was before I was even aware of showbiz or anything like that. I came from a very musical family background. My grandmother, Rose, played the piano very well in those days. When my mother came back, she introduced jazz into the household: Benny Goodman, Harry James, swing and big-band jazz. That was very prevalent in my home when I was around nine or ten.

Did you click on that?

Yes, very much so, especially Glenn Miller.

Would you describe yourself as an outgoing kid or were you more retiring and shy?

I was an outgoing kid until the trauma and then I began to cultivate being different – I wanted to be different from everyone else. I sensed that I was so I developed the philosophy of flaunting it and that wasn't in an outgoing way, it was very introvert. I wanted to be a beatnik before beatniks were ever heard of in Ripley. I was the village beatnik.

How old were you when you started playing the guitar?

I was thirteen, but I stopped that for a while when I became very interested in art, not interested but I was very good at art and I got a scholarship to go to a school in Kingston, and I was travelling from Ripley to Kingston every morning, half working on being an artist in training, and half being interested in music. The music got the better of me in the end. I got thrown out of art school and started working professionally after a year or so with a band.

What sort of age were you when you knew that's what you were going to do?

I don't think I really knew that that would be it for life until I was about twenty, but when I started playing professionally at seventeen, even though you don't care what you're going to do at that age, I didn't care whether I was going to live beyond twenty-one. But I think I was quite serious about it so there must have been an inkling. By the time I was eighteen, I was pretty much a loner in terms of what I believed in to be musical for myself and had to be very defensive of it. I was very serious, very protective towards my musical ambitions. But I didn't come across anyone until I met Steve Winwood who was of the same mind, and about fifteen at the time. It really was that bleak in this country at that time.

Do you believe in a greater power?

Yes.

Does it connect to your creativity?

Yes, definitely. I think it's an inspiration. I pray a lot. Usually after the event or just before I'm about to get involved in something, which is going to be stressful or demanding. And that usually gets me through it. Being an alcoholic I practise the steps, which involves letting go and handing over quite a lot. On a daily basis I have to hand over some kind of problem. So, I have to have a higher power. And I don't really know what it is. I can't say whether it's Jesus or God or anything, just something more powerful than I am.

Do you believe you're here for a reason?

Yeah, I think that's what's kept me alive. I've had a lot of narrow scrapes, and they still keep coming up. Every now and then, I go through a situation which is potentially life taking. And I know that if I give in to that, or allow myself to take that kind of negative direction, that I'm wasting something very valuable.

And that isn't necessarily for my benefit but for the benefit of other people too.

Have you ever felt you've been here before?

No, I don't think so. I may have been but I don't subscribe to anything like that.

What was it like learning to play guitar? What kept you going through the learning period?

I don't know why I chose to play the blues or play rock and roll. I don't know why it settled on me in the middle of the countryside in England to be a messenger, in a way. I've got no idea. I don't really like to analyse it. Maybe I've been handed something to lead on, to carry on in this generation. I often feel a very, very strong sense of responsibility towards that, as if it's something that's not really anything to do with me. So, it would be like carrying a torch. It's more powerful than I am, and I have to kind of be a servant to it.

It's funny. I have to tell you now that, when I first thought of writing about creativity, you were the one that inspired me. Having known you for all these years, I'd always thought you had something special, you were here for a reason, but then I wondered, why would you always drink? Was it the fear of having a sort of God-given gift and how heavy that must have been at times, like touching the hem of God's garment? To numb out feeling special? That's what started it off and then it went on from there.

Very perceptive: that's what it's like. It's like staring into the face of God sometimes. It's very, very frightening. Did you ever see that film about that jazz musician, a saxophonist in Paris played by Dexter Gordon? It was called *Round Midnight*. Someone commented on him because he was always drinking, and they said, 'Why is he drinking?' And someone else replied, 'If you had to stare into the face of what he always has to go through every night and discover those kinds of truths, you would too.' It's like that, it's like staring into the face of God sometimes. It's very frightening. You're kind of naked a lot of the time and afraid of exposing yourself. You're very vulnerable.

When you're playing your guitar, do you ever have transcendent moments, where everything comes together?

Yeah, I can't really explain what it's like, except in a physical sense it's a massive rush of adrenaline which comes at certain points. Usually, it's a sharing experience. It's not something I could experience on my own. It has to be in the company of other musicians onstage and, of course, with an audience. And it's not even just the musicians, it's the whole experience of everyone that's involved in that transaction. Everyone in that building or everyone in that place seems to unify at one point and it's not necessarily me that's doing it. It might be another musician, but when you get this completely harmonious experience where everyone is actually hearing the same thing. Without any interpretation whatsoever. They're all just transporting towards the same place. And that's not very common, but it always seems to happen at least once in a show. And that's what you hope for. You may start out with a kind of framework of songs you're going to do and hope that it's going to happen in this one. And if it doesn't, you wait for the next one. You don't really know what it's composed of, it's just a kind of point where everyone's got exactly the same momentum, a lot to do with actual timing. Beyond that it's hard to describe. You can call it unity, that is very spiritual for me. Everyone is one at that specific point. Not for very long but, of course, the defeating aspect of it is that the minute you become aware of that, it's gone. It dissipates.

Music seems to be the biggest communicator of our time. I suppose the audience picks up on something that maybe they can't express for themselves, but they can feel it.

If someone puts on the radio or you put on a record, it demands your attention, and if you talk over it, you're not going to get anything out of it, and if you're walking around or drinking or doing something that deprives your attention from that music, it's the same thing. What music demands is surrender. Everyone there, at some point, are all going to surrender at exactly the same time to the same thing: musicians and people in the audience.

Do you get that feeling anywhere else in your life?

I do as an alcoholic, because that's part of the programme. You have to surrender, accept what you are and what the day's going to bring in every way. The minute you try to control the situation then you're back on the wrong path, So I have to practise it and it's very difficult.

Do you feel everyone has the potential to be creative or is it a gift?

I think everyone has that capacity, but I think the gift comes in recognising it or being able to channel it. My gift is that I have ten fingers that work, so I have that capacity and that ability, but if I didn't have those ten fingers, I wouldn't be able to play the guitar. Maybe I'd channel it somewhere else. Some people have got the gift of being able to manifest and others haven't. They're blocked in some way mentally, physically or spiritually.

What gives you the drive to create? Do you have to be in a special frame of mind when you're writing?

That's the hardest question you've given me yet. I don't know. In the past I've always put it down to emotional stress, emotional turmoil. But I think that's more like a trigger which sets off something that's actually waiting dormant. It can be triggered by any amount of outside stimulus, such as joy. A lot of people think that it has to be from something particularly nasty or a problem. It can be triggered by something a little out of the ordinary in terms of an emotional stimulus. It's something that makes your day or breaks your day.

Do you have a choice to create or was it something that just happened?

That's a valid question. I think you have a choice. And the thing is that it's all wound up in the craft itself. Because if you don't practise your craft, you deny your choice. You can have all the ability in the world but if you don't actually put it into practice, you're throwing it away. It's like being a singer and not singing, knowing you can sing. A lot of people think they can and perhaps they can, but they don't. So that's their choice.

Are you in touch with the child?

That's difficult at the moment. I'm just starting out again on the road to sobriety. So, I tend to be in a very serious frame of mind. It's kind of early days and I know from the last time I did it that you actually become very attuned to adults drinking. Drinking always brings out the child. And, unfortunately, the nasty child most of the time. But I hope I can get in touch with the child again without having to resort to alcohol.

When you first started drinking or taking drugs, did it affect your creativity, and did it enhance it or block it?

To begin with, drink is very, very baffling and cunning. It's actually got a personality of its own. Part of its trap is to open the doors to unreleased channels or rooms you hadn't explored before or allowed to be opened. A lot of my creative things came out first of all through marijuana. I started smoking when I was about eighteen or nineteen, pot or hash, and that would let out a whole string of humorous things as well as music. Then drink allowed me to become very self-pitying and opened up that whole kind of sorrowful musical side of myself. Unfortunately, after that, the booze becomes more important than the doors it's opening. So that's the trap. I think in a lot of cases people do have inhibitions about expressing themselves. Most people are very shy and very neurotic and nervous about even meeting other people but are fine after having a couple of drinks, and that's the same with being creative.

But anything that distorts your awareness or any mood-altering chemical will actually impair your thinking, because you tend to be just wanting rather than serving. You're not really in tune with anything at all other than your drug, and that works on your nervous system to a point where you are really at the mercy of it, so the only thing you can do is beg and ask all the time. This can happen with any kind of experience. At the beginning there can be an opening up and then you move to the next phase where it all becomes confused, and then the final phase is where the drug or whatever it is has actually got control of you and you've lost that original thing.

What are you feeling when you're playing?

Very, very nervous until the show has started and then I call on some reserve that is waiting inside.

I always relax after playing my first solo because singing and playing the guitar in the band is one thing – any musician worth their salt can do it – but my particular forte is to play improvised solos. Because I don't know until I've done it in front of all these people, and then I find out what sort of shape I'm in. If it's all right, then I can play; if it's not, then I'm in dead trouble because there's an hour and a half to go and it can only get worse!

Are there any particular bands you've played with that you've felt more connected as musicians than with any others? Where you're all on the same level?

I think with Cream it was like that in a different way. In one sense we were all very in tune with one another, probably like The Beatles were, where you're a little unit amongst yourselves. We talked a language that no one else understood. And if we were going to get stoned, we'd all get stoned to the same extent. And the harmony came out of that. And then jumping right up to now, the band I've had and will have again probably with Greg Phillinganes and Nathan East and either Phil (Collins) or Steve Ferrone, their awareness and their musicianship is the best I've ever come across, and their confidence too in me and themselves is the best I've ever come across. They are really very, very supportive too.

What about the music today? (1989)

There's a lot of gloss, a lot of facade, but fortunately underneath the surface there is an incredible amount of good things going on, which kind of supports all the chrome up on top. Consumer taste at the moment are people such as Madonna and all that glitzy sort of thing. It's all kind of forced, but it does rest on something that's fairly strong underneath. People who are interested in music or are interested in what is happening in a communication way will always start out with the veneer and then dip down to find out what's underneath. And they are the ones who'll get the reward. The *Ry Cooder* album, for example, is fantastic but it might not be palatable to the masses, although it's what supports the top veneer.

Have you any idea where the creative force comes from?

Other than within, no.

Have you ever felt there was a purpose to your creativity on a political, social or spiritual level?

I always lean towards the spiritual more than anything else. I don't have any interest in social issues or political issues, but even then I wouldn't choose to express anything lyrically. I always resort back to the music, because it doesn't have words, just a voice that can be understood by anyone.

Suffering with tinnitus and peripheral neuropathy, Eric has had to step back from performing at times over the last few years. However, he has been touring again recently and is set to return to Tokyo's Budokan for a six-night residency this year, which also marks his sixtieth year as a professional musician since joining the Yardbirds in 1963. His most recent album is a concert film and live album, Nothing but the Blues, *released in 2022, which features live performances from a 1994 concert at The Fillmore, San Francisco.*

BUDDY GUY

Blues guitarist, singer and songwriter.

MY INTERVIEW WITH BUDDY GUY WAS ON THE phone – another one of my favourite blues musicians and another one I felt honoured to interview.

'I used to lie and dream a lot of times that I was onstage in front of an audience. It crosses my mind now that every time I looked out at a huge audience, I remembered my dreams, when I'd wake up and didn't even know what a guitar was.

'I've been aware of my love of music ever since I was big enough to know I could take rubber bands and put two nails in the wall and just stretch them. The sound the rubber bands gave was exciting to me. I was doing something like that as far back as I can remember. I recall I was just a normal kid like anybody else, only I would always wander off from the crowd and wind up trying to get some kind of sound out of something.

'The first thing I ever learned to play was John Lee Hooker's "Boogie Chillen". I was lying down outside in Louisiana on a warm, sunny day when I dozed off to sleep. I didn't even know I was tuning the guitar, but I knew what I wanted to hear. After dozing off, I woke up and I thought, this is not a dream – I'm playing "Boogie Chillen". The positions I had my fingers in, I thought, if I turn them loose, I'll never be able to do it again. And would you believe I played that tune for five hours so my fingers wouldn't forget it! I was afraid if I missed that, I would never be able to play it again the next day, because I doubted myself as a self-taught musician at that time. It was no problem; it came again fine. I could play it the next day, because I never did put my guitar down until my mom and dad made me do the home chores. In fact, I sleep with it – that's what I do when I'm out of town now. I've got one I sleep with.

'The feeling I get when I'm playing to an audience is, "Am I reaching you?" Am I getting to these people through communication with my music? And I look out and I see a smile. Something tells me then, you've got it. But there are also days I don't get that smile. My message is not getting to you, so I've got to go back and figure how to get my message to you through my music – and that's what keeps me going with my music.

'I've never experienced drugs, but I've drunk alcohol. I don't recommend drugs and alcohol to nobody, but I think if you're going to do it, you should use common sense. The strong mind is the most important thing that we can use against whatever we deal with in this short span of lifetime we have. When I learned how to play guitar, I didn't have drugs, alcohol or nothing else. I think I was at my best as being a natural person with nothing in me, with nothing in me telling me, "You're better or you're worse." My first drink made me get the nerve to turn my face around to the audience, to not have that shyness, which led me to have one – but only one – before I play. Some people have walked up to me through my lifetime and said, "You've gotta be doing drugs to play like you play," and I say, "My music is my drugs to me.'"

Buddy Guy announced a 2023 Damn Right Farewell Tour beginning in February. At eighty-six, Buddy continues to record and tour around the world.

STEVIE NICKS

*Singer, songwriter, solo artist and member of
Fleetwood Mac.*

I FIRST MET STEVIE AND LINDSEY AT MICK'S AND MY
house in Laurel Canyon just before they both joined
Fleetwood Mac. At the time, Stevie was waiting on tables at a
smart restaurant in Beverly Hills and playing gigs at night. We
were delighted to meet her; she brought in a fresh energy that
was missing in the band, and she was very pretty and very funny.
I remember liking her immediately.

'My mom said that I started singing when I was very young.
They always had music going for me because I seemed to have
such a love for it. Even as a baby in a crib, I wanted music. My
dad's father was a country-and-western singer, so he brought
music into my life as soon as I was able to understand music at
all. I was singing duets with my grandfather when I was four. My
grandfather rode the railway trains across the country and played
in different places. He played harmonica, fiddle and guitar. He
wasn't a great musician, but he was a really good songwriter. I'm

kind of the same way. I consider myself a good songwriter, but I don't consider myself a very good musician.

'I wrote my first song on my sixteenth birthday. I finished that song hysterically crying, and I was hooked. From that day forward when I was in my room playing my guitar, nobody would come in without knocking, nobody disturbed me. My parents were very supportive and wouldn't let anyone disturb me until I came out. They'd even let me miss dinner, if necessary, it was that important. They could hear that I was working, at sixteen years old, and they would leave me alone. I started singing in assemblies at school and in folk groups. I sang whenever I could, for whatever I could possibly find to do; if it had anything to do with singing or music, I did it.

'There were times when I was between twenty and twenty-seven – before I joined Fleetwood Mac – that my dad would say, "How long are you going to do this? You have no money, you're not happy, you work constantly, you work at restaurants, you clean houses, you get sick very easily, you're living in Los Angeles, you don't have any friends, why are you doing this?" And I would say, "Because it's just what I came here to do."

'Sometimes I get a real serious idea for a song. I'll just be sitting there or looking at something, and it will come into my head. Something about those flowers over there will give me an idea. A name will come out, like "Rhiannon". Then, I'm instantly in tune that it's a song. I race to the piano. If I have an idea for the words first, I run to the typewriter. What I have is little flashes; I just see things. Without any speech at all, it just says something to me, and I'll quickly write that down.

[To capture those transient messages from the unconscious, Tony Williams told me that he readied himself to do so at the drop of a hat: "I can be sitting around and a song will just come into my head. I have a couple of micro recorders, and I'll whip one out and sing the idea. If I don't record it immediately, I'll lose it."]

'In the beginning, stimulants made you brave. You're scared to walk onstage in front of a bunch of people. Last night performing at a club in front of only two hundred people, my knees were knocking together. I was holding on to the microphone and my hand was shaking because I was so nervous. The old days to get away from that you have a drink, or whatever anybody does, and you got brave and so you don't have to experience that terrible fear. I get terrible stage fright . . . where I'm very, very nervous. The last ten minutes before I go on, my hands are really shaking to the point of having a lot of trouble working with my make-up or anything. It hits me about fifteen minutes before we go on. I'm almost sick to my stomach and it's difficult for me. It used to be that you'd have a shot of vodka and tonic and you'd calm down.

'But the second I'm onstage I realise that I'm not nervous any more. I think I'm going to be nervous all the way through the song, but I'm not. The second I walk out, and the second I start to sing, it just goes away, and I'm totally confident. I know now that once I'm out there, I'm fine. That's probably why in the old days people did start doing drugs and stuff because they were simply afraid. Then that becomes a habit; you think you absolutely can't do it without it.

'A lot of us realise we're really lucky to be alive. The ones of us who did make it pretty much cherish the fact that we are alive. You have to learn if you can't depend on yourself without chemicals, you might as well stop doing it and go to something else, because it isn't worth dying for.

'As far as being creative, chemicals made you feel that you

were braver, so you were more likely to say more, to write down more, to give away more of the secret or to maybe say too much, and that's the vicious circle of drugs and alcohol. You think it's making you better and in the long run it's not. It's taking away the actual essence of what you started out to do.

'It's hard to adjust back; it's hard for everybody. Some people have and some haven't, and I wonder sometimes who will be the ones . . . I know we will lose a few more and I think, thank God it's not going to be me. Because I'm definitely going to be sitting in my rocking chair on my porch somewhere when I'm eighty years old, and I'm not going to be one of those people who have a TV special on, and people sit around and cry. But it is difficult, and probably will always be difficult to accept this whole life in a different way. Because for so long I lived under that dream cloud, dream-child world of different kinds of drugs.

'I recently wrote six songs when I went home to Phoenix for about fifteen days. I go from writing in my journal to typing out some ideas on the typewriter. I make it into a full-on stanza poem. It's really fun for me because I just put on music that I like, that's got a good beat and makes me feel good, and then I type along to the beat. I just read the words and put it into rhyme and then I'll take that paper to the piano and just start writing, and it either happens or it doesn't. Usually, if I get it pretty complete on the paper before I get it to the piano, then it's usually really easy. If I go to the piano without anything, with just an empty piece of paper and a pencil, then it's harder. But I will do that sometimes. I'll just sit down and play a chord and I'll just write a line, like say, "The white-winged dove", then I'll play a chord, or a couple of chords and I'll start humming something.

'I have all my writing tapes, where you hear the very beginning, where I started with "Gold Dust Woman" or "Dreams", and you hear them evolve. All it is, is a trial-and-error thing, and if you're determined enough. I feel that you have to keep doing it and not give up. I tell people all the time that you should keep a journal, even if it's just, "I had a terrible day today and I don't want to talk about it, love Stevie," or, "I dreamt last night . . ." Even if it's just three sentences, because at the end of five or six days, you would have created a habit and you will find that over a month you have a whole story growing. Whether it's just for your own memories, so you can go back and look at it at any age. Anyone can be creative if they want to.

'If I've done something that I thought was good that day, then I can relax. If I haven't done anything that I feel is very special, then I have a lot of trouble sleeping – I feel almost guilty. Sometimes I'll get out of bed in the middle of the night and go into my office and put the paper in the typewriter and get out my books that are inspirational to me, Oscar Wilde, Keats, Canadian poets, European poets, and I'll just open a page and read something, and I'll say, "Okay, this is my information for today, this is what is supposed to come through to me today," and I'll close the book, so I'll never be able to find that page again, and I'll think about it for a while, and then I'll probably write for one or two hours, then I'll be able to go back to bed. I'll take my writing to bed with me and put it right by my pillow, so when I wake up the next morning, I can read it.

'When you come up with an idea you think is magnificent, or you sit down and play a piece of music that you know is going to turn into an incredible song, you walk away feeling worthwhile. Every day I feel I have to do something, whether it's to write a paragraph or sit at the piano for five minutes or go to the studio for a little while. If I don't feel I've done something worthwhile every day, then I feel worthless. I feel always that I have to hold up my end of the bargain, that I was given something by God, and He asks only that I give Him back something.'

As well as her work with Fleetwood Mac, Stevie Nicks also continues to tour as a solo artist.

PAUL KANTNER

A founding member of Jefferson Airplane and Jefferson Starship, a singer, songwriter and guitarist.

I **FIRST MET PAUL IN A LITTLE 'HEAD SHOP' ON GRANT** Avenue. It was the spring of 1967 and I had recently arrived from London for my six-month trip to San Francisco, with no idea of flower power, Haight-Ashbury or love-ins. I'd recently been introduced to a father and son who owned a head shop and I would often sit in their little den, writing poetry or chatting to their friends when they came to visit and score hash! It was curtained off from the front of the shop. Chocolate George, a Hells Angel, was there one evening, drinking his carton of milk chocolate. Paul arrived the following evening and, after chatting for a while, offered to drive me home to the place I shared with my friend, Judy Wong. As I got out of the car, he asked if he could see me again . . . that was the beginning of my first nineteen-year-old major crush on someone who was always on the road! I met up with him many years later in L.A. as we sat cross-legged on the carpet of a friend's house to interview him for the book. The crush had long since gone but it was nostalgic to see him.

'Stuff comes, and sometimes you can't write it fast enough. Sometimes the song is so good, and you're out somewhere and you start hearing this song. Your one instinct is to go write it down, but if you do that, the song is not the same as just sitting there and listening to it; it comes in and it goes out. And if you try to capture it, you can't. It's like a child's first birthday party. You could spend all your time taking videotapes and pictures, but you'd miss the whole party, 'cause you're wound up with all the buttons and machines instead of just sitting there and enjoying it. Other songs, you can catch. You have your tape recorder or you wake up in the middle of the night. It comes in a thousand different ways: sometimes a word, a line, a musical phrase, or an idea at a time. Other things come just full-blown. I used to try to capture them and you look back and they're gone. So I learned to just enjoy them. After it's done you try to capture it, but don't try to capture it in the middle.

'I was a California, late fifties, early sixties kid who got stimulated by the beatnik movement, early jazz, John Coltrane kind of stuff. We came out of the fifties, which was really a suppressive time. It was a very Nancy Reagan kind of time, where everything was "perfect" in America and nothing was wrong, but all of us could see something was wrong and we didn't know what it was. It was like James Dean in *Rebel Without a Cause*: just these confused children running around, not having the slightest idea what the fuck was going on. The social movement, the folk music movement, came out of this fifties "white bread America". We were middle-class kids with no problems compared to other people in the world. We weren't rich but we weren't poor, [we were] comfortable, we went to college. We were just drifting without any idea of what we wanted to do. All these jobs looked tedious and dull and boring; nothing shined. Then you saw these people making music and social movements circling around them from the peace movement to the civil rights movement. American folk music, Pete Seeger, Kingston Trio, Joan Baez, Bob Dylan – that whole thing before [the return of] rock 'n' roll [in] '61, '62, '63.

'I had taken piano lessons in sixth grade to get out of math class, but it was real dreary and boring. I didn't go back to music till I was twenty-one, when it meant something. It wasn't just music, but [it had to do] with the folk music and the civil rights movement in the United States, particularly in the late fifties and the early sixties, and just seeing people onstage get away with all this stuff, thinking, that looks good. It was as much a social phenomenon as a music phenomenon. It's like John Lennon said, "There's a whole thing going on – and it's also a great way to meet girls." It was a great socialisation process – you're just thrown into this cauldron, very strange people. It attracts all sorts of interesting people, who have something to say, funny, witty, bright, searching, whatever. It seemed to be a better cauldron than my father's office for talking about interesting things and pursuing interesting ideas, just the draw of doing that.

'It's like if you've sprained your ankle that day or hurt your knee, all pain leaves your body and you focus on what you're doing onstage. You just focus in on it and you go into a zone, almost like voodoo. You just do stuff naturally. I like to play with my eyes closed. I have to force them open to know there's people out there! Generally, you just go outside of yourself. It's almost like astral travelling, although you don't get out and look down on yourself but it's just about at the bridge of that. You feel that you almost could. There's this big circle of something between you and the audience. If you play well, they really enjoy it and give something intangible back to you. That charges you up to play even better, which makes them get even more ecstatic. It's like a circle of energy. It's as close as I get to religion, and it's what religion should be about: much more exhilarating, much more unity with the people all around you, much more human touch going on. It's done just through people. It's been done around ancient bonfires at harvest festivals, among people who've worked all season picking crops, in ancient times, dancing and singing, and in voodoo rites, as well as among Christian fundamentalists, where they fall back and people have to catch them.

'In our generation, some drugs got out of control and were bad; some were quite good. It affects people differently. As it goes into artistry, it probably helps people achieve moments that they might not have otherwise achieved. I don't want to put this out as a prescription to indiscriminate drug use, hoping for the creative. You've got to be creative and work at that too. You can't just sit down and smoke a joint or drink a bottle of wine and expect creativity to just happen. You have to have something else before it. Some people use marijuana to loosen them up, some people use alcohol, some people use meditation, some people use jogging. Whatever gets you through the night, in moderation.

'Particularly in our generation, drugs presented a real problem with moderation, and they got out of control, as alcohol did with our parents' generation and some of our own generation as well. LSD was as close to God as I ever got – one step above the rock 'n' roll experience. It adds another element to it and drops a lot of doors that you normally keep closed. You just got close to people in ways our parents' generation wouldn't have even considered, would have been horrified by. [Someone] pointed out at one point that we took it upon ourselves to test ourselves with all these drugs, having no other tests to go through the fire.

'Everyone has elements of creativity. Everybody isn't a great piano player or great singer. Some people have to study it, and some people can't get it after studying for a hundred years. But everybody has some capability of being creative. What does the word "creative" mean? Expressing yourself in some fashion beyond your normal workday. In Nicaragua, when I was there, they encouraged everyone to write poetry. It was a government programme to teach the people how to write, to express what they felt about their life, to examine it, and to see what could be done about it in tangible, practical terms. I have books of poetry from Central America. It's some of the most beautiful and some of the most mundane, but the fact is that somebody who just picked corn all day and went to sleep and got up and picked corn all day for thirty years can all of a sudden write beautiful poetry.

'Today, various different musicians speak for various different groups in society. Before The Beatles – and even with The Beatles – it was like one large body. Then it fragmented, like a flower shooting pollen all over the place for new flowers to grow. Some of the new flowers are pretty ugly and some of them are quite beautiful. There's stuff to be had everywhere. There's just so much more of it, you're almost overwhelmed.'

Paul died on 28 January 2016, aged seventy-four, after a heart attack suffered a few days earlier.

STEPHEN STILLS

Guitarist, songwriter, singer and solo artist.
A member of Crosby, Stills and Nash, he
co-founded Buffalo Springfield and Manassas.

STEPHEN WAS ALWAYS ONE OF MY FAVOURITE GUITAR players, ever since I saw him playing in his band, Manassas, at the Rainbow Theatre in London, 1972. Many years later, in the mid-eighties, my then-husband, Ian Wallace, was playing drums for Crosby, Stills and Nash, and so Stephen would often come round to our house in Sherman Oaks for supper, or we would go over to his house. I met up with him again to do this interview in 1990, curious to know what made this musician tick. It was five minutes into the interview that I noticed the record button was not lit up (every interviewer's nightmare!), but he laughed and started again!

'My dad had a tremendous collection of old jazz records; he was an agent when he was in college. My mom used to sing in the church choir and had a beautiful contralto voice. I started playing drums, then piano, then bass, and a little trombone. Guitar was later in the game; I'd already been playing music since I was about six, but didn't get a guitar until I was fourteen. My dad bought me a set of drums when I was eight, because I was going to tear up the furniture. He even bought a guitar for this kid I wanted to form a band with.

'I'm so far ahead of what I'm doing when playing the guitar that I'm very surprised when I haven't made a mistake. I'm really concentrating, and then all of a sudden, it's so relaxed and so easy that I cannot make a mistake. All I'm doing is creating. You've got to give yourself to the music, give it all up so you can become one with it. There's so much going on at the same time, I'm at maximum output. It's to the point where I can be doing all that and daydreaming at the same time.

'All of a sudden, it's all done. And I try to sing, but I can't, because I'm weeping, because I'm so moved. Somehow, I've got it all right and I've said just what I wanted.

'The peak occurs when everyone else is right there with me and totally concentrating on what I'm doing. I can just barely hint at something that I'm playing, and if everybody is concentrating on what I'm playing, then the rest of the band shifts with me, rather than being self-involved. That hasn't happened for a while because the discipline in music has really gotten out of hand. Nobody pays attention to what people are playing so much; they're all into themselves. I'm from the jazz school, that's why I love playing with Ian Wallace so much, because he'll come right with me. And it's rare. The better the musician, that's all they'll do. They give themselves to the music, rather than showing off. You've got to give it all up; you've got to become at one with it. And the only thing that's important is that the noise you make is really good and fits.

'To experience that feeling, a band of any kind has to be paying attention to what I'm doing and vice versa. That's what made Buffalo Springfield so special. Why this particular group of cats was so good live was that we would get that every night. It's turning yourself inside out and becoming a total player. I experienced it with [Jimi] Hendrix a number of times. The great players know that; they don't even consider themselves a player until they can do that. It really is a one-pointed focus with other musicians.'

Stephen plans to release, for the first time, live recordings of his concert in Berkeley, California in 1971. Known as The Memphis Horns Tour, it was his first solo tour and supported his second album. He hasn't played music on the road since 2018, but he gets together with fellow musicians for special performances. He also jams privately with Neil Young every week.

PART FOUR

'Everyone has the potential to be creative, but they don't all have the drive' –

RONNIE WOOD

JACOB COLLIER

Twenty-eight-year-old producer, multi-instrumentalist and composer, Jacob is recognised by audiences, critics and fellow musicians alike as one of the most gifted young artists of modern times. He already has a seemingly endless list of achievements including five Grammy wins – which saw him become the first British act in history to win four Grammys for each of his first four albums – along with eleven Grammy nominations including Album of the Year in 2021.

THAT NATURAL PULL TOWARDS MUSICAL COLLABOR-ation went on to inform Collier's plans for his ensuing four-part Djesse series of albums. Alongside the upcoming release of Djesse Vol. 4, he has plans for future projects centred on solo piano, orchestras and film scoring, while he has written for a forthcoming West End musical on the life of opera singer Luciano Pavarotti.

Watching Jacob on YouTube conducting the audience as they sang at the O2 was like watching 50,000 people transcend into one enormous, finely tuned instrument: the voice of the people, all together and in harmony. How powerful the sound and I wondered what Jacob must feel as this exciting barrage roars out in harmony, filling the air and creating a connection to every single person in the hall. All eyes are on him as he bounces along the stage, striding from left to right, his arms flailing in the air or lowered down to the ground, while the audience responds, watching his every move like hawks. His angelic choir is guided by his hands, how high or low, fast or slow, he plays them like an instrument. I couldn't wait to interview him – not easy to catch as he travels around the world. But finally, through Zoom, we were able to speak when he was comfortably nestled in his childhood room surrounded by instruments of every kind.

What was your childhood like?

I spent a lot of my childhood in this very room. Actually, it was in this room that I first began to explore music as a language, and have continued to do ever since I was a wee lad. Throughout my life, I've brought things in here to explore – things that weren't always real to the outside world but were intensely real to me. As a child, I had a spectacularly vivid inner world, which I was given a great deal of permission to explore by my mother, Suzie, who raised me and my two sisters largely as a single parent. She enabled me to open my inner eye, or you could say, look in my peripheral vision and reach for things that were slightly intangible. I was given the space to play in this room – my favourite room in the world. My father walked away from my family when I was ten years old. It was hugely challenging for all of us, but looking back I think it created quite an interesting dynamic rift in my childhood fabric.

On the one hand, there was my exceptionally open-minded, strong female energetic force of my mother, which was infinitely inspiring, but on the other, I didn't really have a male role model to parry against, play with, push against or be shown how to hold myself as a young man in the world. Many of those challenges I've had to face by myself over the years. I think, when a child experiences trauma like that, it brings up many different kinds of questions. There's a vividness to such questions, which spring from a lack of something integral. For me such questions ignited a great deal of creative questioning in a sense – and a desire to push and discover on my own terms. I really wanted to find my own voice – to expand, explore and play. Those were the kinds of forces I was dealt with early on, and am still grappling with today, and I'm very grateful for all of them.

Your mother was obviously a great influence in your creativity?

Yeah, big time. My mother still is to this day. She is an astounding musical force of nature in my life, and in many other people's lives as well. She's a violinist by trade, and also a phenomenal conductor. Some of my earliest memories are of sitting on her lap watching the violin being played above me – an amazing feeling. Being a part of the music . . . feeling that music is able to come from around you was wonderful! Another crucial image for me was watching her conduct the chamber orchestra at the Royal Academy of Music in London, where she still conducts to this day. It's been a similar orchestral format for the last three decades, but watching her physically spring into form, and watching musicians spring into form themselves as a result of her physical motion and emotional intelligence, was such a meaningful connection for me to make. You can sit and make music in your own world, and all may be well – but if you really do music, fully and deeply, then you're playing through other people in some way . . . extending each gesture through your own senses, and into the arms, ears and mouths of others. I actually think it's taken a long time for me to come around to that in a practical sense, because I began my musical journey by doing everything by myself, in this very room. I would sit and jam on a bass, a guitar, drums and my voice – layering all the vocal parts myself, one by one.

When did you first start doing that?

When I was five, I got a Casio keyboard called a CTK-611. It was just so amazing for me as a kid to be able to really get to know music through that lens. You've got a hundred rhythms and two hundred sounds, so I had access to all sorts of weird sounds . . . tubular bells, dulcimers, timbales and all sorts of things. I would never have had the chance to mess about with those in real life, but I had the sounds right at my fingertips! So, I think I fell in love with the idea that I could play with all these elements and make them my own, that the art is in the combining of things. Even if there were things I didn't quite understand, they were worthy of being investigated. I believe that children create as many ideas as there are ears to hear them, in a sense, and using whatever materials there are around them. With permission to experiment, they can go all the way.

I grew up listening to many different kinds of music, even at that age. Lots of Earth, Wind & Fire, Stevie Wonder, Bobby McFerrin and Queen, but also Bartok, Stravinsky and Britten. In my mind, there was a constant alchemy between all these different worlds and forces. I packed them into my little Casio keyboard because I could sequence on the keyboard. You could layer up snare drums, bass drums, hi-hat . . . you name it! By the age of seven, I'd got hold of Cubase, which is a music recording software on a desktop computer, and that was a thrill because then I could visually design what I was hearing beyond the little Casio screen. I could move things around with my fingers and things. On my eleventh birthday, I got my hands on Logic, and that was a huge moment – I still use Logic to this day! I also got an SM58 microphone, which is an affordable, classic mic on which I recorded everything for the decade following that. Until I was twenty, it was just this one SM58, me and Logic in this very room. So now, the only limitations were the limits of my imagination.

I think when you're a child and you're given permission to dare to imagine things, as I was – not necessarily at school, but I definitely was at home – there is a kind of dizzying infinity to everything. I could go anywhere! I could move into any genre, use any sound I could dream of, use any musical devices, and my one job was to just make the music that I wished existed. I would think to myself, I wish this sound existed. How can I make that sound? That was what I chased after for so many of my teenage years using Logic, which I still use today. In many ways, my process hasn't changed much. In other ways, it's changed a great deal.

You were so young to be part of this amazing world and, as you say, all the different genres too.

It was fascinating! Even clicking through rhythms on a keyboard, I had bossa nova, rock and roll, classical waltz, polka . . . all these great little examples of things.

Was there a time when you thought, I want to play the piano or the guitar myself?

Well, I didn't get to explore either of those deeply until I was about fourteen or fifteen. I had singing lessons as a young boy, but otherwise no formal training until then. I had lots of experience singing in classical operas and such, which was an amazing time. There was one opera I was in called *The Turn of the Screw*, which is by Benjamin Britten, a chamber opera, and it's actually a pretty horrifying story. My character of Miles, the little boy, has to do some quite musically adventurous things, but with that strange kind of veiled innocence of a boy treble, always just a boy but musically kind of hardcore. I really got a kick out of that experience. I learned how to sing by supporting from my diaphragm, and how to breathe properly. That was the one thing I had lessons on. I remember my mother saying, when I was much younger, 'How would you feel about piano lessons?' because I was spending so much time at the piano. I remember knowing I didn't want that yet, and that I would rather explore on my own terms.

And then later on, in my mid teens, I enrolled at the Royal College of Music Junior Department as a composer, a double bass player and a percussionist, not as a piano player at all. There was one teacher there, Shirley Smart, who heard me play the piano once after class and said, 'You know, you should really meet my friend Kit Downes, who's an amazing jazz piano player.' I remember thinking, that would be something! So I went to meet Kit Downes, and Kit opened a number of doors for me in terms of pianistic possibility – voicings, triads, extended dominant chords, and all these things which I sort of half-knew but didn't really understand with my analytical brain.

I wasn't really interested in music theory at all growing up, and this was an entry point that I felt I could get behind. There was another piano player whom I really idolised at that time, called Gwilym Simcock. I went to him thinking, 'Oh, this is going to be cool, we're going to be doing some crazy extended jazz harmony stuff, and get into a groove'. But in truth, after hearing me play, Gwilym's main piece of advice was, 'Jacob, you should really practise some scales.' I didn't yet understand some pretty fundamental concepts at that time – such as that if you put your thumb underneath the finger as you play a scale it works more smoothly . . . very basic things! Sitting down and doing a bit of scales practise over the following few months ended up being a very important, vivid enlivenment of my piano playing. I think that was the first time I thought, okay . . . perhaps I'm a piano player!

At the same time, I was also doing gigs on the double bass and singing with a folk band that my mother was in, alongside two of her very old friends, an accordion player and a saxophone player. I was beginning to understand what it meant to do gigs – which was great for me at that time. I think between the double bass in the folk band and the piano in the jazz world (which I eventually went on to study at the Royal Academy of Music for a couple of years before I departed halfway through the programme), I cobbled together a kind of understanding of music that I could quantify in a way, a lot of which had previously just been dormant in my imagination. I think, as is always the case, certain things become clearer and then certain things become opaque the more you learn. But discovering – oh, here is major and minor, and diminished, and augmented, and triads and all that stuff . . . I loved the language. In a sense, I also felt that the mystery of it got deeper, and was even more important to peer into and discover that – because that was the reason I first started. It wasn't because I was interested in arpeggios, it was because I was interested in goosebumps.

Did any of your music or songs come to you in dreams? Is your dream life part of this?

That's a fascinating question. I've never had one of those literary experiences you hear about: 'I had a dream where the whole piece appeared in my head, and I woke up and wrote it down.' I've definitely found myself with melodies when in certain physical locations, and with people in places that spark. Or a shape that will begin to take form . . . Usually, it's just the gestation of an idea that can happen in dreams, but then I wake up. Even three weeks ago, I was dreaming very heavily about my secondary school, which was a surprise as I hadn't thought of my secondary school for a while, but there I was, night after night walking the same corridors. I think something must have gone down there that I wanted to return to, and it was actually the thinking about that and those spaces that caused me to write certain music a few weeks ago and imagine music in a certain way. So, I think the life of dreams and the life of the waking time are very connected . . . Though I've never had that crazy experience where it's all there in a flash. I hear about it, and it sounds amazing.

One thing I will say is I've become very interested in the idea of alpha state, the state that you go into just before you sleep and just when you wake up. I've read somewhere that very young children are constantly in a state where they can receive the world with less of a left brain going on . . . more aware. I'm a very late sleeper. I'll frequently go to bed at 5am or 6am and wake up at 2pm. I think one of the reasons for that is I'm chasing that edge. It's the gap between waking and sleeping, where one is so fertile for ideas, that I tend to chase, and I chase my hours later and later, and then I have to do a hard reset. I definitely find myself in bed right before sleep, normally more before sleep than after sleep, and it's when I'm drifting off, that I think, 'That's it! I can join that together with that . . . what if I did *this*?' I think there's a magical zone there. So the kind of sleeplessness of ideas, and chasing that alpha state, is very important for me, and finding ways to bottle those ideas up without imprisoning them. There's an art to that. I think that if you write down everything you're thinking and you over-articulate an idea, it also dies. It's almost like you have to half-articulate the idea so that when you wake, there's still room for it to be imagined further.

I do feel through interviewing musicians and artists, that there's a much more porous connection between the conscious and the unconscious, often the unconscious showing itself through dreams, using dreams as a channel.

I completely agree. There are some days I think when . . . and I've spoken to all sorts of musical friends, artists and people I look up to about this . . . there are certain days where you're in alpha state for the whole day. It's like you're tapped into a higher state of some kind, and it's almost like you have access to different portions of your frequency band. I often think about this. When you buy a good microphone, it comes with what's called a frequency response graph. It's a little sheet of paper with a shape that says: this microphone best receives *these* frequencies, and there are these other ones that it's not so good at. I'm speaking right now into a Neumann U87 which has a very particular high end, so it's quite clear and also quite bright. These mics are actually lovely, but the high mids and lower end can be problematic if it gets really billowy because it can blow up a little bit. I think this is a good metaphor for internal creative conditions.

It's like . . . every day I wake up with a different frequency response, and there's a fundamental frequency that's like the real reality, whatever that is, and then overtones of that. I think all of us in life are constantly interacting with different parts of this. I think musicians, as you say, live a lot of their lives up in the strange upper echelons of being half here and half not here. A lot of us have trouble being in the real world and interacting with the real world in a literal sense. I definitely feel like that to a certain degree. I think that it's easy to confuse reality with the imagination – the line is blurry, which is a process so crucial for writing, creating and performing music. It's more problematic for more ordinary occurrences in life and sometimes the straddling of those two worlds can be very dynamic and difficult for musicians.

That's why it's amazing that you have your room because it's like a womb. That's where you can actually hold it all.

Yes! When I come in here, I always feel safe.

Do you believe in a greater power?

I would say so. I wouldn't necessarily call that power a God, although I'm becoming more open-minded to what that could mean. 'God' is simply a word, and every word is a symbol anyway, not the actual thing it stands for. I would probably describe it as something like the Universe at play.

I think that we as musicians draw, in a particular way, from what it feels like to hold that power within us. I don't believe by any stretch of the imagination that this is an access limited to musicians, but I think that we practise it often. When you step out onstage, you ask . . . how's the Universe today? How can I find that force? It's the part of you that belongs to everybody and part of everybody that belongs to you. I would say it's an abstract, ever-changing force. I think that often it can be a cause for people to come together in astounding, beautiful ways – and can clearly be problematic as well, when mispackaged or mishandled. I think that we human beings are strange, flawed creatures and also very beautiful. I think the way some people have of elevating such power to be this grand paternal lording figure, who makes judgements and organises hell and heaven and punishes for sin . . . I'm completely not a subscriber. I think that living your life for a greater purpose than yourself is the whole point, and can happen whether or not you believe in a God figure. Again, I think that music can give us access to that. It offers us a chance to gather together and then decide what matters the most, once that assembly has taken form. That's a real privilege.

I wonder about the greater power, or as you say, Universe, or whatever one wants to call it. Does that connect to your creativity? Do you ever write a song or put a piece of music together and then get that feeling of being in a zone where it's not even you any more? It's something that's coming through you?

I would definitely say so. Again, I would equate those moments with the moments of alpha state, where I feel almost half asleep, and I don't know how I'm doing this, but I'm doing it. There have been some amazing moments, both in this room and on the stage, like that. I suppose you could call it divine inspiration, that something will occur through you. The 'what if I . . . 'moment – trusting that. That's the magic. I do feel like sometimes people hold too tightly to the idea of 'something took hold of me, and it was a mystery!' because I think a lot of the magic that we hold as humans is in our humanity and it's in our design. But a lot of the good stuff happens when we let go of control.

I have some issues with the idea of God as the controlling figure that we all must fear – but if it's an amount of that which gets you to the place of letting go – the 'I'm being held by God'- if that gets you there, then, hallelujah! Whatever does it for you. That letting go . . . there have been moments in my life that have astounded me internally, and also when I've observed other people in this state . . . it's the most beautiful, unbelievable thing to bear witness to. It sometimes feels a shame to say that a person experiencing that has been blessed by a mysterious force that no one can understand. It's more challenging and more ambitious to think, 'I have access to that too . . . what's my version of that connection, and how do I open myself up to letting go of the control, or trying to make all these elements fit together, so that I may be guided by whatever it is?'

I'm very curious. I was watching you on YouTube conducting an audience, and it just seems to come so easily to you. It's like watching a dance. What does that feel like when you've got that many people and the sound you're creating and conducting is coming towards you like a tsunami of sound? What does that feel like?

It's really beautiful. I feel very big and very small at the same time. I feel big because I'm extending my limbs so far. Sometimes in these big rooms, or outdoors, I have to extend over many hundreds of metres to communicate an intention. I also feel small, because I'm not doing anything musically with my voice. I'm not singing. I'm silent. I think there's something amazing about the feeling of only being able to speak through the voices of others in that moment. I don't have a microphone turned on, or anything. It's just me, my hands and the people. It's such a feeling. I feel like it's a gift that I stumbled across, because I never really planned it out. I never sat at home and thought, I'm going to make a big choir out of my audiences, to organise a way for them to sing in improvised three-part counterpoint, in real time. It was one of those moments onstage where I just . . . had an idea. It happened spontaneously in San Francisco, in 2019. It was the end of the show, during the encore, and I was finishing the song. My audience tends to be quite musical in general – and so they sang this lovely three-part triad at the end of my song. I thought, oh, that's so nice, and then something clicked and I thought, okay, so, you're there, and you're there, and you're there, and then suddenly I realised, what happens if I just move one of those notes up? And they moved to a higher note! Oh! I thought. This is insane. Then I was off, walking them up and down all over the shop. Over the years, especially last year in particular, I've really taken that simple idea and run with it. The truth is . . . you can take it so far out, and people follow if you believe in them. You can even leave one key centre and enter a different tonality entirely. It's a whole different way of creating – and the only job I have is to give people permission, and be their guide. They do the rest. It's extraordinary what people are capable of if they just have the belief that they can do it. If I stood onstage and thought. 'Oh, is this going to work? I don't know . . .' then it wouldn't work. I have to believe it's going to work, and when I do – it really does.

So, you're in tune. You're completely in tune with them.

Exactly. It's a bit like meditation, because I can't be anything other than completely aware of the exact moment I am in – that two-second radius or so. If people are distracted or looking around or whatever, then I have to be even more of a clear magnet to the intention – I play that by ear. There are some gigs, especially at festivals, where I have to reach people all the way in the back, and they're distracted. You can't do that by shouting at them, 'Do this!' because that's distracting in itself, from the music. I have to be really clear and precise, without saying a word. The thing I've realised in doing this is that it feels like I've always known how to do it. For a moment I think I wondered where that came from – and then I remembered back to being two years old and watching my mum conduct the orchestra at the Royal Academy of Music, and I thought, well, of course I know how to do this because I've watched the master at work! And of course, it's a very different world. My mum conducts exquisite classical repertoire, and I'm kind of making my repertoire up as I go along, because these sorts of things haven't been attempted on a mass scale like this before – there is no repertoire. But I've come up with the basis of a language, through trial and error, where 'up' and 'down' are certain motions, and if I want to move an even smaller distance, I use only my wrist, up and down.

I find it so moving that they're all strangers, that they've never met before and may never meet again, and they've come from all walks of life. The reality is that everyone in the world has a voice, a different flavour of voice, and when you bring all those voices together it's the voice of all of us, and that voice is, to me, far more interesting than my own singular voice. The idea of combining all these people together, just for a moment, in a troubled world when moments where we can all agree on things are seldom. I think music does make us a doorway – to open our hearts to things. If you want to change somebody's mind, which many people do, about many things, you need to move them somehow. For example, climate change . . . People have been trying to do that with facts and figures for the last four decades. People are not moved by things like that. It doesn't make any difference to their hearts, but music and art can climb right into the heart, and if you can move people there, and join people together from there, then they can go out and move people too. It spreads. So, I take my job very seriously in that way. I think that as a musician, I have a really amazing opportunity to access the hearts, and therefore minds, of people – the spirits of people. The audience choir feels to me like one of life's most synergistic moments, where we really are a common intention, and I'm as much guided by them as they are guided by me.

I love it. Did you ever reflect . . . 'Why me? Why me, to be given the chance to do that?'

Every day there are moments of that. It's always impossible to plan what's going to be true for you, and it's always hard to know why certain people, certain things and certain events come into your life. I think of myself as much as a conduit for other people to manifest themselves as I do for my own manifestation of myself . . . Increasingly, I'd say. I suppose the sort of illusion, or you could say disease, of the way we think now is it's so individualistic. It's 'I am me, and I have my vision, and I'm achieving all this for me . . .'

I think of the things I've had access to as immense privileges as an individual, but also as opportunities to bring other people into those spaces, give them visibility of those spaces, and invite them in. Pretty quickly, as you rise up in the industry, you realise – no one knows what's going on. No one knows what they're doing. You know that there's no such thing as a professional musician who finally grows up and just knows what direction to take. I feel one of my main motivations is to show people it's fine not to know what they're doing, that it's not a good enough reason not to start creating. No one knows what they're doing when they start. You don't create to be good at something; you create to express where you are and how you see things. I suppose I think of myself as a sort of connective tissue between lots of different things I really care about. There are definitely moments where I think, gosh, what an amazing privilege to be able to stand onstage and conduct an audience, or to accept a Grammy, or to create a song that I love with people I respect. Every moment that my eyes or ears are opened further is a chance for me to open the eyes and ears of other people, and so it doesn't feel like an isolated journey for me. I do take it seriously to share and give as much as I can to the people around me. I can't help it. Over the years, I've loved talking about the process of making music as much as making it, and answering all sorts of weird and wacko musical questions from people all over the world. I think there's a part of my essence that I just can't help but explore. That feeling of learning something new and expanding . . . it's a feeling I get high on. The older I get, the more I get to be a student, really, and the more access I have to things that can teach me deeper things.

How different is the music world today, in your generation, compared to, say, the sixties, seventies, eighties?

I think it's easy for us younglings to herald the sixties and seventies as the truly great time for music, and I don't think that's necessarily fair, but I do think there was something crystalline about it. It was exactly the right amount of technological friction, musical friction and political friction for all that music to be born. We're so grateful for that. It's interesting, in certain respects, how much less friction there is than there used to be – way more access to things, more access to music, access to infinite toolkits, access to people, millions of people at the touch of a button. Then there's also so much MORE friction, I think, just because everyone's in constant crisis all the time, and we're all so distracted, and turned against each other by the media. There's just so much going on, so much to grapple with. It's an interesting sort of paralysis, but also an opportunity, and I think that's what music sounds like nowadays in a sense . . . at least all the most interesting music.

There will always be people who are reverent of things that have come before and don't want to evolve things forward. There will always be people who want to essentially fit in and follow all the rules – to be liked and accepted. I think then there are the people who don't care about fitting in per se, but want to find a way to stretch the existing norm into a new place because they're curious. It's kind of fashionable to be revolutionary on the surface nowadays, which doesn't really work for creating meaningful stories. All these so-called irreverents, who stand for this and against that, where this is wrong and this is right, and all that.It's dangerous, as it can become chatter. Sometimes the most irreverent thing you can possibly do is just be completely present and joyful to be alive, and not try to fight anything – not even yourself. That's the thing that no one wants you to believe, but it's always available to you.

I think there are people right now who are making music I could barely imagine ten years ago. It's so exciting to see. I mean, electronically, the kinds of sounds we can make, the ways we can combine things. As a maker of music, there's just no end to sonic recipes and different kinds of alchemy. If, fifty or forty years ago, you wondered what would happen if you combined the sound of a tubular bell with a vibraphone, to be used as a hand clap, with a saucepan lid . . . whatever *that* sound is, I think it would only have been possible for a very few people to have access to, such as film composers or completely wild maverick musicians who were off their rocker. Now I can make that sound in ten seconds . . . right here! I can hear what that sounds like, and that's such an amazing thing. Nowadays I think it's just a matter of finding different kinds of limitations to push against, but it's all the same questions we're asking; 'Why are we here?', 'What's it all for?', 'What happens when we bring people together . . . why do it?' I think questions are always so much more important than answers, and I believe that music is capable of asking the most profound questions. I don't know, but I wouldn't say music's any better now than it was in the sixties and seventies. It's different. I think a lot of the songs from that time are untouchable and will never be beaten, because we're just not there any more. I think it must have been a ravishingly thrilling time to be a creative person, with all of its own challenges to boot. I think it's of paramount importance to be asking the questions, pushing the boundaries and trying to distil this crazy, chaotic world into salient forms, that can move people. I mean, there's never been a more important time for that than right now.

I wanted to ask you how you feel when on the verge of creating something, but talking to you, it seems like it's ongoing pretty much all the time. Just like a child playing with all these wonderful toys and being curious. I believe curiosity is a big part of creativity.

I think curiosity is so much of it. I've thought a lot about this, the art of courting an idea . . . the feeling when you get on the edge of something. It's like having peripheral vision. When you look at a star in the sky, it's always brighter when you look slightly away from it, but when you look directly at the star, it's slightly dimmer. I often think the same is true with musical ideas, or any ideas for that matter. I would say the same is also true if you're courting a person – if you're calling for a dance. If you run after someone, arms flailing, they may run away and get scared off, and if you're totally absent from them, then they won't pay you any attention. So, it's that fluidity, the in-between zone, where you're saying . . . I am interested in you, but I'm not too interested. I'm not going to scare you away, you're too important. I don't want to define you just yet. I'm not trying to give you a form, but I do want to court and welcome you into my area, and I want to dance. I want to see what we find in the dance. That's what it's like when you have an idea. A levity takes hold – and takes focus. There are some moments, which I'd call my high-alpha-state days, where I have no option. I *must* create. There's nothing I could possibly do that would make any sense, other than creating. This energy . . . it simply must come out. And then there are other days where I'm knocking on the door, and I'm not so inspired. On those days you have to work a little bit harder, and find a way to create some friction.

Again, I go back to the idea of internal creative weather. I could literally draw you a graph every day of my creative frequency response in a number of areas . . . there's my empathy level, my humour level, my irreverence level, my physical health . . . all these different kinds of things, and every day has a different set of sensitivities. One day you can make me laugh so easily, I just get the giggles, yet on another day, I won't feel like laughing at all, I may be really prone to tears – somebody just walks their dog, and I want to cry, it's so moving. On another day, I'm completely disconnected from that sort of reality, but I might be connected to something else imaginary. I'm constantly curious about this process, and I feel like I've developed an antenna for detecting what my curiosity is best expended at. Judging by the weather internally, I'm not going to try and write this song today, it's just not the right day. I'm going to try to do something different that's more suited to my inner space. One thing I sometimes do is the exact opposite of everything I think is good, in the creative process. That can create some really helpful friction.

Say I'm mixing a song, and I think the kick is too loud and that I should turn down the kick, and instead, I turn it up! Or if I think a song feels too short, and that I ought to make the song longer – what if I cut the song in half? Sometimes those kinds of irreverent processes can really enliven the peripheral mind to be like, whoa! That's so weird! I can react to it – it makes me move. Giving myself permission to be very bad at music or be very weird in my decisions can often glean so many more interesting results than just wanting to be really good all the time, to do great music and hope people like it. Everyone needs a dose of 'what wouldn't you do?'; 'what's the ugliest chord here?'; 'what's the worst choice to make?' I think that can really feed things. So . . . When I come to the dawn or edge of an idea, I think I try and discern the flavour of my creative weather, find a meeting point between that and the thing, and then create some friction – like lighting a match – you need a rub, a spark for something to catch on and begin, you can't just stand there waiting. In the same way, just like courting a potential dancer, there needs to be some push and pull for that dance to be alive at all.

I know your mum was obviously a huge influence and supportive of your creativity. Did you have any other sorts of music heroes when you were younger that really grabbed you?

Constantly. I think my original was Stevie Wonder. I fell in love with the songs, and then went on to discover that he played almost all the instruments on them, and produced it all too. I just loved the whole of that scenario. It made me believe that I could do that. Sting was really important to me too. His ability to draw from all these different words adjacent to his own . . . English folk music, for example, or lute music, or country. Listening to those beautiful songs of his was just so freeing for me, and to hear something like Kathryn Tickell's Northumbrian pipes in the same phrase as Dominic Miller's distorted guitar. Bobby McFerrin was also a massive hero of mine. I think he taught me that the voice could be more than just the lead singer, that a voice can be a whole instrument in its own right, and that you can play the voice and imitate other instruments with the voice . . . that you can be an acrobat and describe harmony and chords with the voice in a horizontal way. I really loved him for that. Benjamin Britten is a niche but crucial hero of mine. He's the composer of that chamber opera, *The Turn Of The Screw*, that I was a part of as a kid, and I know every note of that – but besides that I just loved everything he did. Bach too, of course. I would listen to my mum play Bach for hours. I still often hear my mum play Bach, resounding through the house, and think to myself... that's what music should feel like. Earth, Wind & Fire was the most joyous music I could imagine, and Queen was another big one for me. Later on, Joni Mitchell, Bob Dylan, Paul Simon. Just finding my way through all those lyrics and working out how they all fit together was such an adventure.

I remember listening to every Joni Mitchell album consecutively in a row once when I was nineteen. I had a week of bus rides to the Academy, and so within a couple of weeks I did those twenty or so albums. It was an unbelievable experience, listening to her grow up like that. The way that the tone evolved . . . and the increasing sort of cynicism, the ever-changing perspective, going deeper and becoming brave in new ways, meeting Jaco and Wayne . . . I really loved that journey. Another artist I did that with at that time was, of course, The Beatles. I just adored The Beatles. I remember, again, listening to every Beatles album from back to front for a week. I mean, what an education. What an astounding thing to have access to that music for free now, and you just think, gosh, streaming is so problematic in so many ways, and a lot of the head honchos need to pull their socks up and upheave the whole system in favour of artists . . . but then again, if I hadn't been able to stream the whole Beatles discography, or Joni discography, effortlessly as a kid, I simply wouldn't be making this music. I'm really grateful for such pure access to things. I would climb into YouTube of an afternoon and find all sorts of weird and wonderful video clips of people all over the world experiencing music in different ways – recording, playing, talking. They were all my teachers. You can learn anything from anyone – and that was an amazing part of my journey.

With you talking about The Beatles and their music reminds me of being in Maharishi's ashram in India with them. My sister, Pattie, and John's wife, Cynthia and I would sit on the roof of our bungalow with Paul, George and John while they played their guitars and sang the beginnings of a song that would later end up on *The White Album*. John would say something like, 'I really couldn't sleep last night,' and that was the beginning of 'I'm So Tired'. I witnessed many more of their songs coming to fruition while we were there. The songs they created during that time were all to do with what was going on in the ashram.

That's so extraordinary. I have so many questions I could ask. I think it's amazing, as a young musician, to just imagine how music would have felt at that time without those records having previously existed – because we take them for granted now! Like, obviously The Beatles have always been there, right? But naturally they came from somewhere – and you were there for some of that evolution – I just find it so astounding that those materials evolved by their own hands. I suppose I wonder how seriously they took themselves in a sense, because it would have been easy for them to become disillusioned by it all. Did they ever think, in your words, 'Why me?' What was their interaction with all of that to you?

When I interviewed George in 1988, I asked him if he'd ever wondered, 'Why me?' He said he often did. He also wondered how it came about that everybody in the world knew of The Beatles. It was a phenomenon, and it had never happened before. Every one of the musicians I have interviewed has asked themselves, at one point, 'Why me?'

I can imagine. I mean, I sort of feel reassured by the fact that everybody I hear you speak of affirms that feeling of 'Why me?'. It's as though everyone is kind of new again. There's growth in everything – and in a way, everybody's kind of a fraud. Sort of like, I don't know what I'm doing here, but I guess I'll just do the best I can. I think the more people who realise that even the greatest of the greats feel like that, the better – it would hopefully give them permission to know maybe they're qualified enough, as they are.

After interviewing seventy-five musicians between 1988 and 1990, I found the thing they all seemed to have in common was a sense of humility towards the creative process, that their best songs seemed to come from somewhere else, a higher power.

More than anyone else, I hear musicians talk about the idea of the higher power – the moment the universe takes hold. I wonder, in terms of faith, what kind of commonalities you found over the years interviewing people about their experiences. If there's one thing they all have in common, or if there were vast differences across the board.

Willie Dixon, Buddy Guy and John Lee Hooker referred to their higher power in a more traditional sense. They were closer to that feeling when they were singing and praying in church, but there were other musicians who, in their own words, seemed to equate their higher power with moments of transcendence of self, a heightened state of awareness, inspiration. These moments were often experienced while writing songs or playing onstage, where everything comes together, what is now called 'being in the zone'. The ego is out of the way, and you just kind of let go and let it happen.

Well, that's it, letting it go and letting it happen. Exactly. It's funny because I grew up singing in church a bit, and then stopped for a while – I think the audience choir feels like all of what I loved about the church thing, just without all the hymn books, all the talk of good and evil, and that stuff. The value is simply that all these people are all singing together – strangers, yet friends. Elevating each other just by being in the room with each other, and there being a space for everyone in there. It feels like a lot of the great musicians I look up to grew up in the Church, many of them black gospel musicians. There is something that takes hold when you sing in a community that doesn't leave you, no matter which tradition you find yourself in.

One more thing on what drives someone to create: I think there's a certain amount of it for me where I can't help myself, I'm just so curious, I must try things out. And going back to what I said at the start – I think an amount of that comes from having two very different parents who saw the world very differently. Part of a job of a musician is to take the world, whatever world they find themselves in, and alchemise it into something cathartic, something meaningful. As a child, I was faced with a confusing set of forces – like many children are – and I feel very lucky to have found an outlet that has taught me so much. There's a flame in me – to keep pushing and keep exploring. And even something that felt so opaque and empty as an absent father figure could become known through the limbs of what I was making. And all these years later, I still feel the flame, and I know that I'll never stop creating.

So in a way, he was a gift.

Absolutely. And no matter what the world brings – there's always a way to turn it into something beautiful – no matter who you are.

Since our interview I was given the chance to watch Jacob perform at the Bristol Amphitheatre. As soon as he bounced and skipped across the stage, bare-footed and in brightly coloured clothes, a simultaneous roar broke out from the crowd. And then, right on queue, everyone began singing: 'Ahhh'. The audience was all his. He was the conductor and we were the instrument. And then it broke and everyone cheered. The audience was now part of the show. It made me think of the hundreds of times I'd stood on the side of a stage watching bands perform, either Fleetwood Mac, Don Henley, Bonnie Raitt or Crosby, Stills and Nash during the seventies, eighties and early nineties. There always seemed to be a big divide between the stage and the audience until such time when they were all connecting to the groove, when everyone took off at the same time, eyes glistening, bodies moving. These were special moments.

The feeling I got watching Jacob was that the audience were

his friends; we could have all been sitting in his kitchen. 'Would you like to hear another song?' felt no different from 'Would you like another cup of tea?' Not only were the audience connected with him, it felt as though we were all connected to each other, singing or chanting together in harmony. What a fantastic show and what a great musician!

ROSANNE CASH

Singer, songwriter and solo artist.

I CAN'T REMEMBER WHO INTRODUCED ME TO ROSANNE
Cash, but I was very grateful to be able to interview her, even
though it was on the phone.

'I've had psychic experiences from the time I was a baby.
I saw people that weren't there. They call those "imaginary
friends" but they were very real to me. I had dreams that came
true continually. Some of this sounds pretty weird – it kind
of makes me sound like I was a total looney! I've never told
anybody this except my husband and a few close friends. I always
did have dreams that came true and saw and heard people and
knew that there was another world just beyond what I could
see. And sometimes I could see through the veil. It still happens;
it's not stopped. It frightened me for a while. It didn't frighten
me when I was a child, but then it started frightening me
when I was a teenager and in my twenties. Now it doesn't
frighten me any more.

'I wasn't encouraged as a child to be artistic. In fact, I got
angry about that later in life as I realised it. Nobody recognised

131

it, that I had artistic tendencies or that I was the creative type. I don't feel like I was encouraged at all. There was no room for it at school; outside of school, it just wasn't focused. I felt I was very strange. The kind of forums I wanted to work in were unacceptable or unexplainable. So, I became very passionate about music. It inspired me continually. I listened to music all the time. I was very passionate about what I listened to, beginning with The Beatles. I wanted to be a writer, and I always wrote. I always kept journals and wrote really bad poetry. Then I started writing songs when I was eighteen.

'The drive to create is pretty intense to me. It's almost like a survival instinct; it's that primitive. If I ignore my work, I start having anxiety attacks, I can't really sleep well, my eating habits become erratic, I get irritable. It starts taking its toll in a very physical and mental way. So it's almost like the energy is there, and if I don't use it as it was intended, it turns toxic. It turns on me. It's very much a survival thing for me.

'Music today taps into the collective unconscious, just like myths and fairy tales. These are new myths and new fairy tales. Music has to do this, because the collective unconscious is part of all of us. I think that's probably a huge part of the [creative] source.

'The essence of art, if it works, is it should reveal people to themselves. It shouldn't just tap into a vein that's already there and reflect back at them what they are. It should reveal something that's hidden to themselves. When that's working, it has power – power to heal and change.

'We all carry a divine spark in us. I think there is an access point in me, and if I can find it . . . Sometimes it's like reaching through fog trying to find it, and sometimes it's just there; it just presents itself. And if I can get to that access place, there's some kind of source that I draw on that works in writing and painting and music. When that's happening, when the gates are open and it's a free flow of information and inspiration, it's being in an altered state. It's very satisfying. Everything else disappears. It's like I'm part of a river and no matter what I did, I couldn't stop the current right then. It seems that sometimes it's easier to access when I'm writing. When I'm performing and I can access it, it's wonderful, and at the end [of the performance] it's like surfacing, like being part of this river and coming up. It just feels so wonderful. It's impossible for me to contrive it, though. If I can get myself to the access point, then it works, but I can't make it up. I have a few tools that I use to try to get myself there. Sometimes they work, and sometimes they don't. It's elusive.

'I had an experience where I was painting in a warehouse in a friend's art studio one afternoon. Everybody had gone and I was painting. Then I looked around and it was dark and the whole building was empty. I had lost myself for four hours in this experience of painting. I got really frightened coming back to earth – it was a dark warehouse in a bad part of town. So I washed my hands and quickly got out of there. But during the time it was happening, it was pure essence and absolute accessing too. It was wonderful! There were no distractions, there was just nothing else. I don't think at any other time in life is there that kind of purity – purity of being.

'I used to think drugs and alcohol enhanced [the creative process] but now I think they blocked it. Once I got straight, I had a fear that I couldn't write, that being straight would numb out my work. I found that, in fact, drugs and alcohol blocked the access, made it far more elusive. It's not that it can never happen through that, but it makes it more difficult.'

Rosanne continues to tour worldwide with her husband, John Leventhal. She has released fifteen albums, won four Grammys and written four books, including a best-selling memoir. Her album She Remembers Everything *was released in 2018, with further single releases in 2021.*

IAN WALLACE

A former member of King Crimson, a drummer who played with such artists as Bob Dylan, Don Henley, Jackson Browne, Bonnie Raitt, and Crosby, Stills and Nash.

IAN AND I MET EACH OTHER IN 1981 AT CHRISTINE McVie's house in Beverly Hills. I'd come to L.A. with my children to spend Christmas with Christine, and see our friend as well as seeing Mick. Chris arranged for us all to sing Christmas carols that night at the care home in Santa Monica. I was immediately aware of Ian's sense of humour as we all squashed into the van. It was a great evening with Christine playing the accordion, Ian conducting and playing spoons, while the rest of us, wearing our Yuletide T-shirts, sang every Christmas carol we knew to a delighted audience!

'I didn't know what I was going to be until I was fourteen. I was really into music then; I got a guitar, but I didn't know how to tune it. When I was about fifteen, I joined the school jazz society, and they had a local outing to the cinema where Acker Bilk was playing. We sat in the back, the stage was all set up, then the ice-cream lady came up the aisle. I went down to get an ice cream and, as I stood in line, I looked up at the drum kit and it was like the heavens opened and choirs started singing, and Jesus' rays came down on the drum kit. I knew then what I wanted to do. The next day I got all my albums and my guitar – without telling my mother – and took them to the local music store and traded them in for a little snare drum. I used to sit at home with cardboard boxes and things and a pair of sticks and play to old jazz records. I knew I wanted to play the drums. After that, that's all I ever wanted to do.

'Once I've managed to transcend such things as where I am, who I'm playing with, how I'm playing, what the temperature of the room is, how the audience is, who the rest of the band are, that's when the real playing happens. It's very seldom that it happens.

'Once you can stop thinking [about everything], then it's a trance kind of thing. You don't think about anything; that's the whole point: you don't think. Thinking is the thing that comes in the way of so much – that's the Zen thing. It's the thought that is the blockage. Once you stop thinking, instead of it being thought, it becomes existence. I suppose it's what you try and achieve in meditation. It's a feeling of going on to another state of existence. It's like white-water canoeing or something where you're really in control but you're being borne along at a tremendous rate by something that you only just have control of. It's almost like it's controlling you. It's that speed and yet at the same time it's complete tranquillity.

'It doesn't happen very often, though. You can get very close at times. Sound has a lot to do with it. It has to sound a certain way before you can feel comfortable enough to let it happen. I've played some gigs where the sound was so disruptive that there was no way that could happen, just by being so hung up on the sound.

'Hashish was so powerful at first; it opened up all kinds of things. I'd just lie there and fly. Listening to music was just absolutely amazing. You could get into the music so much – every note became a shape – it was really incredible, very influential. It enabled total concentration; it cut off all external influences. You would just get so totally into the sound that nothing else existed. But on the other hand, it took away the desire to do anything about it. After having stopped taking drugs completely, I've realised that, for me, being under the influence closed many of my creative doors.'

Ian sadly died of laryngeal cancer in February 2007.

STEVE WINWOOD

Singer, songwriter, multi-instrumentalist and solo artist who was formerly with the Spencer Davis Group, Blind Faith and Traffic.

I **MET STEVE AT CHRISTINE McVIE'S HOUSE IN 1989.** I can't remember whether he just happened to be staying with Chris for a few days or whether we had organised this meeting for me to interview him. I had always been a big Steve Winwood fan and especially loved 'Gimme Some Lovin'', which he co-wrote while in the Spencer Davis Group.

'Shortly after I turned five or six, I had some music lessons, but I fooled the teacher by doing things by ear instead of reading. That didn't last long, and I didn't really have any training until I was fourteen. Then I got into the Birmingham and Midland Institute of Music as a part-time music student while I was still at school. I did that for about a year and a half before I got kicked out for playing rock 'n' roll and jazz, which, of course, was not acceptable. They made me make the choice – so they kicked me out.

'My father played several different instruments, and my

mother was musical, although she never actually exploited it. My grandfather on my mother's side was a musician, a church organist and a fiddle player. All my father's brothers were musicians, and my father's mother played piano. My older brother was also a musician, and there were always instruments around the house. I was gently encouraged towards music, though I was never forced to learn. But I felt sure I was going to be a musician too.

'Everybody has the potential to be creative; creativity manifests itself in different ways. Some people are lucky enough to be able to channel it directly into one field; probably other people have their talents diffused through lots of areas and can't immediately realise what their true talent is. Often people have a talent without knowing it.'

Steve made his first performance in three years at the 2022 Cornbury Music Festival in Oxfordshire. He was a special guest of The STAKS Band and played a tribute to Gary Brooker, who had died earlier.

RONNIE WOOD

Guitarist, singer, songwriter, member of the Rolling Stones and former member of the Faces.

I HAVE KNOWN RONNIE AND HIS THEN-WIFE KRISSY since the late sixties, early seventies. He knew Mick, Christine and John McVie well, having seen each other playing over the years. I saw a lot of him and Krissy when we were living in L.A., at one point living almost next door to each other in Malibu, but interviewed him at his home in England for the book. He gave me a drawing he'd done of Big Bill Broonzy. I think he has the biggest smile of anybody I know!

'My dad had a twenty-four-piece harmonica band that toured the racetracks of England, and he used to play a kind of barrelhouse piano. My two brothers had already set the mould, both musically and artistically. They both went to Ealing Art College, where I followed them, and they both had bands. Art, my older brother, introduced me via jazz to the first 78s of "I'm Walkin" by Fats Domino and "Great Balls of Fire" by Jerry Lee Lewis. Mum and Dad knew I wanted to follow that course, and they were very good about it. They just said,

"As long as you don't get into any trouble with the law, you can do whatever you want!"

'I first went onstage at the age of nine, playing washboard at the local cinema with my two brothers in a skiffle group. But even before that, I was lent a guitar, and a couple of members of the band – the guitarist and the banjo player – used to give me chord sheets. They used to write out easy chords for me to learn when I was about seven or eight. Then I took it a bit more seriously up to the age of ten. The guy who lent me the guitar took it back, so I had a gap of a couple of years. Then my brother saved up and bought me my own guitar. I was about twelve then. I didn't ever see any reason to stop playing just because my fingers hurt. I was never impaired by the physical side of it. I thought it was something I had to do. It still goes for today. You can never sit back and rest on your laurels, because the moment that feeling hits you – if you stop playing, then it's all over. You have to keep playing and get better. I'm playing for someone higher than me. Maybe it's that person in the crowd, God, or Eric Clapton! I never lose my ambitious drive; I'm always striving.

'I have to be in a certain frame of mind when I paint. Sometimes the urge is so irresistible if you're on an aeroplane or something, that's why I scribble a lot on notepaper or draw on little pads. When you want to do something like a big oil painting, it can be really off-putting if you're sitting there talking to somebody who's come to visit without phoning first. And you're wasting your time, thinking, "Oh, I should be painting!" When they go, you run down and do it. It's the same with a song. If I'm in the middle of a conversation and I get a song, I have to run off and play it into a recorder or something.

'I wrote one of my greatest songs [which hadn't come out at

that time], by just remembering it [after waking up]. I was lying in bed one night and I couldn't sleep; there was this song I just had to put down, and my wife Jo said, "Well, remember it." So I woke up the next morning and it was still there. I was going to punch her if it went! It just goes to show you can do it if you put your mind to it; you can picture a song in a visual way in your mind's eye, if you just have a basic structure to refer to.

'Everyone has the potential but they don't all have the drive within themselves to realise they have something. I made Jagger do a drawing. He always said, "I can't draw." I told him, "Just do a drawing for me." He did one and it was the most fantastic drawing. He may never do a drawing again, but I wish he would. I think everyone's creative, but it's a gift that makes you keep turning the work out.

Ronnie lives in Little Venice with his wife and young daughters. Sober now for a decade, he continues to play with the Rolling Stones and paint prolifically.

PART FIVE

'Everything likes music;
everything that crawls, creeps, flies
or swims likes music' –

WILLIE DIXON

GEORGE HARRISON

Former member of The Beatles, singer, songwriter, guitarist, solo artist and member of the Traveling Wilburys. In 1991 George went on tour in Japan with Eric Clapton, in 1992 he played at the concert for the Natural Law Party at the Albert Hall, and in the same year played at the tribute concert for Bob Dylan at Madison Square Garden.

INTERVIEWING GEORGE WAS FUN! IT STILL FELT, EVEN after all these years, as though I was talking to my older brother. I had known George since I was sixteen, and even though he and my sister, Pattie, were no longer married, I would still see him and Olivia periodically, especially when he was in Los Angeles or Pattie and I would visit them at their home in Oxford. He showed up for the interview at our house in Sherman Oaks, having just spent the previous evening playing with his old friends, Roy Orbison, Tom Petty, Jeff Lynne and Bob Dylan. That night was the very beginning of what turned out to be 'the Traveling Wilburys'.

Tell me a little about your upbringing: how many brothers and sisters, where you came in the family, and if both parents were with you.

Both parents were around, four children and I was the youngest. I had a sister eleven years older than me and two brothers in between. My sister had gone to college and was living in different cities while I was growing up, and with my brothers being older, I don't remember much about them.

How old were you when you knew you wanted to play the guitar?

When I was twelve. I'd heard about some guy who used to go to the same junior school I went to and he had a guitar for sale. I bought it off him. Neither of my parents were musicians, but they did have an upright piano in the house, and my dad, who was a merchant seaman, brought a lot of records and a wind-up gramophone from the States. There was always music about the house. My mother liked to sing and they both liked to dance. I remember hearing them play 'Hong Kong Blues' by Hoagy Carmichael. It was a big hit in 1941. I remember other songs they played, including 'Stardust' and songs like that. I heard them either on the radio or wind-up gramophone. Years later I did cover versions of these old songs.

So they appreciated music?

Yeah, they did and they encouraged me when I said I wanted to buy this friend's guitar. My mother gave me the three pounds ten shillings to buy it. And later when I got a better guitar – a pound down and the rest when they catch you – she signed the contract for me. Because my dad was always out working late or doing shift work, my mum liked the idea of me playing guitar.

Would you say you were an outgoing kid or were you shy and introverted?

I think both, maybe it's the Pisces in me: one half is noisy and the other half is quiet. Just the same as I am now. I had lots of friends. We always had parties and would go to each other's houses.

Around the time I was about eleven we moved from the neighbourhood I was in to one of the new housing estates on the outskirts of Liverpool, where I went to the local grammar school. That was a big change in my life because it was also around that same time when I got my first guitar. It was also at that school when Paul McCartney came into my life and all these other people I met who were guitarists. I would hang out with anyone who had a guitar.

My father had a friend, whom he hadn't seen for many years, but he remembered that this guy used to go with him on the ships and they'd all bought guitars at one time or another. My dad had sold his because there was no work and they needed the money. But this guy continued playing guitar and so my dad called him to see if he could help me, show me a few chords.

This same guy owned an off-license, and whichever evening of the week it was closed, I'd go down there and he would show me how to play my guitar. He was a very nice guy and he was probably in his mid-forties when I was twelve. I'm sure that set a certain pattern in my music because he taught me all these old songs, just chords mainly, of what you'd call dance band music and that's stayed with me to this day. He was a great help, showing me where to put my fingers and how different chords follow each other just by playing songs. So, in retrospect, I think he had an enormous influence on me.

Did you know what you wanted to be when you grew up?

I still don't think I know what I want to be! The guitar was the first thing, and music through the guitar was what I was interested in. I was not a great student through high school but I did manage to make it into the grammar school. Sometimes I think it was fixed for me to go there by other powers, not because I was a bright student, but because karmically I had to meet my destiny. And it was important that I went to this school even though I was a terrible student. I hated school most of the time, especially this grammar school. I had enjoyed school up until the age of twelve, but I didn't like this big school. I thought it was too serious. All through my schooling I didn't have any idea, not a clue, what I wanted to do. I knew I didn't want to be an accountant or fireman; I didn't want to do any of that stuff. And if it hadn't been for the band, I don't know, I'd have just been a bum or whatever, just doing menial work. The only thing that held my interest was music and the guitar and how to avoid getting a proper job.

What was it like learning to play guitar? What gave you the drive to carry on learning? Did it come naturally or did you have to work harder?

I spent a lot of time learning to play the guitar. Even to this day I'm very bad at practising. I find that I can do a lot of things by doing a lot of little bits at a time and by putting it all together until it becomes something substantial. As a kid I did play guitar a lot, even though it was just simple stuff, a skiffle tune or Buddy

Holly's 'Peggy Sue'. You have to learn how to clamp down on those strings while you feel your fingers are hurting, and you have to know how to change the chords without the music stopping. I must have played for a long time to arrive at that. But it was something I didn't think about, I just did it. I loved music and I loved guitars, so it was a labour of love.

Did you have any significant or recurring dreams as a kid?

I used to sleepwalk all the time, going into a sort of trance-like state and then getting out of bed and walking around and waking people up. I remember once waking my dad and talking to him. My father knew I was sleepwalking and having some kind of dream. So they would just put me back to bed. I did that a lot from about age eight or nine until I was thirteen. My brother Peter remembered me waking him up and saying, 'Come with me.' He got out of bed and followed me back to my bedroom, and he said I just got into bed and went to sleep. But when he walked in the room, he saw an old man sitting at the end of the bed. But I don't recall that. After looking at an old photograph album, the old man looked like my grandfather, who died long before I was born. It could have been him. I used to have an amazing feeling. I'm glad I remember this now and thank you for reminding me. It was both amazing, but horrific at the same time. I felt I was a tiny thing in this enormous, infinite space. I felt I was just a vibration and there was a sound that went from being the tiniest, to expanding and becoming as infinite as the sound. The sound got louder and louder, faster and faster. It would frighten me. It really freaked me out. I forgot all about that until after we were meditating at Rishikesh. I also noticed it during the time we were making The Beatles' *White Album*, the album we made

From top left, counter-clockwise: Don Henley [© *Sam Jones*], Mick Fleetwood [© *Neal Preston, henceforth NP*], Hank Marvin, Sinead O'Connor, Christine McVie (centre right, with author centre left). **All photos in section © *Getty Images* unless otherwise credited**

From top left, counter-clockwise: Eg White [© *Adam Campbell*], Lindsey Buckingham
[© *NP*], Teddy Pendergrass, John Lee Hooker [© *NP*], Peter Gabriel

Eric Clapton [© NP]

From top left, counter-clockwise: Buddy Guy, Stevie Nicks [© NP], Stephen Stills, Paul Kantner

From top left, counter-clockwise: Jacob Collier [© *Betsy Newman*], Ian Wallace, Ronnie Wood, Steve Winwood [© *NP*], Rosanne Cash

From top to bottom:
David Crosby,
Bonnie Raitt, Jackson
Browne [© all NP],
Willie Dixon

George Harrison [© NP] and, below, with Paul in India [© Paul Saltzman]

From top left, counter-clockwise:
Graham Nash, Albert Lee, Cece Bullard
[© Maggie Smith], Edie Brickell,
Richard Thompson

right after being in that really concentrated meditation. I used to go into the big studio, the number-one studio in Abbey Road, and it was nearly always empty. When the time came to take a break from recording, I would get inside the sound booth and do my meditation and that's where I experienced that same sound as when I was a kid. I realised then it was the mantra.

I don't know what happened to me when I was a child, if I'd woken up or if that's what made me sleepwalk. In the earlier days, up until I was about twenty-five, I would get feelings of déjà vu. Not a lot, but occasionally, like now say, we'd be sitting here and I'd just be talking and I'd feel I've done this before. I think everybody's had those days. That occurred a lot during that time. I understand it much better now because there's been so many years of meditation and talking to spiritual masters, trying to obtain some knowledge. I understand a lot more about what it is and about reincarnation. I believe absolutely in reincarnation without a question of doubt. Some people are not quite sure and think life is just one limited span and that's it. But not me!

Going back to the déjà vu, I think it's pure feelings that flow through you, that don't get trapped in your intellect or your emotional side. I think the worst barriers between soul and reality – the external reality and the internal reality – is that the expression gets blocked through intellect. I find when I talk to people who are great intellectuals, that they are very often not in touch with their heart, whereas for me I'm still a bit stupid when it comes to having a great vocabulary and the information at hand about statistics and things like that, but I am in touch with my heart. I can meet people and feel like I've known them before and quite often I don't have to go through that period of getting to know someone. I think that's just instinct of being able to recognise other souls that maybe you've known before, and anyway, even if you haven't, you just see a reflection of your own self in them.

I wonder with intellectuals whether it's an incredible effort they make so they don't have to be in touch with their souls. It's like a wall.

There's something which sums it up. After reading the *Bhagavad Gita*, I wrote this tune called 'That What I Have Lost', and in the last verse it says, 'In your mirrors of understanding, they need cleansing, polish away the dust of desire before true light can reflect in.' So, I don't know if everybody's basically a perfect soul. But then souls are encased in these bodies and the body is like a mirror that's got layers and layers of dust on it, so it doesn't reflect the true nature of the person. Some people have less clutter on their mirror, and so you're able to reflect more easily. Intellectuals seem to me to have a layer of intellectual dust on their mirror.

Have you ever felt you've been here before?

Do you mean on this planet?

Yes.

I've definitely been somewhere before. I don't believe this is the first time in 1943 that I came into existence in this body, because I understand more about reincarnation and the whole thing about karma. We are the result of our previous actions. Depending on what we're doing now makes us whatever we're going to be tomorrow, or the next years, or whenever. So I believe I've been around many different places, not like these people who say, 'I used to be Napoleon in my last life,' I don't believe it to that degree. I don't know or have any proof as to who I've been before, or when I was here, or whether it was on this planet or any other planet, but I feel that I'm ancient, an ancient soul, and I couldn't have just started in 1943. I feel I understand more about reincarnation and about karma, that we are the result of our previous actions.

Do you believe in a higher power and does it connect to creativity?

Yes, obviously the power that exists is the meaning of the word 'OM', the complete whole. There is nothing that isn't part of the complete whole and 'OM' is the cause of all causes. And so really, it's God and it's the sound vibration that is in every atom of creation. Whether we know it or not, God is there in everybody, in everything, even in inanimate objects and in the material world. It manifests in different ways, as Maharishi used to say about 'Sap, Sap, Sap'. Everything's made of sap. The flowers have petals, leaves and stems but they're all made out of sap and it manifests in all these different pieces or components.

The sap is the spiritual energy that's within everything. You can manifest it to varying degrees, just like flowers are all different in the garden. It manifests in the manner suited to that person's individuality or their particular karma.

When you're playing or when you're writing songs, have you ever felt it's coming through you?

Well, it does come through you. Again, it's like the barriers between being either clear or cluttered makes a difference in how you write a tune, whether you'll have a difficult time putting it together or whether it's quite simple. Some tunes you can write a hundred verses, with other tunes you can just say it all in one verse and then the rest of the song, lyrically, is hard work to complete. It does come through you in different ways. I believe it's all about how much you open yourself up to it. Like they say in Indian philosophy, 'I am the instrument and God is the player.' That's true, but at the same time it does sound a bit conceited in a way. I like to be inspired and hope that maybe there can be some value in what I'm doing which is greater than just my personal contribution. So in that respect, I believe something else comes through, but then sometimes you don't get much at all, it's just a mundane little tune, and other times it's just a reflection of how you're feeling. I try to write a lot of tunes about spiritual things purely because that's what I was feeling and needed to express myself.

Did you ever reflect, 'Why me?'

Not really, because it would be different if I was a solo artist. It is pretty strange though, having the enormous fame that we had, and still have. When you think that out of all those people, that fame should settle on the Fabs, that the chemistry between the four of us created this big thing that went right through the world and there wasn't any country in the world, even the most obscure places, that didn't know about The Beatles, from grandparents to babies. It just blanketed everything. That amazed me more than anything, because we always felt if we could get a record contract, we'd be successful. But our tiny little concept of success that we had at the time was nothing compared to what happened. And it does make me think that there's more to this than meets the eye. It was not so much, 'Why me?' The question was more like, 'Who am I?' After the LSD experience, it released all this stuff and I would spend time looking at my face in the mirror, and the face kept changing into that of a Mongolian and then a Chinese man, looking and thinking, 'Who am I? Who the hell are you?' I think that really helped because it turns out that

'Who am I?' is actually like a mantra. The Buddhists call it OM. *'I am he as you are he as you are me and we are all together!'* It's like that. I think, in the mystic way, if you get the question right, the question is its own answer. I think if people just sat quietly long enough and meditated, get inside themselves and ask their heart 'Who am I?' it will be revealed.

Do you think everyone has the potential to be creative?

Everybody has the potential, but to simplify it, karma is the accumulation of good and bad actions, like a bank account, say, for instance – you either have credit or debit karma, or maybe you've got a bit of both. You've got some good karma and you have some bad karma. It's whatever you've created. Everybody has potential, but everybody manifests different amounts of the potential.

Everybody is potentially perfect, and therefore, the basic answer to your question is yes, everybody's got it in them to be creative, but superimposed on top of that is the accumulation of past karma, which either helps or hinders one's progress depending on how much we clutter our lives with our actions or how much we free ourselves up.

Sometimes you can be just working away and, no matter how hard you try, it's not successful or it doesn't work out right. Other times it's as if there's a whole supportive energy that it's like they say in the record business, 'We're on a roll.' Sometimes you just have to do the smallest thing and it has enormous results.

Do you consider divine and creative as being the same thing?

Yes, the divine creativity is the creative intelligence of the universe because it is within our soul. At the same time, we have this divinity within us. It's covered in layers of material energy and, although the divinity is in there, a lot of the time our actions and what we do is just coming from a mundane level. We are like beggars in a gold mine. That's what we are. We're like beggars in this gold mine where everything is really enormous potential and perfection, but we're also ignorant with that dust of desire on our mirrors. That could be the heading for this chapter! I don't know where that expression came from but I wrote it in a song, which was called 'Dehradun', when we were in Rishikesh. I never recorded it. It was all about seeing people from the ashram heading for this place on their day off from the meditation camp. I couldn't see any point in joining them as I'd gone all the way to Rishikesh to be in meditation and didn't want to go shopping for eggs in Dehradun. That's what the verse says: 'See them move along the road in search of life divine unaware it's all around them, beggars in a goldmine.'

It was very important for me to find out who I am and why I'm here and where I'm going. It was important because so much had happened in my life at that point in 1966, when I realised I had obtained quite a lot, and yet it all became meaningless. It didn't have any meaning unless I could figure out what the real purpose of life was and where God was. And so those things we've been talking about, such as karma and everything like that, became so imprinted in me.

Is there any connection when you feel more or less creative to what's going on in your life or what the weather's like?

The environment definitely has an effect upon us and how we feel. I tended to write most of my songs in the night, when the world goes to sleep and everybody's quiet. It's also a good time to meditate, just before sunrise, as that's when the creative energy is renewing itself.

Do you have a choice to create or is it something that just happens?

You have a choice. I find, having just finished writing and recording an album, that I tend to work in bursts, a bit at a time. But I still ask myself, 'How do I write a song?' I've just totally forgotten. But unlike some people who think they've dried up, I don't believe we can dry up. I just have to tell myself I've got to do it. Some people are really good about that. They'll set themselves an hour or two every day to write something, but I don't do that. Maybe occasionally somebody will say something or I'll see something and write it down on a piece of paper, and later it'll become a tune. But other times I have to force myself to do it. That's why sometimes it's good having a deadline. I never used to think I could write about specific things, if someone said write a song for a movie, but I've done a bit of that lately. I used to just write and the song would be whatever it became.

Do you think drugs and alcohol block or enhance creativity?

It can do both. If you have a few beers and you get excited, like I did last night, it can be really fun. The music we were playing actually sounded quite groovy. But then, the next day you've got a hangover and you're all messed up. I think with pot, it definitely did something for the old ears. Suddenly I could hear more subtle things in the sound. It's actually better not to smoke pot when I'm working because I need to be clear; my mind can be a scramble at times and all that does is scramble it more.

What do you feel when you're playing?

I'm just trying to concentrate on getting it right, remembering the words, the tune and where to put my fingers. Unlike some people who play all the time, maybe the sort of musicians you've got in your book, for them it becomes like riding a bicycle. More often than not, I have to concentrate because it's all new to me, because I don't do it enough – it keeps me on my toes.

Would you say the closest thing to a spiritual experience is when you're creating or playing or composing?

No. The closest thing is when I don't do anything, it's when I meditate, and then I can infuse that energy into my being. But really, in order to be really in touch with our creative energies, it lies within stillness and any kind of activity. I'm not talking about great masters or great yogis, I'm talking about us mortals who are at the bottom of the hill trying to walk up. I think it's good to go into the stillness and then come out and do activities, although that only applies to me. There are players like Ravi Shankar who are just so inspiring. He can actually go into a state of meditation while he's playing. I've seen him playing where he was so brilliant and yet he didn't even know what happened. Suddenly it ends. He hears the applause and quickly has to come out of this deep meditation, wondering what happened.

Did you feel spiritually connected to the group as a whole?

I think the best way of illustrating that is that even though at that time nobody knew what was going to happen, the thing that everybody does know about in The Beatles' history is that we had this other drummer called Pete and then he got fired, and that's when we got Ringo. But really it was like a jigsaw puzzle. And those four people were the puzzle. It was unfortunate for Pete, but it just wasn't in his karma. It was in Ringo's karma. I was seventeen or eighteen at the time but felt instinctively that Ringo, his spirit, fitted into us.

Did you feel there was a purpose or gifted meaning to your creativeness?

You have to be very careful, I suppose, because in one way we all have a duty to help ourselves and to help each other in whatever way we can, even if it's just to help people get through the day. I think it's important to share experiences or speak out, like Bob Dylan has always done. If he had not said some of the things he said, nobody else is going to say them. And you can imagine what a world it would be if we didn't have a Bob Dylan. It would be awful! But then there's the other side where you can start mistaking your own importance. I think I've been both of those at various times, when you think you're more groovy than you are, and then something usually happens to slap you down a bit. So again, it all has to be tempered with some sort of discretion. And also, if the motive for doing it is just to impress somebody, it's not as good as saying something that just needs to be said.

It was a very sad day when George died on 29 November 2001.

DAVID CROSBY

*Singer, songwriter and guitarist who was an
original member of The Byrds and Crosby, Stills and
Nash. He also performed as a solo artist.*

IFIRST MET DAVID CROSBY IN A LITTLE NIGHTCLUB ON
Grant Avenue in 1967. He wore a hat and a buck-skinned
jacket, and was standing next to Paul Kantner from Jefferson
Airplane, looking very cool. We were listening to a local
musician, called Dino Valenti. Paul had recently become a friend
so I walked over to say hello and he introduced me to David.
The biggest smile and twinkling eyes greeted me. 'I know
George and Pattie,' he said, 'and I could tell you are sisters.' All
I could think of was 'Mr Tambourine Man', my favourite song
by The Byrds. It was not long after this that I saw him onstage
at the Monterey Pop Festival playing with Buffalo Springfield.
Many years later, my then-husband Ian Wallace played drums
for CSN and I would often meet them all out on the road.

'My dad, who was a Hollywood movie cinematographer,
could play mandolin; my mother was quite musical. She didn't
play an instrument but sang in choirs and loved music dearly.

There was music in our house a lot. We had one of the earliest long-playing record players ever made; even before that, she used to have a big old 78 player to play symphonies. She played a ton of classical music around the house, so that naturally inclined me towards music. My brother also played, and we actually used to sing as a family. My parents were very anti-TV, and my mother had this idea that we should stick to older values, so we used to sit and sing around the fire. We'd sing folk songs from a book called *The Fireside Book of Folk Songs*.

'The story is that I started singing harmony when I was five or six years old. I very often write something all in a blurt; it comes out pretty much finished, and it consists of thoughts that I have never consciously thought. They did not ever take place in the verbal personalised level of my mind. Your mind has many levels: intuitive and imaginative are the intelligent ones and the ones where the creative process takes place. They are not necessarily articulate in the way that normal speech is. You have to get the half-calculator mind out of the way for that other mind to really function.

'I've been amazed when that has happened to me repeatedly. Many of my best songs come out all in one blurt, and at those times I have the distinct feeling that this level of me is just a vehicle for some other level of me that has been sitting there cooking this thing up. It often happens when I'm in between waking and sleeping. I'll be going to sleep, and I'll be sort of drowsy and this motormouth mind – the one that's talking to you right now – will kind of shut down, and then BAM! This stuff will start to come, and I'll turn on the light quickly and write, write, write, and play, play, write, and then, "Fantastic!" And about that time my other mind is starting to kick back in and say, "David, you're cool! *Whoaa,* buddy!" The music is the central issue, and there are a number of peripheral issues that will pull you away from the music. One of them is, "Gee, I must be intelligent. Look how many people are listening to me." Or, "Gosh, I'm powerful. I can influence things this way or that way." Or, "Gee, I'm great. Look at all those people giving me all that adulation." Or, "I must be the sexiest thing on earth; look at all those girls wanting me." All of these are mistakes. They are all ways to mis-perceive ourselves.

'I have found the way to keep sane and focused on the central issue – which is creating the music – is not to look at myself in any of these ways. I do not think about whether I am powerful. I do not think whether I'm influencing people. I do not consider myself a hero or larger than life. Those are all mistakes. They are all ones that make you think you are bigger than life, and you're not. What you are is incredibly lucky. You're a human being, regular and normal; you put your pants on one leg at a time, same as everyone else. You've been given a gift, and if you understand you've been given a gift, you work hard at it. You don't abuse it. I did abuse it, but I treasure it now and I work at it. I don't find it healthy to look at myself as powerful. I find it much healthier to look at myself as gifted and very lucky and grateful for it.

'The highest purpose we can aspire to is to call forth in people the best that human beings are capable of, the most exalted forms of the hero: the person who is willing to sacrifice to achieve; the person who has honesty and kindness, a sense of community; who has civilised himself and evolved above the level of combating animals. It can be called forth in human beings, and in that state can transcend all problems that we are faced with. The only way to improve it is to upgrade the consciousness; you can't legislate it.

'Every time that one of us does manage to slip into the mass media a nugget of truth that does in some fashion raise consciousness, we have performed a service, and it's to that I aspire. If I can do anything, I would love to bring joy to people's lives, bring people closer together, lessen the distance between people, let them see the sameness in each other, and let them share a moment. When you write about issues and events, like a Dylan, you can affect things in a wonderful way. John Lennon's "Imagine" is going to be running around this world for a very long time. There are things we can do that will affect our humanity. Sometimes you are given the chance to make a difference, and that is something to be even more grateful for than anything else.

'When I'm playing, what usually happens is that we achieve at its best a kind of gestalt between all the people on the stage, where we feel as if we are part of a larger thing and we are speaking with one voice. That's a wonderful experience, but it happens rarely. It happens more often the better the group is. It used to happen to us quite a lot when [Stephen] Stills, [Graham] Nash and I were singing. We would sing and frequently hit where we knew what we were doing and it worked; we would feel like we were just singing with one voice, and it was magic. Really good bands can do that: I've done it with several people onstage – all of us playing and singing at the same time and we were on it. It felt ecstatic; it's a near telepathic union. I get it very frequently with Graham Nash. Nash and I get so linked up onstage that we'll both start a wrong verse together.

'What initially happens in the drug experience is that you feel the drugs are helping because they will throw your consciousness up for grabs. And sometimes, early on in the process, that worked for me. The problem with the drugs is that, as you become addicted to them, they become so debilitating that the creative process stops entirely. A whole other effect takes place. While I was an addict, for three years of my life, I didn't write anything. I didn't have the attention span or the will; it just shut down, as if it had atrophied. And then six months after I quit, I wrote lyric after lyric, and it's been that way ever since. So much for the drugs and hash creativity theory.'

David died on 18 January 2023, aged eighty-one.

JACKSON BROWNE

Guitar player, singer, songwriter and solo artist.

BECAUSE MY EX-HUSBAND, IAN WALLACE, SPENT A year or so playing drums for Jackson during the mid–eighties, it meant I would often travel with them all in the fitted–out Greyhound bus. I was fortunate enough to stand on the side of the stage each night, watch them playing, never tiring of listening to Jackson singing 'Somebody's Baby', 'Doctor My Eyes' or his politically charged 'Lives in the Balance'. It was a great show and he's a great songwriter. I was thrilled when he agreed to be interviewed and found him to be an unassuming, thoughtful and gentle person with a political conscience. He, like many others of that time, represented the Southern California sound.

'My father was a real good piano player and grew up playing a pipe organ. He liked Dixieland but could play a number of things. He also got jobs playing for the silent movies. When my father had a party, the whole house would fill up with people, the loudest people you ever heard – he and his friends were great revellers – and there'd be four or five guys playing. My dad would say to me, "If you want to have fun, play an

163

instrument because you always go to parties and you're always indispensable." He wanted me to play the trumpet, and I played it for two or three years when I was a kid. I loved the trumpet, but then when I was ten or eleven, I realised that I wasn't going to whip out a trumpet at a party. It would be cooler to sit down at the piano so people could come around and sing.

'I was thirteen when I started playing the guitar. It was something I could do by myself when everyone else was surfing. I used to take the guitar when a group of us would go surfing at Huntington Beach. I would eventually end up sitting on the beach, playing guitar because I was so skinny, so little. My friends were all bigger than I was. In those days, wetsuits were very rudimentary, big things that the water went sloshing through, and it was cold in the wintertime. I would wind up sitting there, just having been washed up on the beach exhausted. Eventually someone said, "Hey, if you're not going to surf, if you're going to sit there and play the guitar, I know a lot of guys who would want this spot in the van." So I decided to just stay home and play guitar; inevitably one thing takes over from another. So music became my big interest when I was fourteen.

'There was an experience when I was trying to write. I hadn't written in a while; I was about nineteen. I did at one point kind of surrender. I thought, "*Okay*, I know it's not me that writes this stuff, so I'm at your service." It was like a little prayer. I then wrote something that I felt was my first song that was very good. If you have a flash of inspiration, it comes from within you.

'I think there is something like a current. To tell you the truth, it's something I believe without spending too much time thinking about it. Mainly I spend a lot of time standing in line trying to get a little of it, trying to tap into it. I guess you could sum it up that it's like a current of electricity outside of you that also exists inside of you, and it's something you can direct in a clever way. It's not something you can consciously do, but if you were blocked, you would have to unblock. There are always creative people who are just plugged in; they have their finger in that big socket.

'When I was fifteen years old, I started to play the guitar. Some of my friends were playing bluegrass. They turned me on to a whole bunch of really great folk artists – Sonny Terry, Brownie McGhee, Jack Elliott – there was a record called "Blues, rags, and Hollers". Then I heard Bob Dylan. I thought he was cool, and I'd try to play some of the stuff he was playing. I was impressed by his wit and his attitude, which was a real carelessness like, "This is who I am and what I am and this is what I care about." He would talk about things that really mattered. There was this wisdom and passion in what he talked about. The most appealing thing was he didn't give a fuck about what anybody else thought, and there was this wit and this comedy. They always called him Chaplinesque. As he began to make more records, he would change, but we were all changing too. By the time he came out with his third or fourth record, he was no longer folksy, he was writing these really interesting songs about experience. There's a great phrase in Dylan's "Subterranean Homesick Blues" in which he says "hanging 'round an inkwell". To me, it's one of those phrases that really meant *everything*, because you really can't stand around waiting for inspiration. You can try to be a disciplined person and be in shape to handle inspiration effectively when it happens. If you stand around looking for it, it never happens.

'I always thought [the drugs] enhanced [creativity] at the time, but you pay heavily. All these drugs have their effect; they change your perception about things. I used to smoke a lot of grass when I was first starting to write songs. I didn't have the sense that I was using it for anything then. Out of all the drugs that I took, the experiences that I'm consciously aware of valuing are psychedelics. In the mid-sixties, when people began turning on to psychedelic drugs, it was revolutionary. It was something that had been talked about by Aldous Huxley. It was a scientific thing; it was a breakthrough. When I took it, I was really careful; I set up the whole experience. I've never been able to understand people who did it every day or took it casually, or do it and go to a concert or something.

'When I started doing coke, it was for fun and was always very casual. Then there was a time when I used it more and more. While I was doing a certain record, I would go and score my coke and try my best not to get involved in a conversation. Then the first thing that happens, you get loaded and begin to talk. I would think, I'm going to get home and play my piano. I was very young. Eventually you wind up years later, you're doing coke, and you have no such priorities. And you're sitting there remembering all the times you stayed up actually intending to write a song and you wound up solving the world's problems and feeling terrible at eleven o'clock in the morning and wrecking the next two days because you can't recover from it. It turns out I had to stop using any kind of drug.

'Sound really means something; it suggests something to you. You have to find out what that is, and at the end you've got a song. Or you might think of a phrase that evokes all these feelings that suggest something to you. It really means something to you personally but it wouldn't mean that same thing to anybody else, unless you said it in the same context that would bring the feeling about.'

At the time of writing, Jackson was touring across Japan, Australia, New Zealand and Canada with a full band. The tour began in March 2023 and continued through April 2023. His most recent album is Downhill from Everywhere, *released July 2021. The title was inspired by a quote from oceanographer Captain Charles Moore, who said, 'The ocean is downhill from everywhere,' pointing out that everything humanity produces or does winds up in the ocean.*

BONNIE RAITT

Guitarist, singer, songwriter and solo artist.

I MET BONNIE AT A STUDIO IN L.A. WHEN I STARTED going out with Ian Wallace in 1981. My first impression of Bonnie was loving her naughty sense of humour, but that was before I heard her soulful voice as she sang into the microphone, almost bringing me to tears. Ian played drums for Bonnie for a couple of years or more, so I got to see a lot of her. She and Rob Fraboni came to Hawaii with us. Bonnie had recently stopped using drugs and alcohol and was on the brink of recording her hugely successful album *Nick of Time* when she discussed this change in her life during our interview.

'For a while, especially in the so-called disco and Reagan era, there definitely was a turning away from moral and political content, at least in pop music. Progressive radio all but disappeared, and even Jackson Browne had trouble getting his songs on the radio.

'Then the punk movement came along and blew the lid off all that cultural and moral complacency. Groups like The Clash, U2, Midnight Oil, artists such as Peter Gabriel, Sting,

Springsteen, and especially the emergence of Tracy Chapman, all broke through with some great soul-inspiring music of conscience. People started to get sick of all the homogenous formula pop and began to appreciate the more home grown sounds of folk, blues, reggae, world beat, and especially rap. Springsteen and U2 are the most unifying people I've seen since The Beatles.

'While I was born and raised in Los Angeles, I spent my summers at a very progressive Quaker camp in upstate New York. It was co-ed and inter-denominational with counsellors from all over the world. My introduction to being spiritually and socially conscious came primarily from there and my Quaker background. I lived from summer to summer, when I could spend those two and a half months hanging out with people who were more into the peace and civil rights movement – the kids of UN people and liberal lawyers – instead of the beach-party, showbiz, politically conservative world L.A. was in the early sixties. The counsellors at my camp were very much into the folk music revival that was going on at that time: the Kingston Trio; The Weavers; Peter, Paul and Mary; Joan Baez; and later Bob Dylan. I naturally idolised my counsellors, who were all playing the guitar and learning folk ballads and protest songs. So, I decided to trade the piano for the guitar. I didn't take lessons, I just taught myself.

'When I was about fourteen, I heard a record called *Blues at Newport '63* and immediately fell in love with the blues. I had always loved any kind of soul music – Ray Charles, Ike and Tina Turner, Motown and Stax, all the stuff we lapped up from the radio. But now I had to choose whether to spend my allowance on the new Bob Dylan, Beatles or Muddy Waters record.

'Back in California the guitar became a sort of haven for me, a little safe place to go. I was longing to live back East and be a beatnik and a folk singer, but I was always too young. I wanted to go to Mississippi and march in the civil rights movement. I kind of lost my childhood at some point, being so alienated from the L.A. scene, and I became very serious in my dream of saving the world. I was so angered and frustrated over the plight of black people and the injustice and the horror of Hiroshima. I wanted to hurry up and get in the Peace Corps, so I could "fix" things, as if things were my fault. I think that attitude did a lot for misdirecting what would have been a more carefree adolescence, and less problematic adulthood, for that matter.

'Playing the guitar and singing alone in my room made me feel very much in touch with my spirituality. For me, creativity, music, spirituality and political conscience were all peripherally connected in me and to the times. Music was serving a political-social function of uniting people and questioning what had gone on before: "We Shall Overcome", "The Times They Are a-Changin'". There was a social movement reflected in the music.

'I see a swing back to spirituality in music, because I think that there's a great sadness and emptiness today in people's lives. The despair and hopelessness has to be countered by hope and a throwing away of old models. The human spirit has always found a way to pull itself back together. We have to change our own lives first, internally and spiritually.

'An incredible exchange of energy goes on onstage, where you're almost transported. For me, the spark comes, very emotional, from the shared experience of what I'm singing about. It's the band, when we really lock in and the audience knows you're locking in. I wish I could lose myself more when I play by myself. It's easy to do with an audience, but I tend to be too self-conscious and judgemental when I'm alone. The audience is more unconditional, as if the channel is more open.

'That's probably why a lot of people did use drugs after the show because it was just such an incredible high. When you come off stage, what else are you supposed to do? You can't just hug everyone in the audience. I was anaesthetised by drugs and alcohol and also the lifestyle. At an early age, I became "Bonnie Raitt" at a time when I was still very unformed. I had to crystallise this personality before I was really ready to do it. At that point, the schism between the young girl and the professional person made it very difficult and insulating for me. The responsibility for being rewarded for something I didn't feel I deserved made me hide behind the alcohol. I got sucked into the lifestyle of a "rock 'n' roll blues mama". It was also a very exciting, dangerous and rebellious thing to get involved in, celebrated by all the cultural heroes we in the Woodstock Nation looked up to, as rejecting all the violence, hypocrisy, greed and shallowness of the "straight" world. It was an affirmation of real human values to adopt the counter-culture drug lifestyle. I couldn't wait to get out of school and drink and stay up playing music all night.

'But aside from having all that fun, I got out of touch with the person who's underneath all those layers. I built myself a personality. I think it worked in the beginning, but then as I got older, it didn't serve me as well. I think the lifestyle encouraged the music somewhat. I don't think it always got in the way. It's just that the drugs and alcohol part of it became physically and creatively debilitating and started running me at the end. I managed to put a halt to that and got in touch with why I'm here in the first place, a spiritual centre, and how important it is to be clear and to be able to open that up.

'I am right on the precipice of being about to create something new, to come from this new being that I am. It's exciting but terrifying. I'm afraid of being mediocre, which, if you're a little bit loaded, you don't have to worry about. I think too much and judge too much, and alcohol suspended that for a while, so it actually freed me up. Now I have to tap into a wellspring I haven't seen yet. I think if you're getting closer and closer to who you really are, who you really are has an awful lot to say.'

Bonnie continues to tour around the world as well as keeping faith with her lifelong commitment to social activism. Her song 'Just Like That', inspired by a news story, won a Grammy in 2023 for Song of the Year.

WILLIE DIXON

Blues, R&B songwriter, singer and bassist.

I WAS FORTUNATE ENOUGH TO MEET THIS GREAT BLUES singer, known as one of the most influential figures in the development of classic urban blues. He was a prolific songwriter and is credited for writing over 500 songs. I met him at his family home in Los Angeles. With the help of his walking stick, we crossed the room and sat together on the sofa and began the interview. He was gracious and friendly and we spent a long time chatting even after the tape had been turned off. It was not long after this interview, on 16 October 1990, that I saw him onstage at the 'Blues Festival' in Madison Square Garden. As he limped across the stage, leaning heavily on his cane, the crowds cheered. As soon as he started singing, his body swayed and, as one song followed another and the temperature rose, his feet started tapping, almost dancing, as he held his cane in both hands, Fred Astaire-style! He died fifteen months later.

'My mother sang in church and so did my dad, but never in the choir or nothin' like that. My father sang in the fields in Mississippi, and he sang just about some of everything and anything his mind came upon, like most of the blues artists and most of the people around that time.

'I've been writing practically all my life to a certain extent, because my mother used to write poems, mostly about spiritual things. I learned how to write poems, and I was thinking as a youngster I would get a chance to make poem books and sell them, but after I made so many, nobody was interested in them until I started to make songs out of them, kind of popular songs. I couldn't get them sold or nothing done with them, so I began to turn them into blues. My mother was a devoted Christian [and so thought the blues were profane], but my father – they called him a kind of an outlaw – he didn't care because he felt that Christianity and all those things was a lot of baloney and brainwash. So he would sing the blues, and she would sing spirituals, and I began to weigh the both of them. Eventually, I decided with the blues.

'When I was about twelve or thirteen, I was taught a lot about harmony from a fellow named Theo Phelps, who had a group called the Union Jubilee Singers. I joined the group and we would practise singing and go to all the little country churches and city churches and have singing contests all over everywhere. I sang bass all the time, so it taught me a lot about the bass lines. We rehearsed at his house and, in learning how to sing the various parts of harmony, it did me a lot of good because I could always use it in arranging things as I became older. Our group finally got a chance to sing on [radio station] WQBC in Vicksburg in the 1930s. That's when radio first came out. We sang every Friday evening, and that was a big event in our life.'

Willie, who founded the Blues Heaven Foundation to honour

and sustain the blues tradition and its makers, formulated a very interesting theory about the role of blues music in our society:

'I feel like the blues is actually some kind of documentary of the past and the present and something to give people inspiration for the future. The blues is the greatest music on the face of the earth. Everything likes music; everything that crawls, creeps, flies or swims likes music. They enjoy it; it attracts their attention. Most people like rhythm because they can dance to rhythm and it gives them an uplifting feeling. But blues has wisdom . . . it's always been there. If it wasn't for the messages that the drum had in it years ago, we probably wouldn't have the type of communication that we have today. So the drum was giving a message, and even today in musical sound, you get a good sound, then you get drums that you know are trying to tell you something, but here comes the wisdom and they all wait together. This is why the blues has more than the rest, because it has an understanding made with words along with the good feeling and the message. And you can get this understanding and learn to communicate with it and have a good time.

'People who try for anything can gain knowledge from it, and it all depends how much you try to think or try to involve yourself in something. If you involve yourself in something and think about it more, the more ideas can come to you. As these ideas come to you, you can understand them better.'

Willie died on 29 January 1992. He was seventy-six.

PART SIX

'To be creative you have to make illogical connections within your being. You have to pull strange elements together to create something new' –

RICHARD THOMPSON

GRAHAM NASH

Singer, songwriter, guitarist and solo artist who was a founding member of The Hollies and Crosby, Stills and Nash.

I **HAVE A HAZY MEMORY OF MEETING GRAHAM IN THE** sixties. We are sitting at a table in a noisy restaurant with a few other people, me a shy seventeen-year-old and Graham sitting diagonally opposite me further down the table. All I can remember is him catching my eye every now and then, bringing me out of myself with a big smile across his face. Many years later my then-husband, Ian Wallace, played drums for Crosby, Stills and Nash. I would join them for a few days at a time on the road. One night after the gig, when we were all congregated in one of their hotel rooms, Graham came up to me and said, 'I know you are a fellow seeker.' I felt we had an invisible bond.

Tell me about your upbringing.

'I was born 2 February in 1942 in Blackpool, about fifty miles outside of Manchester. My family actually lived in Manchester, but during the Second World War they evacuated all the pregnant women to a town outside the main bombing target areas. Manchester and Liverpool were connected by the Manchester Ship Canal and therefore it was one of the trade routes where the north of England got its food and material. It was a target of enemy bombing, so they evacuated the pregnant women outside of the main cities. My father was an engineer, a foreman in a moulding company in Blackpool, and my mother took care of the family.

'I had friends who played guitar and seemed to have talent, but they were dissuaded from their destiny by parents, who said, "You've got to get a real job; this will never last. Go to the factory like your grandfather did, and his father and your father and get a gold watch at sixty-five."

'I think my parents recognised something in me that they encouraged instead of deflated, and I'll always be grateful to them for that. I was always encouraged as a boy to follow my natural instincts; my mother and father instilled in me that if I followed my heart, I would come to no harm. Neither of them were musicians, although I found out about six months before my mother died that she was living her life vicariously through me. She had ambitions when she was a young woman of going on the stage and performing.

'At thirteen, I had a choice of a bicycle or a guitar. Fortunately, I chose a guitar.

'There was absolutely no doubt in my mind that I would be a rock and roll star, no doubt at all. I would practise my autograph at school. I would draw the latest Fender guitars and little stacks of amplifiers. When Allan Clarke and I first met, we were five years old. I distinctly remember in Mr Burke's class, the door opened and this old lady came in with a young boy and the only available seat in the class was right next to me.

Allan and I became good friends from that moment and we sang in the school choir. We became used to standing in front of the school, singing; it was no big deal at all, in fact, it was a thrill. I continued to perform with Allan and at the age of thirteen I knew that I would be a hit. I don't know why; I don't know what that was based on. I knew that Allan and I had something that pleased audiences, and we obviously translated that to mean that we could make it out there. I think that was also seen by our parents, which was the reason why they encouraged us.

'I wanted a guitar desperately when I was thirteen, after listening to Tommy Steele and Lonnie Donegan in his skiffle groups. They were my inspiration. When the skiffle craze hit England, everybody wanted to get a guitar. My mother bought me a little acoustic guitar which was ten pounds from Barretts of Manchester. One Saturday night we went down and we sang three songs in a working men's club, sandwiched in between the juggler and the comedian and we tore the house down. We knew what the audience wanted so we sang "Worried Man Blues" and "Guitar Boogie". We were given ten shillings each. In 1955, for two young kids, ten shillings was a fortune.

'At fourteen, I was able to go to nightclubs with Allan Clarke, who later, of course, formed The Hollies with me. We would go to nightclubs and be there until eleven at night with strippers and burlesque people and comedians and jugglers. My mother or father would always be there to make sure that we didn't drink. They didn't know we were sharing the dressing room with strippers. Then at sixteen, Allan, who did not pass his eleven-plus exam, went to work. I passed my eleven-plus exam and went on to a grammar school. So, we were separated for a while and, because he had time at night instead of doing homework, he joined a rock band.

'The next time I saw him, which was about four months later, he had this black electric guitar and a small amplifier, and the world opened. This was big time. He had his own electric guitar. So, I got an electric guitar. Every Sunday at the local pub, agents would come down to have a pint and check out the local talent and make bookings for them for various clubs throughout the north of England. And that's how we started. One day this guy came up to us and said, "You guys are pretty good, but you need a bass player and a drummer." We'd never entertained the idea of anybody joining us so we thought about it. He took out the very first Fender Stratocaster that I ever saw in my life and it was a beautiful object. It's a wonderfully designed guitar, and to this day it's a phenomenal shape. I'd only ever seen Buddy Holly with one at the London Palladium in the mid-fifties and pictures of people playing them in a movie called *The Girl Can't Help It*, or *Rock Around the Clock*. I was thrilled. And when he picked it up and played every Buddy Holly lick and every Everly Brothers lick, he was in the band. So, then we had a band together that went through various other amalgamations and ended up being The Hollies in 1962. I was twenty years old.

'One of the clubs that we played at frequently was the Cavern in Liverpool. In early '62, The Beatles were auditioning in London, and in early '63, their record became a hit. So then, all these A&R guys would come up from London to check out the north of England rock and roll clubs. They figured, that if these Beatles can make it, maybe there's other people up there who are also talented. Ron Richards from EMI came up to the Cavern one day during a lunchtime session. I distinctly remember it because I had no strings on my guitar because I couldn't afford them and kept breaking them at an alarming rate. And that made him chuckle. We stood out from the other people and he offered us a contract. In 1963 we went down to London to record, and our first record was a hit, "(Ain't That) Just Like Me" by The Coasters. We did a cover version and we never looked back, and The Hollies ended up having eighteen Top 10 records.

'I left The Hollies in '68 feeling very frustrated and misunderstood. They were basically drinkers. The Hollies were good working-class lads from the north of England and thought nothing of drinking a pint and having a good time. I wasn't so much of a drinker. When The Hollies first came to America in '66, I was introduced by Cass Eliott (from The Mamas and the Papas) to David Crosby. Cass turned me on to Crosby and acid and grass in the same month. So, my entire life changed drastically. And consequently, The Hollies and I started drifting apart in our thinking and in our writing. I was beginning to write songs that I thought were more insightful, deeper, not the normal pop songs that The Hollies were famous for recording. In '68 I left England and came to America, and I never went back. I've been, of course, every couple of years to check [on] my family, but I've been in L.A. since 1968.

Any unexplained psychic experiences?

I once saw a golden city in the clouds from my bedroom window. We lived in a two-up, two-down, which was two rooms downstairs, two rooms upstairs, with a bathroom at the end of the yard, outdoors, no hot water, that kind of cheap, working-class housing that was thrown up to provide the factory with bodies to work in. And I remember sitting at my bedroom window. It was a stormy day and the clouds opened. I can remember looking down Skinner Street and across to Isaac Street, and I saw what I thought was a golden city. It was very fleeting and it was obviously night. I used to hallucinate a lot when I was a child. I think every child does. I think you know the cracks in the ceiling, because it was a pretty old house, and they would turn into railroad tracks and ocean liners. And I would play a game where I would make animals out of the folds in the bedspread. I was always hallucinating. I always saw faces in the shadows, crocodiles in the clouds.

Do you believe in a greater power?

Absolutely. This world is too crazy not to believe that so many wonderful things have happened. There's obviously something that drives the mechanism of this universe. I don't believe it's an old man with a big beard, and I don't believe it's the Virgin Mary either. But I do believe that there is an energy that one can tap and call upon. Every choice I've made throughout my life has brought me to this point and has been a very simple choice, either things are right or they're wrong.

Does this greater power connect to your creativity?

There's no question about it. It's been very strange for me as a creative musician, because there are times when I don't believe where it's all coming from. I've had this ability all my life to observe a situation and internalise it and then externalise it. In younger days it was with jokes, but in my later life it came out musically. With some of my best songs, I have a memory about writing them, but the memory is of not remembering what state I was in when I wrote them. I go into a void, and it's very still. There are lots of times I don't remember writing the stuff I've written. I know I wrote it because it's on the paper, it's by my bed, or on the piano. It's in my handwriting too. But as to where that comes from, I have no idea. People have asked me all my life, how do you become a songwriter? How do you become a sculptor? How do you do these things? How do you take these photographs? Well, it's part of the same process. When I'm taking a photograph, there's no doubt in my mind when to push the button. It all comes together; the composition, the light and the moment. That's when I press the shutter.

I think that what I do as a creative artist, whether it be photographs or art or sculpting or music, is centred on something inside me that is different than most people. And they're just by-products of the feelings I have inside. Taking a picture to me is as difficult or as easy as writing songs. To me, it's all tapped from the same source. I can't really explain where that source is, which makes me believe that there's an external power that I'm tapping into that channel that is opening up.

Do you have to be in any sort of frame of mind or any frame of emotion before you can feel that channel opening?

I have to be moved. I have to be physically moved before I write. For instance, the last song I wrote, which was probably 'Try to Find Me', was written about the kids that had cerebral palsy. It was for the Bridge Benefit. There was me and Crosby, Stephen and Neil, Springsteen, Robin Williams, Tom Petty, Don Henley and Nils Lofgren. We all got together and did an acoustic concert at Pilgrim's Place in Bill Graham's place up in San Jose. Seeing the children in their wheelchairs and seeing a little girl crying because she wanted to get out of there, and then seeing another little guy in his wheelchair moving slowly towards her to make her feel okay. Later, feeling that emotion made me come back that same night. I was lying in bed and thinking about the situation, thinking what a drag it must be to be in a prison like that. To have a mind that works inside a body that doesn't. And then all of a sudden, the words come and the music comes. I go down to my piano, and this beautiful song that came out of nowhere has been born.

Most of my songs just take a matter of hours to finish, but 'Cathedral' took me four years to be honed and crafted. I think it's an important piece of my music. 'Wind on the Water' was a little like that too. That was a wonderful experience of sailing with David and coming across a blue whale. David's boat is about 55–60 feet long from bow to stern, and the whale was much longer than that. It had a blowhole bigger than this table. It was a tremendous experience.

So, you have to be moved to write?

Yeah, I have to be physically moved. Physically I can be anywhere because I have a pencil in my mind that is writing all the time. I'm finishing verses and choruses and tacking it on to this bit internally so it's almost like a conveyor belt where they drop off the end, seventy-five, eighty per cent finished. I can be anywhere. I thought that I would need space, peace and quiet, but when you have three kids, that's a fallacy. That doesn't exist. It's nice to be alone and to be quiet but it's not absolutely necessary for me to be able to create.

Do you believe you're here for a reason?

Absolutely. I'm here to feel good. If I can make myself feel good, I can make other people feel good. If I can reach myself with some of the stuff I write. If I can please myself with some of the sculpting I've done or pictures I've taken, I know that I stand a good chance of pleasing other people.

There's a painter friend of mine, an older guy from

Czechoslovakia. He was showing me some of his surrealistic paintings one day. One of them was on a big canvas and was called 'To be remembered'. That was the title of the painting. He looked at me because he knew of my own creations and he said, 'You'll understand this, Graham.' And then I realised, I'm probably creating pieces to affect other people, to be remembered. To leave some mark on this planet.

Have you ever felt you've been here before?

Oh, yeah. All my life I see people in various stages of spiritual growth. And I think very often that this life, this thing we call life, is a circle that we're on that gives you the opportunity to learn lessons throughout your life – how to treat people, how to treat yourself, how to relate to the environment, how to how to deal with life itself. And it's a series of lessons that I think you have to learn. And if you don't learn by the time you die, then you got to come back and until you have, then you can get off the wheel.

I often meet people for the first time and feel I've known them before.

What was it like learning your craft? What gave you the drive to learn to play guitar?

Initially it was obviously hard on your fingers because your fingers weren't used to making a D chord and your fingers weren't used to pressing strings down. Physically, it was difficult for a couple of months until you get calluses on the ends of your fingers and your fingers know where to go. It's never been truly difficult. I've always managed to be shown in an elementary lesson and then take it from there. For instance, Stephen Stills showed me how to play a D and an A chord on the piano, and then I took it from there. It's never been really difficult. What has been more difficult is realising that when you've finished writing a song that is one stage of the development of a piece, when you put it down on the record, on plastic, it's finished, it's over. There's nothing you can do to change those millions of copies of the song that are out there. And with that comes a certain responsibility to say something that is worth saying, something that can help other people deal with a very rough life. Say something that can hopefully make things a little less lonely and make people feel that they're not crazy by thinking the same thoughts that I'm thinking, and realising that once it's down on tape, on record, that it's unchangeable. You can't recut it and rewrite the second verse, there are a million copies out there and that's the way you did it.

So, there's a certain responsibility to get it right?

That's the most difficult part. I think it's knowing when to let go, knowing when to feel that the piece is finished. I would change bits of every piece of music I've ever written if I had the chance. But you can't. So, you have to recognise the point of I've pushed it as far as I can push it. This is it. It's done.

When you're playing your guitar or creating, do you ever feel what psychologist Abraham Maslow described as a 'Peak Experience'? Can you describe that?

It's an intense enjoyment that somebody else will love this. There's an intense joy in finding a chord progression that is beautifully linked to a melodic refrain which is totally linked to great words. That is one of the greatest pleasures for me in creativity. It's very hard to write simple songs. 'Our House', for example, is an incredibly simple song, but it's difficult to write for everybody. And sometimes I wish I was the kind of person like Maslow who didn't write for anybody but himself and is incredibly complicated and brilliant. I want to talk to people. I want to communicate. Maslow obviously communicates to a great many people. I think Elvis Presley communicated to more people. It just happens to be the art form of the time. I've saved myself fortunes in psychiatry bills because I talk to everybody and I talk to myself. It's not like I'm alone and isolated without any forms of expression. I have thousands of forms of expression every single day, every breath I take. I'm looking at the dewdrops dropping off the end of these leaves as we're sitting here. I'm looking at the pattern of the leaves shaking. And it's beautiful to me. I can express myself and find myself incredibly lucky like that. I don't know who I'd be if I didn't have the outlets I've had. I'd probably be crazy.

What are you feeling at the height of your creativity?

The feeling is one on a human scale that I just created something that really gets me off and I'm so excited. I want to go to Susan and I want to play her this new thing that I've written. I want to go to Crosby and share that experience. On the other hand, it's kind of scary because I have no idea where it came from because I'm not a trained musician. If anything, I'm an observer of life and I have this ability to translate that into an artistic expression. I don't want to question it in case it isn't there. In a way, I'm waiting to be found out that I don't know anything, that I've been scamming all these years. That's part of my rational feeling. I don't believe that that's the case but there are moments of weakness when I think, these people think you're some big shit. You know what? You're not. You're just a person who has his weaknesses and his bad side. I have this ability to get outside of myself.

Do you get more excitement from playing your guitar or writing songs?

The composing part is the most exciting. The rest is just my hands working.

It's the ideas that excite me more than anything. It's when I manage to put a great idea with a great melody and great chord structure that moves me when I say to myself, 'Fuck! That's good.' It fits, it all works. I don't play that well, so experiences on that level are from composing. I can see when Neil and Stephen are playing their guitars, for instance when they're playing a solo, they're out of themselves. I can definitely see that in other people. I don't have that experience myself. My experience on that level comes from actually composing; creating something out of nothing.

Did you ever reflect, 'Why me?'

Yeah, a lot. I mean, I could still be in Manchester, in the mill, but something in me made me strive for something I believed in. Which through parental encouragement and opportunity, I took total advantage of. All my life I knew I would be doing this. I must confess that it's gone on a little longer than I thought. It's been twenty-five years since I got my first record that was a hit. And in this business, that's a long time. But I feel I'm getting better and I feel I've got a lot more to offer. I still have an insane drive to create and express myself. It will never stop because I don't know what it is, I don't know how to stop it. I've never had a writer's block.

Are you aware of your creative abilities as a power?

Yes, very much so. And the power is enabling and shaking people and waking them up. I use my music to reflect the times that I'm going through, to reflect some of the things that happened to me, to express my outrage at some of the stuff that's going on that is unforgivable. To express the love that I feel, and the joy. And that's a great power to me. I think it makes people less lonely. It brings people together. It can change the world.

Of all the work that I've ever done, the greatest creation in my life are my three children. They're by far the greatest thing that ever happened to me. They contain everything that I am and hope to be. Everything I've been through is compacted in their tiny bodies.

Do you feel that everyone has the potential to be creative, or do you think it is a God-given gift? Did certain people have that gift?

I can look at myself and I feel differently than I do about Beethoven or Mozart, for instance. There are certain people who obviously have a God-given gift, and they were put on this earth to do nothing but that. Especially in the case of Mozart. With myself, I think I have a glimmer of creativity that I exercise the muscle of. Creativity is like a muscle. From the hallucination process that I've been through all my life that we talked about as a child, you take that ability and you work with it. I think creativity, to a large degree, is like a muscle that must be exercised or it withers.

Do you believe that everybody has that potential?

I think everybody has that potential, but I don't think that everybody is the same. Like I say, in Beethoven and in Mozart's case, I think they were a direct channel to what we shall refer to as God. I don't believe they have that power, even though I see glimpses of it. They have a sustained flash and burn out very quickly.

Is emotional turmoil an essential tool to your creating?

No, not necessary. I don't believe in the pained artist syndrome, where it's absolutely necessary to go through emotional turmoil to be able to create. I feel that being in touch with your emotions and being able to feel emotionally is vitally important. I don't believe that you need to create unhappiness in your life to be able to write from.

Is there a connection when you feel more or less creative to what's going on in your life?

I think my entire life is a song. I think my entire life is creation. I'm creating all the time.

I think my emotional and physical eyes have to be open. And it's tough sometimes, because I feel haunted by things that need to be said. And very often those feelings get triggered by a phrase or something that I see or a feeling that I feel, and I'm haunted until the song gets out. It's one of the reasons that I hated about John Lennon dying. I'm working on eight different pieces of music at the moment that no one's heard and won't hear until I complete them to the point where I can then externalise it on paper, and on an instrument, to be able to show somebody. How many songs did John have in his head? Important songs that we will never get to hear. That was the saddest part of his death.

Do you ever feel any spiritual force within you where your creativity is?

I can separate my humanity from the state I'm in when I create. And that's what makes me wonder, who am I to be doing this? Where is this coming from in me? There's part of me that feels totally normal like everybody else on the planet. But when I get into this creative state, I'm not the normal Graham Nash. And that's when I start to question, who is this? Where is this coming from? And that's when I have to say there's a channel opening to a greater power.

Do you have a choice to create? Or is it something that just happens?

It's happened both ways in my life. There are times when I've created out of nothing. There are times when I absolutely had no choice but to do it. That's a part of what I was saying earlier about being found out, because for a lot of my life I'm just trying to deal with life and get the best out of it. And then there's this other part of me that's not so sure what that is or who that is. One side of me is going, 'Boy! If only people knew how normal I am,' and the other side of me I know is different.

Are you in touch with the child in you?

Oh yeah! I'm still waiting to grow up!

What part do drugs and alcohol play in creativity: do they block or enhance?

Alcohol has never enhanced anything in me. I've been drunk

many times in my life, but I don't drink now. Alcohol has done absolutely nothing for me. LSD has opened a gate up for me, and there's a sign on the gate that says you already knew. Acid only reaffirmed what basically I already knew; that I am just one small speck in this giant madness. I try to do the best that I can. We're all a part of the same energy and we're all basically from the same point of creation. Weed, I used to love it, but I don't any more. For years I used to think it would help put me into a space where I could dream, where I could space out. I don't think it really enhanced the creative process. Cocaine absolutely did not, it blocked it and most other things. Coke to me is a number; it numbs you out to everything.

I stopped snorting cocaine and taking drugs in the same moment and never went back and never went through withdrawals. I used to smoke a lot but I was always in control. I don't have an addictive personality and I believe I have an addiction to beauty and have an addiction to the creative process, but not to drugs.

Did you ever feel a deep connection while playing with CS&N?

Oh, absolutely. I felt it much more with David and Stephen than I did with The Hollies. Especially with Crosby. I felt so linked to him musically, which I guess is spiritually as well. I know when he's going to make a certain mistake and I make the same mistake so that to the people listening we're both doing the same thing. I look at Crosby and we both smile at each other. That's how close we are.

Do you feel that the music today represents the unconscious feeling of the masses of our time?

Very much so. I think that in this world of turmoil and chaos, where the kids can't see a future, where the kids wonder, why get married? And why have kids? Because a lot of the people can't even get a job. A study was done in Connecticut about ten years ago. It was with 1,000 children and 80 per cent didn't believe they'd live to see the age of eighteen because of the nuclear holocaust. Put all that together with environmental pollution and they can see the poison in the atmosphere, in the earth and the water. And when you see the destruction of the family unit, with so many divorces and a scattering of people and a family. It is reflective, and I see it reflected in popular music. It is chaotic, especially things like the punk movement, rebellious, and it's very interesting. The music of the popular culture is totally reflective of what kids believe is happening now.

Have you any idea where the creative force comes from?

It's the question of the unknown channel. I know the channel's there but I don't know where it leads to, or if it comes from the desire to express myself. I think that combination of physical happenings in my life are the creative process, the desire to express the things I see and the ability to tap into the channel that allows you to create.

How do you feel on the verge of creating something?

I feel moved before I create. When I create, it becomes very still and time goes very quickly. It's like I'm suspended for that moment and that moment will last for an hour. But when I come out of that moment, it feels like it was only seconds long.

Do you feel there's a purpose to your life on a spiritual, political or social level?

Yeah, and they're all connected because I'm me. I cannot separate myself and the way I live my life from my writing or from my sculpture, or my photography. I think life itself is the art piece. The picture of my life will not be finished until I'm dead, and possibly because hopefully the music I created will be affecting people's lives way after I'm dead. To me, spiritual, political and social are all connected. It's my life.

Graham releases a new album, Now, *of original material in May 2023. Alongside his music, Graham has developed a parallel career as a photographer and has published books of his photographs as well as his artwork. An exhibition of his work opened in summer 2012 in New Jersey which showcased his skills in both media.*

ALBERT LEE

Guitarist and songwriter who has played with the Everly Brothers, Eric Clapton, Emmylou Harris and many others.

I MET ALBERT WHEN HE WAS PLAYING WITH ERIC IN 1978. Eric and my sister Pattie lived very close to our cottage in Surrey and so I would often go with my children to Eric's local gigs and got to know the musicians that played with him. Albert was highly respected as a guitar player and I got to know him and his wife Karen when I moved back to L.A.

'When I was about thirteen or fourteen, a friend's brother lent me his guitar. I learned to play the basics on it, and from then on the piano [which I'd been learning to play] took a back seat. I was really crazy about the guitar. I used to borrow guitars from various friends; in fact, I played for two years before I actually owned one. I taught myself just listening to records – Lonnie Donegan, then all the early rock 'n' roll that came along, Elvis, Buddy Holly and The Crickets. As far as guitar players go, I guess it was the guitar player with Gene Vincent, Cliff Gallup, that really made me want to play, to really learn about guitar.

I learned a lot from him, just copying his solos. They were very intricate and jazzy and had a lot of scales. It was a good way to practise, learning the scales.

'I left school when I was fifteen, and all I wanted to do was play music. I wasn't sure what I was going to do, but I wanted to do something with music. When I left school, I wasn't quite good enough to go professional, but a year later I was. At sixteen, I did my first tour, and I've been on the road ever since. Once I discovered the guitar, I really didn't have any other interests.

'I'll be playing something really fast, it'll just go by, because I play the guitar very fast and I don't have time to think of every move I'm making. It seems as if I'm skating over the fingerboards. I believe it's in the subconscious what's happening there, between my mind and my fingers. I might not be fully aware of what I'm doing. I could be thinking of something else, totally, but I'll be playing it.

'It works so much better when the band's in tune and it works as one. Then it really lifts what I'm doing, otherwise I'm just really going against the grain. I may be doing something dazzling, but it will sound stiff to me if I'm not playing over a perfect sound bed. It's exciting when you play with musicians and something comes about that you're not really expecting. If things aren't going well, no matter how well I play, it feels like I'm trying to push a car uphill, all bogged down. It can really take off when everybody is going in the same direction. There are those magic moments when the rhythm section has the perfect sound and groove, and you're able to just ride along, like riding along on the crest of a wave. It can lift you up.

'It happened often with Emmylou Harris and the Hot Band. It was a particularly good time for me, because I think I was really in tune with that band. It was my kind of music, and it was a band where everyone really listened to everyone else, which I rarely find. That band in particular was very sensitive to other musicians.

'I've used [drugs] to get me through that period where you're just slogging away at something and you really haven't got that initial excitement that you had at the beginning. I haven't taken any pills for ages, but when I've taken uppers I've been up half the night with them. I felt the nerve endings were raw and you are very in touch with your feelings; I know a lot of people who write like that, who stay up all night. Even without pills, though, just being up all night can get your nerves feeling like they wouldn't normally.

'It's taken me a long time to realise this, but I can play so much better without even one beer. I really can operate better if I'm totally straight. It is a lot of fun after having a few beers. It puts you in a different place than you would normally be in, but you're obviously sacrificing a lot of things by putting yourself under the influence of whatever you want to use. I haven't really done much coke over the years, I'm glad to say. I consider myself lucky that way; I don't really have an addictive personality. Like all musicians, I've tried most things. I can take it or leave it. I think back to ten years ago when I would occasionally have some coke before I went onstage; it was absolutely stupid. I'd get onstage and I'd be rigid. You could tell; I'd be playing really stiff and I'd think, what am I doing this for? I soon learned that was a mistake.

I like old rock 'n' roll – that's as raucous as I like to get. Tastes change as you mature; you begin to appreciate other kinds of music. I love listening to thirties and forties music. Some of the music today leaves me wondering; it worries me when I hear heavy metal music. Are its listeners getting their aggressions out by listening to that? It puzzles me. I guess going through adolescence, you feel you have to make a statement.'

Albert Lee continues to tour with his band in Europe and the US as well as release albums, the most recent being 2019's Gypsy Man – A Tribute to Buddy Holly.

CECE BULLARD

Singer, songwriter who has performed with such artists as Rita Coolidge.

'**D**URING A PEAK EXPERIENCE, IT FEELS LIKE I'VE LEFT my body. It's like you're dizzy and light-headed and yet right there. My hands just seem to throb, like a pulse almost. It's the best feeling in the world, bar none. It took me a lot of singing lessons before I finally connected with that feeling. The first time it clicked and I connected, I nearly fell down, nearly fainted. I went white and had to sit down, and I started crying. It was such a release of emotion. It was more than physical; it was as if I'd been trying to put a round peg in a square hole and suddenly it just went, and it just shocked my whole system. It doesn't happen often.

'When I'm blocked, which is caused by tension and fear – fear of success, fear of rejection, and all those things tied into your creativity being involved in [the music] business – the flow seems to stop and I just jam up. That's when you have to meditate or something and have faith, which I can't live without, and release all that negative energy and try to let those feelings of creativity come through.

'I want people to benefit from what I've learned about not being negative, not letting this century bog us down. I want to make people feel better about themselves and that they can change the world – as corny as all that sounds. We can make a concerted effort just by being the best we can be. Each person can do something so important on an individual level, that's what I want to tell people. You affect everything around you. That's the kind of thing I would like to express in music.'

Cece released a jazz EP in 2021, My One and Only Love, *and has been singing for the last ten years with a classical group called the Angeles Chorale, and occasionally as a soloist, doing concerts around L.A. three or four times a year.*

RICHARD THOMPSON

Guitarist, songwriter, singer and solo artist. He was formerly a member of Fairport Convention.

'**M**Y FATHER WAS A MUSIC FAN; HE'S A GREAT JAZZ fan and played a little guitar in a police dance band. So, there was a guitar in the house, plus his record collection – fifty per cent Jimmy Shand and fifty per cent Duke Ellington and Django Reinhardt. My musical taste is still fifty per cent Jimmy Shand and fifty per cent Duke Ellington and Django Reinhardt. I think childhood is a big influence on life: what you hear when you're three or four years old really tends to stay with you. About ten years ago I did a version of a Duke Ellington song, and I did all the parts on the guitar. I realised I hadn't heard this song since I was eight years old, but I'd remembered every single part, got the whole arrangement completely down. Amazing.

'I found rock 'n' roll very exciting, even at the age of seven or eight. I wanted to play the guitar as long as I can remember, because Elvis had a guitar and Buddy Holly had a guitar. I actually got my hands on one when I was ten.

'I was very introverted and shy, so often instead of having friends, I'd sit at home and play guitar. I felt like a social misfit all through school. Guitar might have been a kind of revenge: "Well, at least I can do this; they think I'm nothing." I was going to show them. It wasn't the whole thing, but there was some element of trying to acquire acceptance and respectability by playing the guitar.

'There are people who use music in a spiritual way in our world; it's absolutely their way of elevating. It does something to the human heart. This is the extraordinary thing about music, that whatever you're experiencing, it communicates to other people. It's not just this thing – "Oh, this is me having this great time musically" – that is communicated to the audience. It's a collective something or other. The way people respond to music when those exhilarating moments happen – it's a thing you remember all your life.

'When you inflict your creativity on other people, say an audience, you're very aware of what you can do to an audience, and there's a responsibility that goes with that. To some extent I find myself having to be moral. I express a morality in my music; there's a certain amount of propagandising in almost any kind of music, and that's okay. There's understanding that you don't want to feed people darkness or negativity. I write what's considered heavy-going kind of songs, but I don't see it as negative. I see it almost as a social necessity. Society is complex and strange and dark, and things happen. Being onstage you almost have to hold something up to the audience and say, "I know you don't want to look at this, but this is something we're all going to look at now, and after we've looked at it, we'll all feel better, won't we." It kind of works, it works for me and it works for the audience. Something's happened through singing it, through stating it, through letting it out in the room, and then sort of closing it up again. Mass catharsis!

'Not always the most popular music satisfies the collective unconscious of the most people. Popular music is basically crass and appeals at a crass level. It says something for people. There's a futuristic feeling with writing, where you're dealing with what's about to happen. I think a lot of the less commercially successful writers are really tapping into the collective unconscious, but people won't realise it for another ten years or so. The audience is slightly behind. I don't think someone like Madonna taps into the collective unconscious; I think she calculates, extremely cleverly, and she figures out her symbology and the right moves.

'The Peak Experience is very hard to talk about because you're not really there when it happens! It happens on most shows I play. You get inside the music to such an extent that you almost *are* the music, or the music's you. You're thinking about it but you're not thinking about it. It's almost a flashing backwards and forwards of intellect and intuition: one minute you're thinking G flat, seven five, and then it's gone and you're doing something that you're not aware of. You're just sort of flying along, and then you have another conscious moment where you think, "Oh, yes, two bars left."

'The same thing happens with writing. It seems to go backwards and forwards. There are times where you're thinking logically what you're doing: okay, two more lines here, and that's got to rhyme with that. And then suddenly you've got six verses written, and you don't know how it happened. It's odd, and I wouldn't like to be writing a book about it myself! It's too hard to figure out. It's the time when you're not there that things happen. It's when your ego moves out of the way, when you create the space that the music can actually come in and through. It's what we musicians live for, those magical moments.

'Drugs and alcohol work differently for different people. I don't think they helped me at all, quite the opposite actually. There's a balance to writing, and any sort of drug upsets the balance, except coffee, of course! I can't remember having written a good song while under the influence of anything. I've written songs about being drunk, but only while I was sober. Different people have different tolerances, though. Some people have written great stuff; *The Rime of the Ancient Mariner* was written under laudanum, a tincture of opium popular in the nineteenth century.

'To be creative, you have to make illogical connections within your being. You have to pull strange elements together to create something new. You have to weave something new out of different strands of the world. Drugs can help you get into that frame of mind, but they don't give you the overall view. There are states of mind that you have to reach. Drugs can help you do this or they can destroy your ability to do it. I don't think I've taken any drug, alcohol or anything for fifteen years. I'm certainly much happier. I'm just trying to use what little brain I have left!

'I can write anytime. I take notes while I'm sitting on a plane or in an airport. I jot down observations, lines, hooks. I'm really happy if I can say, "This month I'm going to write from six to four, whatever it is, office hours." Three months is paradise. That's the most creative for me; not only do you get the tap turned on, tap's a bit creaky at first, you have to oil it and give it a good turn before it starts to flow, but once it's flowing and I'm doing it every day, it seems to have some cumulative effect and I can really get rolling. That for me is ideal, and I can only write when I'm well. If I'm ill, I can't write at all. I can write if I'm comfortable, even if I write uncomfortable songs. My last drug is coffee; I find coffee is a wonderful elixir. A cup of coffee and I'm ready.'

Richard's album 13 Rivers *was released in 2018. In 2011, he was awarded an OBE for services to music. He published a book in 2021 called* Beeswing: Losing My Way and Finding My Voice. *He continues to tour with his band.*

EDIE BRICKELL

Singer, songwriter, who mostly collaborated
on an album with Steve Martin.

'**YOU FEEL LIKE A PRISONER IF YOU DON'T CREATE;**
you're jailed up inside of yourself. You've got to let that
out. It's there and it just needs to come out. It's freedom, the
desire for freedom.

'Sometimes you don't even know what your songs mean.
They just come out, and it can be a year later, and you think,
wow, I get it now, because you can look back on your life and
see more clearly than at the time when you experienced it.

'If you think of your creativity as a pool of water, then
drugs would be like throwing a rock in there. It creates ripples,
and it gets a little bit out of focus. It changes it. Sometimes
it's interesting and sometimes it's good, but sometimes it's not.
I think too much of it will block up the water, will dry it up.
You can have a balance, so I'm not against it, but I'm not for it all
the time. I think you should be in touch with being straight too.
I don't think you need drugs to be creative.

'Everybody has the potential to be creative. That's why there are so many unhappy people – because they won't do it, they won't let go. Everyone has their own particular gift. You just have to accept it, "Okay, this is it," then let it take over. Trust it, believe in it. Once you believe in it, it's there for you and you're there for it.

'I was just lucky enough to stumble on to the path and stay on it and not be so scared. There is fear involved, but once you get over that, you realise what you're doing and your abilities, your potential in life, then it turns into excitement.

'Letting go of fear, that's what creativity is. It's just all possibilities, creative ways of overcoming fear. The more fear you can release, the more you can allow yourself to be creative and take steps in the direction of your heart. I think you have all the answers right there for you. There are so many means of being creative. Creative is just being yourself, really, letting go of that fear to be who you are.

'Usually, the house has to be clean, to have a nice environment to create. I can't stand a crowded, cluttered environment. I like sparse settings.

'Sometimes you get that locked-up feeling in your chest, where it's all blocked there, black. Creativity frees you up, you feel like an open channel. I'm really lucky to do what I do – and grateful.'

In 2021, Edie and the New Bohemians released an album called Hunter and the Dog Star. *Edie has also worked both as a solo artist and in collaboration with other musicians, such as Steve Martin and bluegrass band Steep Canyon Rangers. She lives in Maui with her husband, Paul Simon.*

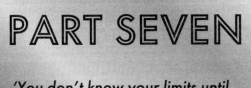

PART SEVEN

*'You don't know your limits until
you've gone to the edge'* –
PHIL COLLINS

ATTICUS ROSS

Atticus Ross is an English musician who lives and works in Los Angeles. He is best known for his musical partnership with Trent Reznor, both as a film composer and a member of the band Nine Inch Nails. He has received multiple awards for his endeavours, including two Academy Awards, two Golden Globes, two Critics Choice Awards, two Grammys, an Emmy and a BAFTA amongst others. In 2020, he was inducted into the Rock and Roll Hall of Fame alongside the other members of NIN.

In addition to the above, Atticus has produced, remixed and written for multiple other artists as well as scoring films both on his own and often alongside his wife Claudia Sarne and brother Leopold.

INTERVIEWED ATTICUS JUST RECENTLY OVER A ZOOM call, him in his studio in L.A. and me in London. I hadn't seen much of him over the last few years, but had followed his success, often through his son – my grandson – Wolf. I met Atticus and his family many years ago while he and my daughter were living in London.

How different is the music world now compared to the eighties and nineties?

I can't speak to making music in the eighties as I started professionally in about '92 but I presume those decades were fairly similar. Different music but same kind of model. As an artist, even an experimental one, you could earn a living making music. The great change – or in modern speak, 'disruptor' – was the internet. Napster followed by torrenting decimated music. I know how hard it is to make a record and I believe music has *worth* and musicians should be *paid*. The saddest thing that happened was people started to believe music was free. And it was. I'm not going to lie – I was torrenting like a maniac. I'm not proud of it but there was a sense of, if you can't beat them, join them. If I'm going to be broke, then I may as well own every piece of music that was ever created. That is literally how crazy torrenting was; the best sites were *far* better organised than iTunes, with *far* more music available. But another way of saying 'free' is 'no worth' and music *definitely* has worth. Unfortunately, this went on for far too long before the record companies got their shit together and the damage was done.

Then came Spotify – not exactly a saviour. As I understand, a creation with the record companies. Pretty sure there weren't any artists in those establishing meetings or anyone fighting the musicians' corner. Pretty sure there was no interest in hearing that side of the equation. Anyway, the rest is history – Spotify emerges with its meagre royalty plan and all-you-can-eat buffet. It succeeds primarily on the basis that it's less hassle than torrenting and a simpler solution for the general public. Since then, they've been joined by Apple Music, Tidal, Amazon and whatever others. Spotify set the model and the others fell in line – it never occurred to anyone that *maybe*, with a more generous split for the artist, that platform would garner a groundswell of support from the community they trade on.

Whilst all this is going on, journalism is suffering a similar fate – what once we paid for is viewed as 'for free' and the combination of the two starts to take a toll.

Obviously this happens over time, and this may be an oversimplification, but in effect we lose the traditional gatekeepers; with the loss of the old model record deal and artist support, plus the reviews that once mattered so much, so began, in my view, a cultural erosion. I know some may say it's democratisation – now anyone can upload a record – but the problem with that is too much music. It's so hard to get noticed.

When I was growing up, the *NME*, *Melody Maker* and *Sounds*, along with an assortment of fanzines, were like my bible. *Sounds* and *Melody Maker* are long gone, the *NME* turned into clickbait, as did *Rolling Stone*, and we're left in a place where any new band or artist needs to be inextricably linked to marketing themselves on social media for any chance of attention. I know that I probably sound like an old fart but I'd go as far as saying that social media has changed song writing. If you have to self-promote and your format is limited to fifteen or thirty seconds or whatever, naturally you conform to the opportunity. Think of a song like 'Pictures of You' by The Cure. Fifteen seconds *doesn't* get you very far. So, are we losing classic songs like that?

I don't have the answer.

I have felt a little more optimism over the last couple of years but I'll give you a recent example of the conundrum:

A friend of mine, Dave Sitek, who was in a band called TV on the Radio – a phenomenal band, part of the New York scene of the early noughties that gave us Yeah Yeah Yeahs (whom Dave produced), The Strokes, LCD Soundsystem, etc. – recently sent me his work with this girl who I thought was amazing. In my mind she ticked every box; great song writing, great look, obvious talent... 'authentic'. It was so good that I asked him what he was doing with it, and when the response was 'floundering', I offered to speak to my lawyer. I was amazed to hear, and I semi-quote, 'You could literally walk into a record company with *The White Album* and they wouldn't even listen to it unless the social media metrics had hit a certain level.' And to me that's just so depressing. Essentially, music alone is now not enough.

Do you know Eg White?

I used to know Eg in London in the nineties but I haven't seen or spoken to him for at least twenty-three years. From what I've heard, he's become an extremely successful and sought-after songwriter and producer. He was always very talented, so it's no surprise.

That's another way the business has changed: in the nineties, the song-writing stream was a pretty narrow one, one you might have heard about but was confined to the edges of pop stardom. In 2023, it's the main thoroughfare – I'm sure Eg is a one-stop shop but it's certainly not unusual to see multiple writers on one song. Perhaps it's a good thing in that more people are able to express their creativity and more musicians are able to make a living. But viewed through a nineties lens, it's obvious where the judgement comes from; in yesteryear an artist was expected to write their own material.

Worst case nowadays is you might sometimes see fifteen to twenty people on a song because it's gone through various different stages, like, this person's done the beat and this person did the top line and this person wrote the verse, and that person did the bass line. It's almost like an equation that's put together from different people. In that scenario I feel like music can become 'product', and that's where I'm out. Maybe I'm old-fashioned but I still view music as art, and art requires vision and heart.

Anyway, I am certainly NOT suggesting all pop stars don't write their own material – in fact, Trent and I worked with Halsey, who is incredibly successful, pretty much as big as you can get in the US, and it was a great experience. Halsey wrote all the lyrics and melody – super talented – and Trent and I did the music and production. It was something different for both parties, and out came an album that I'm incredibly proud of. Halsey was nominated for a Grammy and I think I can speak for everyone when I say it was a lot of fun – we all learned a lot.

That said, we've got a young artist staying with us right now – Neneh Cherry's daughter – who's out here doing sessions. 'Sessions' in the 2023 sense of the word. The label sends her out into different scenarios each day, working with different songwriters and producers to see whom she clicks with. She writes her own melodies and lyrics but I don't get the sense the hunt for the right collaborator is particularly fun . . . there are good days and bad days, but it's endless. Add to that the pressure of keeping up social media each day . . . it's tough. And it's VERY different to my experience of starting out.

How has it changed for you as far as song writing, compared to then writing for film scores? And are you doing more of that now?

My life is divided between doing records and doing film scores, but it's much more weighted towards film scores at the moment.

Nine Inch Nails has always been about storytelling, in my opinion, so the jump to writing music for film, although incredibly intimidating at first, felt like an organic part of our musical journey. Even before I met Trent, I used to listen to his records and be taken to 'a place'. A record like *The Downward Spiral* or *The Fragile* is a cohesive statement – you start in one place and end in another and along the way experience a visceral emotional journey. And going back to your first question, the notion of the album as a body of work is something else we've largely lost in how people digest music today . . . and that's sad as those kinds of records were written as a whole. One song follows another for a reason – think of Pink Floyd's *The Wall* – meal best served whole, no question.

Anyway, I think it'd be fair to say Trent and I share a certain sensibility and the last twenty-three years working together has been a wild experience. To get back to your question, I think one feeds the other and vice versa. The songs feed the scores and the scores feed the songs – we bounce between both worlds. There's no question that writing music for film has taken us to places we'd never imagined and what we've learned on those explorations has provided a new depth to the vocabulary we can use for NIN. And to go back to the notion of storytelling, writing for NIN goes beyond 'is this a good verse or chorus' – it's more like, what are we trying to say with this song? And how do we want you to feel when you're listening to it? So moving into film felt organic in the sense that we're in service to a story, this time someone else's, but it's still about how you feel when you are experiencing it. In fact, I think our strong point has always been focusing in on the emotional heart of the story and finding the best musical approach and language to communicate it. And the way we've approached films is that each movie is a unique story, so each score should have its own unique identity, whether that be through choice of instrumentation or different ways to treat and effect the instruments, or sound collage or whatever it might be. And that process is always informed by lengthy and ongoing conversation with the director. It's a collaboration, in the truest sense of the word. Writing for NIN we are in charge, on a movie we are in service; whatever the director might have imagined, our goal is to ten times better it.

There's a version of film scoring where the composer comes on board toward the end of post and applies the score – a bit like wallpapering the house after it's built. Our approach has been to become involved very early, often even before a camera's picked up so that the music can act as a foundation for the house rather than a coat of paint at the end. The music becomes part of the DNA of the story – like another character in the film, if appropriate. The scores that really have inspired me are things like *Taxi Driver*, if I hear a piece of that music, I think about that film, and if I see a bit of that film, I think about that music. They're indelibly connected. That's the goal. I'm not saying that we hit it every time, but we're aiming for it and we're going to put the time in to try.

What I CAN say is no record or score has ever left the studio any less than the best it can possibly be at that point in time. It's always the best we can do.

When *The Social Network* came out, it became this big thing.

But that wasn't how it was when we were making it. That was the second film I'd done; I'd literally just finished my first film, *The Book of Eli*, for the Hughes Brothers and then we did *The Social Network*. So, it wasn't like either of us had much experience. We were faced with a choice: should we do some kind of crash course and 'learn' about making film music or should we rely on instinct? We chose the latter and I'm glad we did.

There was never an intention to be doing something just to be different. It was simply that that approach felt like the most effective and appropriate way to tell that story. When the film was being made, I'm not sure that Sony had huge expectations considering the subject matter and the absence of a big star line-up. And then it came out and got all these amazing reviews . . . I think they had to rush to catch up to something that had taken off.

And then, for us, it just became very psychedelic. In 2023 I have some experience in this world, but at the time it felt super weird, to be at the Golden Globes or the Oscars. Amazing and unexpected but nonetheless definitely weird.

I think that those early films established a process that we've continued to refine. Just getting better at storytelling – or not better, but getting deeper into it as an art form. And as I mentioned, what's interesting about film music is it's taken me to places that I very much doubt I would have ever visited making records. For instance, with a film like *Mank*, [David] Fincher wanted it to feel like a work that had been sitting on a shelf undiscovered since 1940, a companion piece to *Citizen Kane*. Suddenly one's faced with a challenge wondering, can we can live up to it? It's simultaneously exciting and terrifying. Herrmann-inspired with a big band and orchestra. Add to that the pandemic, so every musician had to record themselves at home. No challenge equals no experience and these have been incredible experiences. It's been humbling – it's taught me how little I know about music and how much there is to learn, and how music is a lesson that never ends. That's one of the things I love about doing films. It's an intense collaboration for a period of time, but there aren't really any rules. There's no rule to tell you how you're best going to tell a story sonically and I think that's very freeing. I'm incredibly grateful that this avenue opened up, because, as we talked about at the beginning of this conversation, how different it is being a working producer in 2023. I don't know if I'd enjoy it. Film has allowed production to be a choice rather than a necessity. We just did a couple of songs with Fever Ray. I don't know if you know Fever Ray? Karin Dreijer is their name and they were in a duo called The Knife, an incredibly influential and important band, as is Fever Ray. Anyway, Fever Ray's last album was called *Radical Romantics*, and it came out this year. It was an extremely well-reviewed piece of work. Karin is a true artist – someone who's expressing themselves without any compromise and making great progressive music. It's probably not going to go to the top of the charts because the top of the charts has become a different place now.

It's interesting because we did an instrumental album in 2008 called *Ghosts*, and we wrote another instalment at the beginning of the pandemic, which we gave away for free. A song from the first *Ghosts* collection was sampled by Lil Nas X for a song called 'Old Town Road'. We're in the studio one day and we get a call: 'There's a new artist called Lil Nas X, he's sampled your work and is going to release this song tomorrow. Is that okay?' And we say, 'Yeah, that's fine.' Management work out the appropriate splits and, knowing he's an unsigned artist and how hard it is to get noticed, we kind of forget about it.

Next thing you know is he's having a monstrous hit – in fact, 'Old Town Road' was the first time I really became aware of TikTok. That's where he blew it up. It was already a hit when Columbia signed him. It went on to be the longest number one of all time in America and it was the fastest-selling to diamond, which is ten times platinum. So, me and Trent were credited as producers and songwriters on it because it's our music.

Why I mention it is we were afforded the chance to experience streaming from the vantage of the top 1 per cent. Even if you're in a position of relative success, streaming is really designed for that top 1 per cent . . . like many things in the world of 2023. I don't know exact numbers but my guess is the top 1 per cent take 90 per cent of the money. It's sad because we're losing the middle – great, well-known bands are faced with having to have a side gig, give up or simply stay on the road. Touring is exhausting, and to endlessly be on tour to support yourself isn't necessarily the way everyone wants to live. But options and opportunities have lessened and we're paying a cultural price, in my opinion. And what's crazy is there is more money in the music business than EVER. I read an article about the head of Universal taking a yearly bonus that was more than the entire amount of money generated by sales and streaming in the UK that same year . . . you tell me – does that sound right, or even vaguely fair?

As you say, it happened organically, but it seems to be a better time to be writing music for film scores than doing what you used to do.

It's impossible for me to put into words how grateful I am for the way things have turned out. I don't take any of this for granted, we all have dreams and the fact that many of mine became a reality is humbling, to say the least, and not to sound corny.

Whether it's film scores or records, the fact that I get to do what I love every day with and for people I care deeply about – it's pretty wild.

And to answer your question, yes – film music has taken me on some extraordinary and rewarding journeys but I don't think we're done with NIN. In fact, I think that when we do come to the next one, it'll be a big swing. And having this other career in film means we're able to support however long we need in the studio. Plus we have our own studio, so we're not beholden to anyone or anything. When I think of newer artists, particularly the left-field ones, I really do feel for them.

It's an eye-opener to me. Having interviewed you, and Eg White a few weeks ago, and hearing about how different things are nowadays, it seems so much more complicated.

Well, a band like Depeche Mode probably wouldn't get signed today. I mean, they're doing however many nights at the Forum; they're a huge band. We played with them in Madrid with Queens of the Stone Age. A massive festival in Madrid in 2018. Would any of those bands get signed today? You know what I mean? Maybe I'm wrong, but I just don't know that any of those bands would be able to fit today's format. Music used to be about rebellion and identity, and it seems like the position of music in people's lives has changed. It's more background. It's an addition. When I was growing up, the bands I liked defined who I was and how I dressed, what my identity was, everything about me. And I knew nothing about those bands, they were like aliens. I felt like they were people totally out of reach. And I'm not saying that's good or bad, but it just felt so mystical and amazing. Now you can see, 'Oh, here's what I had for breakfast today.' I don't want to see what David Bowie had for breakfast. Know what I mean?

Who were your heroes when you were growing up?

I was always super into music especially because Dad (Ian Ross) had Radio Caroline. From a very young age we had a jukebox that had everything you'd think a jukebox in 1972 should and would have. I would have been two. We lived on Westbourne Park Road. To begin with I was into Fats Domino and Jerry Lee Lewis, and Elvis – that type of thing. I'm talking about very young. And then The Beatles and the Stones, James Brown and Sly and the Family Stone. I'm talking about while growing up, before I was ten or eleven. And then as I got a bit older and we moved to America I started to find myself more, in terms of music as identity. Then I was into bands like The Police and The Clash, Joy Division and The Cult. It was just such a vibrant time for music, and so I had that, which was more like guitar bands. I was also spending every day in a nightclub that was based around disco music. So, I knew that whole world intimately, and loved that music. I think my understanding of groove, which has always been very important to me, came from then and spending time with the guy that they bought from New York, Disco Danny, who was a DJ. That was the first time I'd ever seen a Technics 1200 and he taught me how to mix and all that kind of thing. Going back to storytelling, if you're a DJ and you've got a night ahead of you in somewhere like Flippers, whatever year that was, you've got to tell a story with your music to keep people engaged over that period, that night. Music is powerful and you are dictating the journey. Babies may be being made because you dropped a particular couple of songs, in a particular order at a particular point in the evening. So I think the art of a great DJ is, in a sense, storytelling. And that magic is beyond the technical abilities that were required, which again have changed now because it used to be mixing records with two decks instead of a computer. I'm not knocking anyone; I'm just saying that it was different then. And then for me, my punk rock is acid house, which started in clubs like Shoom, Spectrum, Heaven and The Wag. That was the kind of music that I could have that my parents wouldn't understand. Then it turned into raves, which the UK press was up in arms about. That was the music of my generation that our parents hated and didn't understand, and you need that. Or you used to.

I could keep going but I'd be here all day listing the bands.

When did you start playing music?

My story is that I was out all the time in music and experiencing music, but I didn't feel that I was a good enough musician until I got clean when I was twenty-two. So, what had happened was I'd managed to get a degree from the Courtauld Institute while strung out the whole time, and I moved to New York and worked for Annina Nosei before moving into curation at one of Julian Pretto's galleries, who had three spaces in Soho. I curated one of them and lived in the back. I moved to New York because this girlfriend had taken me out there for the weekend and it just blew my mind. I mean, London was great but New York in the late eighties was just unbelievable. It was incredibly fulfilling in terms of art and music. There was this kind of collision of artists and musicians, including what was the birth of hip hop. People would argue that the birth was earlier than that, but it felt like this real force in 1989, 1990, which was exactly when I was living there. It felt like all music interplayed and connected at that point – it was an incredible time until it wasn't, personally speaking.

I moved back to England in August of 1990, to get better. I was in Weston-super-Mare for several months and then, when I came back to London, I didn't have anything and, in a sense, having nothing was freeing. I didn't see it like that at the time, but I had just enough to buy a drum machine, an 808, a record deck and a keyboard that had ten seconds of sampling time. And that changed my life forever. Me and my brother and a friend made a song. It was literally the first song that we made that got us a development deal at Island. A development deal in those times meant you're not signed to make a record, which we never did for Island, but we were given enough money to live on, and I'm talking about just to get by, but to do music all the time. That's what really enabled me to commit my life to that. And of course, when that ran out, there was a bit of a time polishing furniture and other shitty jobs for a couple of days a week to support making music until the next deal. But what happened was that through the nineties I was pretty much always signed, never had a big record, but like I was saying about the industry then, it was so different because you could be making music that wasn't going to be a number-one pop song but was being signed by record companies because whoever it was in the A&R department felt this could be a great band or an interesting band or whatever it was. And it felt like every record company had a roster of acts that probably were never going to be number one, but they were interesting artistic acts who were trying to push the form forward. And a huge part of my time over that decade was working for other people as well.

I worked for this guy called Tim Simenon, who was part of

a big musical transformation in the early nineties in London. He had a band called Bomb the Bass that I was in for a bit, but he was already super successful. Tim's first single came out in '89 and went to number two, which was amazing considering the type of music – club music. He was basically a DJ who turned into a musician and became this huge producer. And I worked as a programmer for him. He had a great studio, which at that point in time – he was a couple of years older than me, say twenty-five – was unusual. Instead of paying for studio time and watching a clock tick money away, we could work whenever we wanted for however long we wanted. Him and another guy I worked for and eventually produced, Barry Adamson, they taught me a lot. Then I started my own band, 12 Rounds, with my now wife, the extraordinarily talented Claudia Sarne, and we signed to Polydor and then Interscope and then Nothing. It felt like an exciting time and it was a learning period. I feel like everything has been a learning period and I'm still learning but the experience that I had in the nineties was very special. When I look back at the nineties, it seems like a golden age for music – in retrospect, there was almost a classic record coming out every month. And I feel like that world I grew up in, of making music and being able to survive, has kind of disappeared. It isn't here any more. I don't know, maybe it'll change. A lot of people have tried to do a lot of things. When Trent designed Apple Music and Jimmy (Iovine) sold Beats to Apple, they went up there with the intent of trying to make a service that was artist-friendly.

I think it would be interesting for you to talk to some younger musicians to get their perspective. Maybe I'm wrong but it's definitely different . . . All I can speak to is, there used to be a way to be an artist in your early career and survive.

If that has disappeared, we should all be very sad. And things should change.

What gives you the drive to create, or what gave you the drive to keep creating? What is the drive?

For me I was just obsessed with music, and I still am. Although that obsession has somewhat changed in the sense that I think, when I was younger, I just had to be making music all the time. And in a way, there was something I could hear in my head that I wasn't actually able to get to come out of the speakers until I was in my early thirties. Which is different for different people. But the sound that I could hear in my head, that I was always striving for, I just didn't have the ability to make it. I'm not saying that there weren't good things, there were lots of good things through those years. But when I was able to imagine something in my mind and get it to come out of the speakers, that felt huge. If I'm honest, there was also some competitiveness and I wanted to be able to live for and from music. I knew if I did anything else, I'd just be being dishonest with myself. This was what I needed to do, and it did feel like I needed to do it. There wasn't a plan B or any other option. I think everybody's journey is to do with talent plus the right circumstance and the right time.

It's almost like a sense of destiny.

I was never motivated purely by success, but I wanted to be able to make a living from what I was doing. And as I said, because that's the way the music industry used to be set up, in one way or another I have been able to do this since my early twenties. But when things turned and became very successful, that was out of my control. I did not compromise and always stuck to the vision of what I wanted to do. Coming into contact with Trent was obviously a huge part of that turning point, followed by the ventures into film. But the kind of directors that we work with want us to be artists as well. So that's another very fortunate position to end up in. I'm not saying that there's some kind of autonomy, like, okay, fuck it, I want to do this kind of music so I'm just going to put [it] on your film. Not at all. It's all about what's right for the project. But it's been yet another opportunity for some intense collaborations with some incredibly talented people – directors, writers, editors, producers, sound teams . . . the whole world of it.

That's amazing. Do you have to actually see the film to compose the music, or is it enough to talk to the director and find out what he wants to make the film into?

You end up working to the picture, but our process is usually that we spend time with the director and the script. Ideally this is before the camera has been picked up. And during that time, through those conversations and reading the script, you have your own film in mind and we start creating music that isn't meant to be necessarily for a scene, it's just building the world of what this story feels like and sounds like. It's kind of impressionistic and we'll send stuff to the director during that period. It's not meant for a particular scene in the script, it's more to see if it fits the story emotionally speaking and to hone in on the choice of instruments. It's actually making music that feels very free. You find that through the director saying, 'I hate this,' that it's just as valuable as the director saying, 'I love it' and, 'This feels right.' Although loving it is clearly preferable.

Once the film is shot, then it will transform to traditional scoring to picture, but the advantage is the palette is already established. It's a longer process but it's a more creative and fulfilling one.

I think, if you're writing about creativity and you're writing about music, it's hard to ignore the challenges of how the world works now. It used to be that creativity was enough, but now you have to be a marketing person. That's what bothers me because I'm the last person who would market myself and say, 'Oh, I'm great.' It just feels totally at odds with who I am and what I believe a musician should be. There should be a kind of mystery to that person. I admit that could just be nostalgia or me romanticising, but that's what I enjoyed from artists; this idea that they were mysterious beings who operated on some other plane. That's true for any kind of artist, whether it's a painter or someone who writes songs or books or makes films or whatever. Understanding how much things have changed and how hard it is nowadays, and to get the perspective from a younger artist, that would be an interesting part of your book. Maybe I'm totally wrong about ALL of it . . . maybe it's better. Who knows?

JOHN MAYALL

Blues singer, guitarist, keyboard player and songwriter.

JOHN MAYALL WAS THE FOUNDER OF JOHN MAYALL'S Bluesbreakers, a band that had counted among its members some of the most famous blues and rock musicians, including Eric Clapton, Peter Green and Mick Taylor. Mick Fleetwood briefly joined Peter Green and John McVie as a member of John Mayall's Bluesbreakers.

I saw John play over many years during the sixties, when Mick (Fleetwood) would play at The Flamingo in Soho. John would often either have Peter Green, Eric Clapton (or even Mick for a couple of months) in his band. Since then, I have seen him in L.A. occasionally and was fortunate enough to interview 'The Godfather of British Blues'.

'My father was a musician, and I was exposed to all his record collection at an early age. He had guitars around the house, so when I was big enough, I started to get the rudiments together. My parents split up when I was about eleven, but I did see him. His record collection was really what started all my musical interest.

'I was brought up listening to jazz, and Django Reinhardt, Eddie Lang, Lonnie Johnson, Louis Armstrong, Duke Ellington, people like that. I know I became *obsessed* with boogie-woogie, so anything that was going on with boogie-woogie piano, that's really what led me into my own exploration of American black music, and that drew me to the piano. I spent a laborious couple of years learning the left hand to do this, and then learning the right hand. That's how I did learn to play the piano, through trying to do boogie-woogie.

'We are spokesmen through music. We do have a voice that people listen to, and you can get messages across. People do listen to words of songs. On the album *The Chicago Line*, I wrote a song about stopping drinking ["Give Me One More Day"], which is basically telling people, "Don't destroy your lives. It is hip not to drink." I think there are quite a few musicians who are also taking that stance, and it's great. People who admire you will listen to that, and you are an influence. If you can just reach a couple of people in the audience that one night, then you've accomplished something.

'It's a very exhilarating thing when you play before a live audience or just between other musicians and yourself. The interplay you experience is something you can't really explain; it's just something that takes place. That's why I never play at home; I've never practised or picked up an instrument when I'm not playing on the road. So, when I get together with this band – when we go out and do shows – the peak comes instantly. You're a part of something that you create as a band and individually. I like to savour the joy when we get together and that spark that happens. It's always a surprise. The blues is not music you set down or play the same way any one time, it's always different, a creative process, an improvisation, something that takes place almost beyond your own control.

'The only drug I've ever done is drink. I've had seventeen years of drinking. I didn't start drinking until I was thirty-five and already established in the music business; it was something that was the thing to do. I had never had a drink before; it was the novelty of it. Everybody was drinking in the seventies so I joined in, and that took over for quite some years. I stopped drinking five years ago. I've never smoked a joint, never taken pills or cocaine. I don't think that any kind of stimulant can possibly be of any use to anyone. They can delude you. I've found after having the experience of using alcohol in the middle period of my musical career and seeing the contrast between the beginning and now, that now is a completely different focus. Everything is a lot clearer. You can actually get to the point and play better music because you know what you're doing. You're not getting blunted in any way.

'Perhaps everybody has got a potential to contribute something. It's just a case of whether they will recognise it within themselves and have the courage to go out and say, "I'll develop this and see if I can do something with it," rather than just get nailed in a slot and get stuck with that for the rest of your life.

[In addition to the courage needed to find the creative path, an artist also must fearlessly face creative challenges throughout life. Tony Williams described his continual attempts to take his own creative expression a step further: "I'm always reaching for something." That's what I think my mandate is, what my role is. I am supposed to be reaching for things; I'm not supposed to just be repeating what I've done. I can repeat things and I do, but it's no good unless I'm in the process of reaching.]

'Creativity for me starts with a desire to create something, and be inspired by something, or have a need to do something. For instance, when my house burned down, there was obviously work to be done, so something will always present itself where you have a challenge and you get inspired to meet it. That's where the creativity starts to come in, when you start using your imagination to what it can be and then see how close you can get to that. It starts off as a need. For example, when you get an opportunity to do an album, there's ten songs that need to be done right there, so that starts you: "Okay, I need ten songs, what are they going to be about?" Then you start breaking them down into sections and keys and stories, etc.

'Once you've got it mapped out like that, you can concentrate on any one specific song and, depending how your inspiration might go, you might work on just one song if you're in that particular mood. Sometimes, having got the subject, a couple of lines will just come to you and you build on that, before the music. The music might come first, but first of all comes the idea of what you're going to talk about – the story, the emotion – that needs to be put into words and music in its final entity. Get your subject first and that will lead you where you're going to go, certainly lead you into the musical mood, and then you just have to put the words together to express it in a story-like form.'

John announced his retirement from touring in 2021 at the age of eighty-eight. He says he will continue to do the occasional show near his home in California, and special appearances further afield from time to time. His 37th album, The Sun Is Shining Down, *was released in 2022.*

TERRI LYNE CARRINGTON

Jazz drummer and composer.

'**M**Y FATHER'S A MUSICIAN; MY GRANDFATHER WAS a musician; and my mother is musically inclined – she studied piano. My grandfather passed away before I was born, but his drums were in the house; my father plays saxophone. I started playing saxophone first, and when I was seven, I switched to drums. I'm an only child, and my father wanted a son to carry on the musical tradition in our family, so when I decided to play, he was really happy. I started taking lessons when I was eight.

'My dad and his musician friends – (jazz stars) Illinois Jacquet, Roland Kirk and Clark Terry – encouraged me to play. Jazz drummers would come into Boston, where we lived, and ask me to sit in with them: Elvin Jones, Art Blakey, Buddy Rich. Beginning when I was ten, I was a special guest in Clark Terry's band with Louie Bellson, George Duvivier, Jimmy Rawls, Eddie "Lockjaw" Davis, Garnett Brown and Al Cohn.

'In the last few years, I've come to feel like I encourage

people – women and younger people – with my playing. And that's really what it's about for me. People come up to me, and I can see it in their eyes; they really feel encouraged, like it's something they always wanted to do but didn't. Or they see something in me that encourages them. I started seeing what a deep effect you can have on people, when they see you and admire you, that they can do something.

'Everybody's life is different, as well as their capacity to deal with things. I think there's a lot of heartache in this industry, with very sensitive people, and they hurt a lot. Everybody's capacity to deal with pain is different. Some people turn to drugs to escape. I don't think you can criticise that. I know it's abusive, and it bugs me, but for the most part so many of the great musicians were drug addicts. Maybe they would have been better if they hadn't been, maybe not. But who knows? I can't do drugs, because I'm pretty spaced without them. I have to have all my senses.'

Terri Lyne Carrington serves as the founder and artistic director of the Berklee Institute of Jazz and Gender Justice and the Carr Centre in Detroit, Michigan. In 2020, she was one of four recipients of the NEA Jazz Master's Fellowship in honour of lifetime achievement. She has written a non-fiction children's book in the form of an illustrated poem and has won many awards, including three Grammys. She was the first female musician to win in the Best Jazz Instrumental category.

ANTHONY KIEDIS

Songwriter and lead singer of the Red Hot Chili Peppers.

'**B**OTH MY PARENTS WERE VERY ENCOURAGING towards my creative talents. I moved in with my [divorced] father when I was eleven; it was an incredible change for me, because I went from a very backward Midwestern culture, where they're not really aware of what's around them, to Hollywood. There, it was much more the epicentre of culture, and there were a lot more things happening.

'My dad was very crazy: he was concerned that I become well educated, and he always gave me great books to read, as well as little vocabulary tests and things like that. At the same time, he was very much a hippie/gangster/playboy/over-the-edge party maniac on the Sunset Strip, and I wanted to be just like him, so I followed his every footstep. He was a graduate of UCLA film school; he was very together as far as that was concerned. He led the wild, unrestrained, reckless life, but he encouraged me to do creative things. When I would write a paper, he would always want to read it, and he really enjoyed my writing. And that's pretty much all I did until I started acting – when he started acting, I decided I would do what he was doing. There was never any suppression from my parents.

'There are some times when I sit down to write and it takes me hours and hours to hash out a few verses because I'm very meticulous and very much a perfectionist, and every syllable has to have a fluid connection with each other. Then there are other times when I can sit down and I can just start writing and writing and I will have written three or four verses or a complete song in half an hour or fifteen minutes. I think some of the best songs I've ever written came out that way.

'There's also the thing that happens to me when I lie down to sleep at night. I start getting insomniac energy, and one line will come into my mind and I say, "That's a beautiful line. I'm going to get up and I'm going to write it down." I write it down, and I'll go to lie down and try to fall asleep. And then another line will come to me and I say, "I'd better write this down," and it can happen for hours and hours. Then when I wake up in the morning, I've got a really beautiful poem.

'I don't really go into writing songs with the idea that I've got this purpose to educate or anything like that. But sometimes I'm overwhelmed with feelings strong enough on a political, social or environmental level, where I'll write something that ends up being purposeful.

'There was a time when I felt a great deal of anger towards the police and Ronald Reagan, just towards the whole structure of the American government spending too much money on war and so little money on education, paying so little attention to the minorities and the under-privileged, that I wrote a song called "Green Heaven". It was basically about the difference between life above land and life below the ocean, and how there's an incredibly spiritual and intellectual society of sea mammals – mainly dolphins and whales – that have such a harmonious way of life. Even though they have the capacity for anything, basically far superior to the knowledge of man, and their communication is much more advanced, they seem to live in a very beautiful, peaceful way. Then there's man who's above the land, just making a mess of the planet, making a mess of people, very inconsiderate, very selfish and greedy. So, I wrote that song and that ended up as being fairly purposeful in terms of letting people know they didn't have to buy into the Reagan philosophy.

'In our live shows there's some kind of miraculous energy that happens between the four of us that gives us a sort of superhuman energy to propel us through each show. It's fairly apparent to the viewer and the listener. Most of the shows that we play, it would seem as though it would be impossible to play like that night after night, but we continue to play with intensity. Just the very energetic, explosive nature of our band is consistent.

'People ask us how we keep it that way, and I think it's a combination of the chemistry created between these particular four people in the band. It's also a combination of the chemistry with the type of music that we write. The combination of those two things gives a very strong stage euphoria, something that I'm very grateful for and I live for. Sometimes it's such a great feeling it's hard to deal with when the show is over because it's almost like the downside of an artificial high.

'When I'm onstage singing, I'm completely unaware of anything around me, except for [Chili Peppers] John [Frusciante] and Flea and Chad [Smith]. It seems as though I feel like I'm in some sort of psychedelic, swirling cauldron of hardcore funk when I'm singing. I just try to stay within that space throughout the show. It's always when I can make a complete connection with everybody in the band that our music sounds best, like when it's four people all aiming for the same musical point, and so I just really try to stay focused on the music and the band, and it feels great. It's not an egotistical sense of invincibility but I feel like nothing can harm me during that time; I have no anxiety or fear or worries really, for that moment while I'm playing, which is a nice thing. That's on a good night, of course.

'Every time I get together with the band and we write a song, there's usually so much love involved and so much happiness in the fact that we're creating something that we all desire so much, it all seems mystical to me. I get a sense of euphoria that I never experience any other time in my life. And since every song we've ever written seems to have held up over the course of time, I would say that it isn't a false feeling when it happens and that it's legitimate.

'It's a strange thing. When I first began writing songs with this band, I was taking drugs and alcohol and it didn't really seem to bother me, depending on the combination of whatever kind of drug or alcohol I was on. Sometimes I would find a combination where I could work under those conditions, but then very quickly it got to the point where any time I was under the influence of any drug or alcohol, I had no inspiration to write an honest song. Anything I did attempt to write just seemed very empty and meaningless, and it basically went nowhere. I could sit down and be stumped for hours at a time trying to write something if I was under the influence, and so it became a very negative element of the band – the fact that any of us were taking drugs and alcohol. When we stopped, it was just like taking off the handcuffs and anything we've written since then has been the strongest stuff we've ever done. And it's much more fun this way as well.

'By experiencing life to its fullest – the extreme spectrum, emotionally speaking – that's what gives me the creative impetus. That's what gives me feelings on the inside, just awareness of the world really. Sometimes I feel most creatively inspired when I'm outside. There was a time when Flea and I took a special trip to the south of Mexico just to write songs for an album we were about to do. I would go and climb over these cliffs and sit in the rocks by the ocean. As I sat there, I had very little distraction from people or from cities or anything like that and I was able to just feel what it was that I feel about the world and write it down. I think other creative sources are just your emotional centres. When something happens in your life that really stimulates a specific emotion, I think you're inclined to write about it. If you're really feeling good about this or that, you might be inclined to write about it, or if something is a real bum-out in your life, then you'd write about that.

'There are times when I think I have a very positive influence on the world through what I do. That makes me feel like I have a reason to be here, a purpose, to a certain extent. Having gone through what I've gone through in life and being able to put out a positive message in reference to, say, somebody on drugs, through my music, it may help somebody else who's dying a slow, agonising death, to give them hope and some encouragement. That makes me feel I have a purpose. Any time I can do something for somebody else, I feel like I have a reason to be here.'

In 2022, the Red Hot Chili Peppers released their 13th studio album, Return of the Dream Canteen, *with Anthony on vocals as ever. Since 2000, he maintains he has stayed clean after his struggles with addiction, and his most recent songs offer a more reflective side. He and the band were inducted into the Rock and Roll Hall of Fame in 2012.*

PHIL COLLINS

Singer, songwriter and drummer, who played in the band Genesis and is also a solo artist.

INTERVIEWED PHIL WHILE I WAS LIVING IN L.A. I HAD known him for a number of years as he used to live near Guildford in Surrey, close to where I lived with my children, and also close to where my sister, Pattie, and Eric lived. So we all saw a lot of each other in those days.

'I had a pretty normal upbringing. My dad used to have a little boat, and he belonged to the yacht club with about one hundred other people who had boats. Because of that, they used to put on dinners and dances, and a couple of times a year they'd put on pantomimes, and I would play in them, usually as Humpty Dumpty. Apparently, I was given a little drum when I was three and took to it. When I was five, my uncle made me a small drum kit that fit in a suitcase. I would play these shows, and so I was exposed to that kind of thing from very early on until I was eleven or twelve. My mum started an agency to book kids for commercials and TV, so I started going to auditions. When I was fourteen, I got the part of the Artful Dodger in *Oliver!* That's when I moved from my grammar school to stage school.

'All along, though, I didn't want to do anything else but play the drums. I'd bypassed all the train sets and stuff. I knew from a very early age that I didn't want to do anything but that. I used to come home from school and just practise and play, although I realised I couldn't do that professionally until I was grown up. Other kids would be playing football more than I did. All I wanted to do was sit at the drum kit upstairs and play along with my records.

'At the time, that was a lot different from my friends, who had no interest in music at all. I used to be in my own little world. I always used to play in front of the mirror because I had read that it was good to watch yourself play so you don't look down at what you are doing. I would put the record player on as loud as it would go and play along with it. It must have sounded terrible downstairs where they were trying to watch television. I remember sitting in the living room and playing along with the television while everyone else was trying to watch it. When I was fourteen, I started drum lessons – I'd taught myself from the age of five – thinking that as this was what I wanted to do in my life, I should try and do it properly. I decided I'd do the pop group thing when I was old enough, then after that finished, I'd probably do sessions or go into a big band – that seemed like the kind of thing to do in your late twenties, early thirties – and then I'd end my days in a pit band, like an orchestra pit.

'I used to go home with all the orchestra musicians in *Oliver!* I was in the show on the West End for seven months, then I started being asked to do other things. At that point, when I was sixteen or seventeen, I told them I didn't want to do any more acting. I just wanted to play the drums and I was finally old enough to get into a professional band. My mum and dad weren't very happy about that, especially my dad, because he liked showing me off at the office – "My son's on the West End stage!" as opposed to being in a rock group. There was deathly silence around the house for a couple of weeks.

'You can have the feel for [playing music] and then cultivate it into something more; you can't buy it, or learn how to do it. Some of the most famous drummers, like, say, Carl Palmer, someone like that to me is a very unnatural drummer. He was taught, and it just sounds like it when I hear him play. There are other guys out there, you can tell, who just picked up a pair of sticks and started playing. Without putting down Carl Palmer, I've never heard anything from him that sounds convincing to me, and yet there are other drummers who can do far less but move me far more – like Ringo, for instance.

'It's so easy to get diminishing returns. I have [used drugs]; certain albums are a bit of a blur, not a blur that I don't remember anything; I just wish that I hadn't been so uptight. I know myself now, I know my capabilities, and I know I can't do it, so I don't do it. I haven't smoked for years. Coke and stuff, I just cannot function on that.

'An experience I had with smoking: it was about 1978 and we were playing in L.A. – one of the Forum gigs – and a guy came up to me and said, "I've got this Hawaiian stuff, just one puff, you don't need any more." So, of course we had two puffs, we went onstage, and there's a song we used to do, most of the Genesis songs were more story-oriented, so if you lost the thread, you lost it. So, I started this song. I was standing there and the verse was coming at me and I thought, "God, what am I going to sing?" And just at the last possible second my mind took it away and I knew what to sing. I was in a cold sweat. I vowed from that point, no more.

'There is probably something in most people that just never gets tapped, or they don't think about it, or they don't have the opportunity. For example, every year the Prince's Trust used to hold a holiday camp for a week in Norfolk. There were four hundred kids there, between the ages of fifteen and twenty, from Liverpool, Manchester, Aberdeen, Edinburgh, and so on, all potential football gangs. The purpose was to encourage any natural talents they had. They were taught how to apply themselves, how to get on with other people, how to apply for a job. There were all kinds of different workshops they could go to throughout the week.

'I was a trustee, so I'd go up there on the last day. I'd get all the musicians together in the music workshop and form a band for that particular day. Some were musicians, but most of them had never touched an instrument before. They were encouraged to pick up something and play, and from there maybe they would take an interest in it. We learned a couple of songs which we'd perform that night. There was one guy there, very introverted, and during the week he had plucked up enough courage to get up and sing in front of these four hundred kids. He'd never done anything like that before. The reception this bloke got was absolutely fantastic because they'd seen him get strength through the week. They knew what he was going through, and they went mad.

'You sort of push yourself to the edge to see if you can do it, because you want the challenge: if I can learn from it and see if I can pull it off. I had this terrible feeling after *Face Value*, the first album, that that was all I had. I thought, "Will I be able to do this, or will I get up there and nothing happens?" I'm scared as well, so I have to keep going to convince myself that it isn't all gone. It's a personal challenge each time.

'When Tony, Mike and me – the guys in Genesis – go into the studio, we have nothing written. Nowadays we just keep all the songs we've written for ourselves and we go in and just turn everything on and start playing, and we improvise and improvise for days until something works. I'm taping everything and we'll listen back to it and say, "That sounds interesting. What happened there?" And we'll develop that into songs, so to do that, you have to have no inhibitions, to sit down and not be afraid to play badly, because if you're playing safe all the time, then nothing really new happens. You have to have the knowledge that the other people involved don't mind that I start to sing out of tune, if I'm going to try and sing a melody that isn't written. Just try and go for things that you might not be able to reach. We all know we've got to let our trousers down without worrying about it. And that's like a chemistry that you do get in certain bands, and that's what makes the band great, at least the experience of doing that. It's very enjoyable because you're creating something out of nothing.'

Phil has been dealing with health issues since a spinal injury in 2007 left him with nerve damage, which seriously affected his ability to play drums. His son, Nic, joined Genesis as drummer on their final tour but Phil, who remained as lead singer, played the final gig in a wheelchair. Nic continues to tour with Mike and the Mechanics.

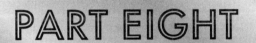

PART EIGHT

'You have to be able to go out on a limb. What keeps people from being creative is the fear of failure' –

JONI MITCHELL

JONI MITCHELL

Singer, songwriter, guitarist and solo artist.

PETER ASHER INTRODUCED ME TO JONI, AND TO-
gether we set up a time and a place. It might have been a
room in Peter's office. We sat facing each other on a small sofa
with no one else around. I felt very comfortable in her presence,
captivated by the stories she was telling or her answers to my
questions. The more she got into her stories, the more her face
changed. At one point it seemed to have morphed into a Native
American. It was surreal – quite subtle but distinct.

Tell me a little bit about your upbringing.

From infancy I favoured my father or maybe it was because
I saw less of him and I think that he and I had a lot of spirit
connection. I emulated his walk when I was toddling. I would
walk behind him and swing my arms. He was in the Air Force
so he would march for me in his uniform and I would imitate
him. Because there was no son in the family, I think my father
blessed me with a lot of things that ordinarily he would have

given to a boy. He taught me how to make bows and arrows out of red willow and whistles and how to play cards at a very early age. He taught me, or tried to teach me, all the things that he enjoyed to pass on.

Was he musical?

Most weekends he played trumpet in very small hamlet dance bands. He had some classical training and he taught for a while, but he couldn't interpolate. He couldn't improve it.

Was your mother musical?

My mother's mother played the piano, but she was stuck out on a farm. She was a frustrated poet and musician. Both my grandmothers were musical. I think where I got my drive from was that both of my grandmothers were frustrated musicians at a time when it was unheard of for women to contemplate a career in music. My paternal grandmother came from Norway, and it's said that all of her children say she was a saint. She raised a large family under tremendous difficulties and she was a total giver and not a guilt-laying self-denying person. But everyone came before her in that way. The last time she cried in her life – and her life was very hard and impoverished with many children – was behind the barn in Norway. She cried because she wanted a piano. She told herself, silly girl, you're never going to have a piano, so just forget it. She never cried again in her life. So, I think the repression of that desire had to come out sooner or later. So, it came to me.

When did the love of music come into your life?

In my early childhood, because I was creative, I was a painter. I had difficulty playing with the children in the neighbourhood, because I couldn't get in on their games, and they couldn't get in on mine. It was difficult when I finally did find friends. My best friend was a boy named Frankie McKittrick, who is a classical piano prodigy, and he could play a big church organ when he was seven or eight. His feet could hardly touch the pedals in the church in Mount Vernon. So, he was quite prodigious in classical music. And the first record that I rushed to the radio to hear was, oddly enough, a Rachmaninoff tune. It was in a movie at that time called *The Story of Three Loves*. I think it was a tribute to Paganini. It's a beautiful, passionate melody. That was the first record that thrilled me when I was about seven.

The next record that thrilled me I heard when I was about nine at a birthday party for Helen Lafreniere. Helen's mother was not very well, maybe she was an alcoholic. I just remember that the lower part of her lids was pink and swollen and exposed. Either she was crying a lot or she had something wrong with her. She made the first pink cake mix with icing that I'd ever tasted. And while we were eating this cake, they had the radio turned to the French station with Edith Piaf singing 'Les Trois Cloches', the story of Jimmy Brown, and it just made the hair on the back of my neck stand up. And that was the next thrill. Then of course, in the fifties, rock and roll hit with a storm, and prior to rock and roll, I loved Louis Jordan, 'House of Blue Lights'. 'The joint was jumping to do good boogie.' Boogie woogie. In my teens, I wasn't an active musician until eighteen, but from thirteen until seventeen, I went to dances whenever I could. I mean, every weekend.

The town I lived in was a small Third World town. It was Battleford, northern Saskatchewan. The mail still came at Christmas on open wagons drawn by horses with sleigh runners, but it had pretensions to European classicism. There were a lot of Irish people who'd settled there, and Scots and Welsh. And so, there were a lot of music lessons taking place in the town. And a lot of my companions, since mainly the kids were athletic, were sticks-and-stones throwers. They were hearty, robust and physical. Not very creative. Creative people in the town generally studied classical piano or classical voice. I had a lot of friends who were considered the singers. I was always considered the painter, but I was in association with child musicians. I spent a little time in a church choir. I chose descant because it was the pretty melody, it was the melody which had more movement. Some people say I have difficult melodies. Some people even say there's no melody at all. But in fact, there's more melody than there used to be and I think that comes from my experience singing descant. So, you go very high and then you drop down to create a harmony under another. It has more movement than a normal melody.

I loved to dance and I think that was because it was partnered. Dancing in the fifties taught me about drummers because you're dancing with a guy but you're not wiggling next to him, like the dances now. Each person feels time in a different way, so some guys rushed, some guys were laid-back, some danced on the bright side of it and you had to make them look good. You have to correct their time without being pushy. I think that would give me a lot of rhythmic experience, which I tapped into later. When I was eighteen, I began to write my own music.

Would you describe yourself as shy? Or were you outgoing?

It's hard to remember what my personality was like as a child. I've alternated between introversion and gregariousness all my life. Certain events would push me inward. For instance, I had polio when I was nine. Initially, that was a very inward-making experience, but I can think of moments in the hospital trying to get out of there when I was extremely gregarious to get my spirit up and to get well. I mean, the raising of good spirits is very healing. So, I used to sing. I had a captive audience, this cripple boy that couldn't move, I would assail him with Christmas carols, kind of show off.

Did your parents encourage your creativity?

Yes and no. When I was about seven, because Frankie McKittrick played the piano and hearing him playing, I used to have dreams that I could play an instrument. They were very thrilling dreams. I used to dream that I was driving a car or playing an instrument, which seemed like wonderful adult accomplishments. And so, I begged for a piano at the age of seven, and I was given piano lessons. I think it was on a Saturday morning, but whenever it was, the time of my lesson coincided with the broadcast of *Wild Bill Hickok*. This was very bad because we were all into cowboys and Indians. And plus, the piano teacher, Mrs Levin, used to rap my knuckles because I could memorise, play by ear quicker than I could read. I was a slow reader, but I was fast at watching my hands and listening and I could get it quickly. And so, she made the educational process extremely unpleasant. She used to play duets in competition with my father for piano and trumpet, and I think she had a crush on him. Therefore, she didn't like me. I mean, that may be childhood imagination, but I always felt, she likes my dad, but she doesn't like me.

So, I gave that up. I quit, I refused to play, but I still used to sit down and compose my own little melodies, and I even wrote them down. I found one the other day called 'Robin Lock' and it was a written composition. I can't even read now. I think I was seven. But that's what I wanted to do, I wanted to compose. In that town it was unheard of, it was considered inferior. The thing was to learn the masters and play them. That was it. But if you were wanting to invent something on your own, it was thought ridiculous.

Did you know what you wanted to do when you grew up?

I was always going to be a painter. I knew I could make up music, I would hear it in my head and so I'd sit down at the piano and pick it up and write it down, and there it would be. I could always do it but nobody seemed to think that it was anything worth doing; it was discouraged.

And then when I quit piano lessons in my teens and I wanted to buy a guitar, of course, my parents thought I'd just pick it up and then quit it. So, they weren't very supportive and I had to buy my first guitar.

Your drive must have been very strong.

I guess we call it a drive. It was just more of a thrill. It was like, 'Ooh, this would be great to do.'

Did you ever have any psychic experience as a child or any significant or recurring dreams?

I think that the psychic part of my life – if I did have it as a child I don't recall – began in earnest in heavy doses when I crossed the border into the States. I can almost remember the day that it began. Maybe it's the day I was aware the synchronistic events in my life became more frequent and I learned to trust them, to follow them at all costs. To say my path here is speaking, and when it speaks, it's stronger in a louder way than anything else.

The day that I recall it beginning was when I was playing at the Philadelphia Folk Festival and I was standing in the wings about to go on. I turned to a friend of mine, David Ray, and I had this funny feeling. It wasn't like nervousness or butterflies in the stomach, it was a feeling like a plummeting from a great distance. It wasn't like fainting, I had never had an experience like it. Anyway, it took all my attention and made me look kind of glazed over and he said, 'What's wrong?' I said, 'Oh, it's the strangest feeling. I can't explain it. It's like I'm falling to earth.' It was a mysterious, spiritual, grounding feeling. It was like childhood's end, a major shift in my perception was coming around. And after that, I would go for weeks leading a fairly normal life and then I would hit a pocket and it would happen again. It was equivalent to a gambler's streak of luck, only rather than it occurring in something as regionalised as a deck of cards or the roll of dice, it would happen again, like wishes coming true, but really quickly, within a month or two days. I could give you specific examples.

Incredible! What age were you when this started happening?

I was in my early twenties.

That's when you became aware of synchronistic events?

Oh, yeah. A lot of it suddenly.

Did it frighten you?

It did. Initially, it made me feel the presence of God. And even though I had abandoned Christianity at a very early age because the Sunday school teacher couldn't explain to me the story of

Adam and Eve. I'd said to her, 'Well, if Adam and Eve had two sons, Cain and Abel, and Cain slew Abel, then Cain was alive and Cain got married . . . Who did he marry, Eve?' The woman was horrified and they dismissed me. That, and other reasons such as the pretensions of the Church and the phoniness of the whole ordeal. The lack of genuine Christian charity in the community was transparent to me at a very early age. So, I tried to educate my parents, who were appalled. I wouldn't go to church because of this. It took many years for them to see that the Church was corrupt. But anyway, when the synchronistic events began to happen, my first thought was to attribute it to God because it was too giddy-making to attribute it to myself. It would mess with my centre. That was bad because I became a root without a church, I became a sort of born-again Christian on my own. By the time of my first couple of records I was an avid Bible reader, but that, too, fell away.

Do you believe in a greater power?

I believe in a great spirit. My philosophy. I've combed philosophy books and religions looking for truisms or things that applied to my experience and found them all fairly hollow. I found one idea which runs through all of them, in one point or another. Its history, which is widely maintained in North American Indians, seems to be one of the oldest spiritual ideas. It's a circle with a square in it. You find it called the philosopher's stone in some books, but nothing much is said about it. You find it on old Chinese pots. You find the symbol in Japan and China and all through the Christian world on windows and things and the meanings pertaining to it vary. The teachings are based on the I Ching. It's a fantastic idea and it's the hub of my spiritual faith, so to speak. I interpret it differently than anything I've ever really read about. Carl Jung used it for personality categorisation. North American Indians address the four directions, the cross within the circle. But they all have different interpretations of what that means. And some of them do it by ritual and have lost the depth of it at this point, as have many ideas in almost any religion. Lost their essence and the power of it. I have this diagram and to me it is a living thing and I believe in it in terms of communication because all religions are divisional, they divide people: you're a Buddhist, you're a Catholic, but sooner or later there will be conflict because of that difference. With regards to my playing, first I was a folk musician and then I was a rock musician. I was the queen of rock and roll polls, and then suddenly I was a jazz musician. And for that, for playing with jazz musicians, I was pretty much excommunicated from the rock and roll community. They didn't play my music on the radio anywhere. Too divisional.

Would you say that greater power, or Great Spirit, is connected to your creativity?

Oh, absolutely.

What was it like learning your craft? What gave you the drive to carry on through the learning process?

Ideas. From the very beginning, I've always said I'm quitting. If you listen to my early songs, there's always references. 'I'm gonna make a lot of money, and I'm going to quit this crazy scene.' There's an early song called 'Urge for Going', which originally was inspired by the idea that – this was before I had a recording contract – I had developed my craft at the tail end of the dying of an idiom. By the time Dylan and Baez and the folk boom was on the wane, that was at the time that I became professional. So, I didn't expect to stay in the business. I thought, I'll play these little clubs, they're folding now and, when they've all folded, I'll go back into womenswear and paint, so I'd have my day job and my passion.

When you are playing or singing or composing, do you ever experience what is called a 'Peak Experience'? What does that feel like?

To me, a peak state is the equivalent of a Zen state, where the ego is nicely anaesthetised. It's the absolute elimination of self-consciousness. That's what ego is, it's you watching you, right? And then it goes to sleep. I get that more from painting than any of the other arts. When I paint for long hours, my mind stills. If you hook me up to a meter, I don't know what you'd find. It's like a dream state. It goes very abstract. The dialogue is absolutely stilled, it's like Zen, no-mind. You hear electrical synapses, which could be cosmic electricity snapping and occasionally up into that void, in the Zen no-mind, in the nothingness comes a command, 'Red in the upper-left-hand corner.' There's no afterthought, because ego is the afterthought; you paint red in the upper-left-hand corner, and then it all goes back into the zone again. You achieve that sometimes in music. I think I achieve it in the loneliness of the night just playing my guitar repetitiously. The mantra of it, the drone of it will get you there. In performance you're going down deep in and then you're coming back out to receive your applause. There is more self-conscious art form in performance because people are applauding you.

What about writing?

Writing is more neurotic. It's a more dangerous art form psychologically speaking. It's the opposite of Zen mind because there you have to make the mind crazy. That's why a lot of the great writers use stimulants. *Alice in Wonderland* was written on opium. All the great Welsh alcoholics. And drugs. Because writers need to screw on a different head, and sometimes they get lost in the different head. The thing with writing is, you need to create a chaotic mind, overlapping insanity almost, overlapping thoughts. If you want to have any depth to your writing you have to plumb down into the subconscious. And there's a lot of scary things down there because it can be like a bad dream. Sometimes if you can extricate yourself from it and face up to it, you come back with a lot of self-knowledge, which then gives you greater human knowledge. It's worthwhile. The spiritual aspect of it, of course, is always cutting through your own bullshit. I mean, rock and roll, generally speaking, is not about cutting through your own bullshit, it's about self-aggrandising, being bigger than life. 'I'm a fantastic lover, baby, choose me.' It's more like that. It's a popularity poll and the bulk of pop music is written in that way.

But with more spiritual or literary concerns you're concerned with the human adventure. To know yourself is to know the world, everything good, bad and indifferent is in each one of us, to varying degrees. And so the more you know about that, the more you know about which is external. So in that way, the writing process is fantastic psychotherapy if you can survive it. But it is tricky. You're grinding the wheels like you have the concept, maybe it's vague at first of what it is you want to say. For instance, I have a song called 'Furry Sings the

Blues'. In Memphis, Tennessee, when I was there, I met a cop who had been the photographer on the scene when Martin Luther King was killed. And I had this game at the time. I had been doing it on *Rolling Thunder* and I continued on my own trip. It was my kind of a survey of cops. Whenever I saw a cop, I would go up to him and hustle him for his badge, just for the sport. It was really quite an interesting experience to see how overtrained they were; how much of their person was left, how much of the person was allowed in that particular precinct and so on. Would they pull a gun on me? Would they think I was crazy? Would they comply? And there were all sorts of different responses. Well, this guy had been through a lot and was pretty deadpan and very, very serious but the corner of his mouth kind of enjoyed it. I made a deal with him, and the deal was a trade. He would give me a badge and I would give him some records. So, we picked him up in the limo the day after the concert, and we drove him to this record store. He was [a] very emotionally repressed person but it seemed as though he was almost enjoying himself. He loved the attention. He said, 'There's something you must see before you leave town on Beale Street.' So we drove in this black limousine. It was so surrealistic.

The inner city of Memphis had been levelled with ball and chain and these cranes were standing with the ball, the wrecking balls dangling all around like a kind of a grove of them. The ground was broken shards and rubble, all nicely levelled. And then there were three blocks of Old Beale Street, which in its heyday was the nightlife of the black community, fanciful old wooden buildings with wooden shell-shaped entrances all boarded up with the old advertising painted on the side of them like a ghost town in the middle of the city. And on the street, there were three thriving modern businesses: two pawnshops, a movie house and a modern concrete structure called the New Daisy. Across the street was the Old Daisy, which was this fantastic wooden clamshell building, and you could just feel the atmosphere. Bourbon and the gin, the laughter, the dancing, feathers and sequins. So we go down the street – this is a very long story to tell you all the details, and it's almost like a novella. But we ended up going to visit Furry Lewis, an old blues musician living in the area. When it came time to write the song about that experience, it was so dense with imagery that for me it was so thrilling that it was hard to sift through it. And there came one line, though, that was in answer to your question, like a gift in that when it flowed out, I drew back and I said, 'Thank you.' Thank you to the room, because it just came out and said so much I felt, so economically, and it seemed I'd been grinding the grey matter, like trying to get this thing to come. And maybe I then just relaxed. Whatever it was when it poured out, it did seem like it was a gift.

It had the sound and the language in it and the sound was right and the content was right. It was, 'Pawnshops glitter like gold tooth caps in grey decay, they chew the last few dollars off Old Beale Street's carcass Carrion and Mercy, blue and silver, sparkling drums, cheap guitars, eyeshades and guns aimed at the hot blood of being no one. Down and out in Memphis Tennessee.'

It came as a chunk. It just poured out. There are pieces in a song that just seem to pour out in spite of you. I mean you're the witness, but the language does seem to come from some place else.

Did you ever reflect, 'Why me?' Why me, that you got listened to, you got noticed?

I think I'm more arrogant than that. I think in the beginning I didn't have much confidence in my work. When I first came to make my record, I felt so out of sync with what was in vogue that I didn't think they'd hear. It wasn't so much, 'Why me?' I think I know my role. I'm a witness and to document my experiences in one form or another. I think, 'Why can't they hear?' instead of, 'Why me?' Because I feel, for instance, with the making of the *Dog Eat Dog* album, America was in a very dangerous place. I felt it was ripe for a Hitler. It was such an ostrich state. The press was not being honest to themselves or others. Everything was declining. The standards were sinking. And in the midst of all of this, there was this frightening patriotism. It was like the death throes of a number-one power who were unable to admit that. Nobody holds back in England and nobody holds the championship forever. Maybe it's because I'm a Canadian living here and I'm able to be more objective. I feel like Paul Revere. It was alarming to me, so I made an alarming album.

But it was dismissed and occasionally ridiculed, and yet what it contained all became newsworthy stories several years later. It was very frustrating. I wanted them to listen to it, to hear it and change and move right now and not to wait. I was so glad two years later when the veils came off the corruption of some religions and politics, when the corruption was being exposed and the rottenness was being exposed, and people were able to look at it. Oh, that was good.

Did any of your music ever feel mystically inspired?

Oh, yeah. Shadows and Light. Synchronicity again. Charles Mingus had given me a puzzle. He'd given me a song of his to set to words, even though it had a life of its own already as an instrumental. It had been around for several years, and he was dying. So, I was racing against time to write this for him. It was called 'Goodbye Pork Pie Hat'. It was an instrumental tribute to Lester Young, who everybody says was just an incredibly sweet man. Charles assailed me with all these stories about Lester Young and the travails of his life and the difficulty of it. And I had everything pretty much finished on it, but I couldn't get an ending, and I had just got word that he was very sick. My boyfriend and I were coming up from Soho to uptown on the subway, and it was Don that said, 'Let's get off here.' So, we got off the subway a block early.

It was coming up on midnight as we came up out of the subway in the steam coming out of the manhole. We were in the forties so we were near the hooking area. Two blocks away we saw a circle of black pimps. You could tell, because they all had the same white hats on with black bands. They were all circled around something, there was something in the middle they were looking at. It was a tough area and my companion was black. I saw the image and said, 'Oh, let's go there.' But he was a little more cautious and approached this coolly. We came up to them and in the middle were two young black boys popping, and this was before Michael Jackson's moonwalking, so it was a first of this robotic dance that I'd ever seen and they were quite young and incredibly impressive. There was one guy among the pimps who slapped his knee and said, 'Yuck, yuck, looks like the end of tap dancing.' So, we stayed and we watched them

From top left, counter-clockwise: Atticus Ross [© *John Crawford*], John Mayall, Anthony Kiedis, Phil Collins, Terri Lynn Carrington

From top left, counter-clockwise: Joni Mitchell [© NP], Michael McDonald, Randy
Newman, John McVie, Steve Gadd

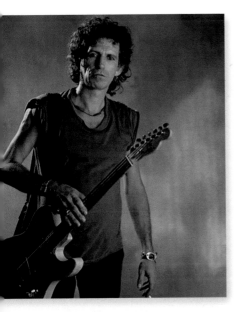

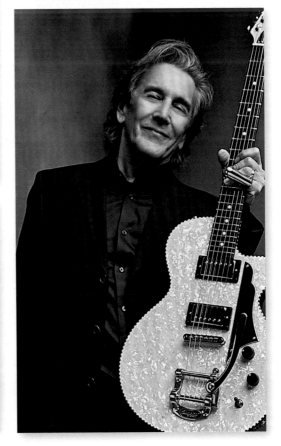

From top left, counter-clockwise: Keith Richards [© NP], Tony Williams, Rick Vito [© Brad Stanley], Koko Taylor, Bernie Larson

From top left, counter-clockwise: Ringo Starr [© NP], Phoebe Snow, Frank Foster, Mike Rutherford, Steve Jordan

From top left, counter-clockwise: Jeff Lynne, Peter Frampton, Stephen Bishop, Sarah Warwick [© William Bazlinton]

Peter Green [© Getty]

From top left, counter-clockwise:
Ravi Shankar, Paul Horn, Nancy Wilson,
Robert Burke Warren [© *Juliet Lofaro*],
Huey Lewis,

From top left, counter-clockwise: Billy Burnette, Vernon Reid, Ice-T, Kirsty MacColl, BB King [© NP]

dance for a few minutes. I looked up in the bar next to where they were gathered at a red-and-black striped canopy that came up to the kerb. Next door was a bar and it said in red script, Charlie's. 'This is the ending of the song,' I said. All the way on the subway I'd been saying, 'I can't get the ending.' He says, 'Get off a block early, let's get off here.' We come out and here is the last verse of the song. So, I'm thrilled and we start to walk away. Now, this is where the thing got really seriously mystical. I took one last look over my shoulder and you know what it said on the red and black marquee? The name of the bar where they were gathered: The Pork Pie Hat Bar. Months later, I went into this place and it was quite a vision inside, because there were pictures of Lester Young blown up, black and white, all around the room and at the back, all the pimps were playing either chess or backgammon, and they were so cool. The room was full of smoke. It had basically a red and greenish blue lighting effect and it was very dark. The only other light, the brightest light, was the light of the jukebox, which was loaded with jazz, and up the central aisle, tap dancing, was the guy who had said, 'It looks like the end of tap dancing.' So, things like that happen all the time. It's magical!

Here's another one. This summer, Gloria and I travelled around the world; it took us about three months. We did six interviews a day in every country so we were gone for a long time. We had a wonderful time. And coming back I had post-partum depression. It was the end of a cycle. You have to get kind of depressed to kick back and to figure out where you go from here. They kept saying they want me to do this, I have to do that, I'm supposed to do this . . . but what did I want to do? It took me about three days and I finally said to my husband, 'I got it! I know what we're supposed to do.' This is the words I said:

'supposed to'. 'We're supposed to get in our car. We're supposed to load up with super-eight film and cameras, and we're going to drive to the Lakota Indian Reservation. I don't know how we'll get on, we'll wave the white flag and say, "We've come in peace, here are some cameras, here's some film, here's how they work. Go into the Black Hills and shoot what you love about them. When you run out of film, come back. I'll give you some more and I will make a film and try and help you."'

I had this idea on a Tuesday and the following Monday I was talking to Gloria on the phone, so it's six days later, and we were interrupted by a phone call. She got back on the line and said, 'You know who it is? It's the chief of the Lakota Sioux.' I said, 'Call me back and tell me what he wants.' He'd heard the song 'Lakota' and wanted me to come in March with himself and the other chiefs of the Lakota on the Black Hills, and they were all going to speak, and I was invited to be a dignitary and sing my song among the speeches of the chiefs in less than six days. So, I said, 'I'll be there.' And as soon as we got there, the children, who only have sticks and stones to play with, became attracted to the cameras. So, they shot most of this stuff, which I turned into a video. The difficult part was the embarrassment of saying, 'We're here and we want to help.' But when the chief of chiefs called, I thought, 'This is the stuff.'

Love it. [We laugh.] Do you feel that everybody has the potential to be creative or is it a gift?

I think some people have more potential than others, but the gift is evenly distributed. For instance, if you're too rational, you're not very well equipped. You need to be able to surrender to the mystic to be good, to be great, to have one foot in divinity, which is the only place that greatness comes from. You can be good; you can write a nice song. I mean, there's a lot of nice songs on the radio that don't have one foot in divinity. They can even be huge hits. It depends on your standards of creativity, what that means to you. I think it comes from an urgency to communicate. The gift can be developed in people. Supposing they're not creative at all and they're struck down by an automobile or some great tragedy can bring out the creativity in a person by shock. But if you're too reasonable, creativity won't come around you because then you're not intuitive. And it requires a great deal of intuition. You need a bit of it all. You need to be emotional, otherwise your work would be chilly; if you're too emotional, it'll be all over the place. You need rationale for linear architecture or orderly structural work, but if you stay there too long, the stuff will be chilly and merely intellectual and icy. You need some clarity to make the thing pertinent. Dylan will write a song and it'll have real abstract passages, but then it'll just have a direct phrase, like, Bam! He'll directly communicate, and then he'll go back into something more surrealistic.

To be creative you have to be able to go out on a limb. What keeps people from being creative is the fear of failure. In creativity, the accidents and the coincidences and the mistakes, that's the hard part. That's what keeps people from being creative, they're afraid to fail, afraid to take chances. They may even be considered creative by some people, but at best, they're just copycats. They hear that, they like it, they'll make something like it. They can do that, but to innovate you have to have a certain kind of fearlessness. I think it helps if at an early age you got used to being shunned and you survived that. That's helpful. If you had to fight for some things in your childhood then you know you can stand alone.

What state are you in for the best background for creativity?

Well, it depends on which part of the creative process.

When the synchronicity began to happen, I tried to find out something about it. What Carl Jung said about it was that synchronicity comes on the cusp of any strong emotion. In his survey it could be anything. With my synchronistic events I have to bottom out. What happens is I lose courage; I lose heart and I'm sinking. I get to the point where I'm uptight and I'm nervous. At that point you surrender those things. Then I think, of course, they have to live a more dramatic *chiaroscuro*. They have to have higher highs and the higher highs are a pendulum swing. So, with it come the lower lows, so why make it sound like mental illness. Why make it sound so clinical? It's not that bad. We can handle it. You swing high and you swing low. They tried to discredit Jaco Pastorius, who was a great innovator. Upon his death dozens of people have come up to me and said, 'He was manic depressive.' And they say it with a sad mouth, manic depressive, like a bad taste. And I say, Christ, how abysmally out of touch these people are with life.

To experience the low time must be a very important part of it.

For me, it is. Because depression is very misunderstood. Depression in a way is a good thing. What it is, is it's a swing to the west on the wheel of the cross; it's a lack of clarity therefore, and anybody with any clarity will say, 'Oh, they're sick, because they're opposites.' What it is, is you're overwhelmed with information and choices and you can't decide what to do. But beyond a crossroads, sometimes you have so many directions that you could go in and it's overwhelming. In its overwhelmingness the body slows down and drives you, like any normal animal, to curl up in a corner for a minute and in that introspective state, which is an anti-social state, you mull and mull and feel low. You find you have ten bad choices and all the roads are unattractive. That's how synchronicity always saves me because I just say, these are all bad choices and I give up, but I may sweat for a week and be in a dark mood, until I surrender. Right away comes choice number eleven and it is not a dull choice. It's a thrilling one.

Do you have a choice to create or is it something that just happens?

That's the way I entertain myself and always have since childhood; despite not writing or playing the guitar, I would be painting. I just have to do it.

Are you in touch with the child in yourself?

Yes, you have to keep the kid alive; you can't create without it.

Do you think drugs and alcohol enhance creativity or do you think they block it?

Both, especially at the introduction to a new drug or the introductory period. They all screw on a different consciousness and any change of consciousness is refreshing. So, the contrast between going from straight to pot, which is a 'south-west' drug, tends to make you tactile and sensual and warms the heart for about the first fifteen minutes, then it starts to fog you over. So, you've got about fifteen minutes of really condensed creative thought. And then, depending on the strength, it can flatten you. If you smoke that on a regular basis, you'll just be flattened and it's anti-creative. But if you've got stuck, like you're getting too 'north-east', take some pot and you'll swing into the opposite direction, then ideas will open up. Cocaine is a very 'north-east' drug. It gives you intellectual, linear delusions of grandeur. It makes you feel really smart and it can create great insanity very quickly. Insanity, by my definition, is a chaotic mind. Too many thoughts overlapping. For a writer, that's a lot of choices. It can be very good, epic thought, but it can take over, and then it's anti-creative almost immediately. Sake for me is a very warming elixir, but with all these things you can't do them two days in a row before they become deteriorating. I think they have to be done with a spiritual, ritualistic prayer.

You're dealing with the real McCoy when you're straight. Stimulants are a desperate measure for when you have no inspiration so you try creating with the addition of something artificial. But in the straight mind the little shocks of daily existence can be enough. You go out the door of your house in one mood and you run into something that either elevates or depresses that mood. That change of mind could be the stimulation needed for the creative process.

The straight mind is ultimately the best because it's the long-distance runner of them all. With the other ones, the road is too dangerous and it can burn out and kill your talent quicker than anything. I know great works of art that have been done on stimulants. Absinthe was Van Gogh's crazy passion.

Would you say the closest thing to a spiritual experience is when you are creating or composing?

For me, the spiritual experiences are synchronicity. For instance, in live performance, synchronicity is the beauty of everybody being really Zen, everybody not only hearing themselves while they're playing, but hearing everybody else and creating spontaneously. This happens more on record dates than in my performance, because by the time we get to live performance, the music is somewhat dutiful. When you're in the studio, you're still in the searching mode, so you're dealing with the unknown. Therefore, luck has to come into it and synchronicity is good luck or rather bad luck. I've had bad synchronistic experiences.

Do you feel the music today represents the unconscious feeling of the masses of our time?

First of all, people are so led and the business is so hyped. In my lifetime, I've seen the business hype up to become phoney twice, and we're on the tail end of a very phoney period where you can take a pretty boy or a pretty girl and they don't have to have any real musical talent at all. First you had rock and roll. It's fiery and it's interesting. Then you had the second generation of it, which was like Fabian. Elvis was pretty so they thought, if you just get a pretty boy (like Elvis), they can make a singer out of him and put him out there. There was a lot of that just as we were coming into the eighties, fabricated punk bands that are not necessarily pretty, but they had a look the other way. Some of them managed to develop some talent after the fact, even though they were thrown into the industry without it. A lot of the masses have to be told what they like. I mean, I think they like it more if they're told they should.

As a result, for instance, you take somewhere like Brazil. They're very sophisticated rhythmically. The whole culture is very sophisticated, regardless of IQ, which I don't believe in or any graph that you might conceive of that is a range of intelligence. All of them seem to be able to absorb and relate to very sophisticated polyrhythmic patterns. In America they don't have that, in the white culture so to speak, but they do in the black culture more so, and the two have influenced each other. But basically, in the history of white rhythm there's been funerals and marching on to war. Whereas in the African culture it's as complex as our oriental calligraphy where figures mean spirits and somebody who hears that doesn't just hear beats on a drum skin, they get a picture. Whitey hasn't even scratched the beginning of what rhythm can do. I wish they could. I've been trying to explore more complex rhythms, and I think it frustrates me because I'm in a white culture where basically they don't get it. I have a lot of fans in the black culture who do, or Italians. When I was in Italy last, I was driving down the street and this guy yelled at me, 'Joni, the rhythm, number one, the rhythm *fantastico*!' It's different. It's almost like three-quarter time and it gets four-four time.

From time to time somebody gets it and that's a thrill. Harmony is the audio depiction of emotion. A major chord represents a fairly happy, nice groove. A minor chord is a fairly simplistic depiction of tragedies, guaranteed to bring sweet sorrow to the heart. Beyond that, most people can't handle a lot of harmony in this modern age. I know my emotions are much more complex. I might be feeling the way the world is going is basically bad, so there's a minor chord to how I'm feeling about the world at a certain time, but with a glimmer of optimism. So, to that minor chord, you add a note which kind of majors it, but it's major and minor at the same time. You get into these hybrid emotional depictions, which for years have been referred to as Joni's weird chords.

That's a great way of explaining it . . . [both laugh]. Have you any idea where the creative force comes from?

I can't think of any stable and one way of describing it. You have these electrical switching boxes down your spine, right? You have seven chakras. I have had the creative force come during the awakening of any one of them. Maybe you get inspired when you get a lump in your throat, inspiration comes through the opening of the throat chakra. Maybe it comes from the third eye. Maybe you feel it in the guts. Maybe it's genital. Maybe the nucleus of the music begins with kind of a genital excitement, which is like the *Dirty Dancing* kind of groove. The net with which you capture the creative force is made of the threads of your alertness. If you could walk through the world with the same attentiveness that you played a video game, for instance, so nothing could bomb you, that's kind of Zen-mind. If you're playing really well at a video game and you say, 'Oh, gee, I'm playing really well,' that'll get you, right there, because that's the entrance of the ego. Up until then, you haven't even had an ego. You've been in no-mind, and no-mind time is huge, but the entrance of one thought in time is small.

To make yourself attractive to creative inspiration, you have to train your ears to be as alert as possible and your eyes as alert as possible, especially me, because I'm working in both the visual and the audio arts. So, it's essential training, basically, it's a finer tuning. You've got a quicker eye and a quicker ear, and a stiller mind. Not that I always have a still mind, as I say, I have to enter into chaotic mind to make poetry.

One last question. Have you ever felt there was a purpose, a gifted meaning in your creativity on a spiritual, political or social level?

I've been apolitical until recently. *Dog Eat Dog* was a kind of a political awakening; it's always been too complex to me. There are obvious things, like Hitler was a monster, and we all agree. Something that overt, you can really see we are on the side of the just fighting against evil. But a lot of times war is evil on both sides and the leaders are both corrupt in one way or another and one system is basically as bad or as good as the other. It's hard for me to take a stance. On a spiritual level or human level, I have felt that it was perhaps my role, on occasion, to pass on anything that I learned that was helpful to me on the route to fulfilment or a happier life. Anything that I discovered about myself, even if I had to reveal something unattractive about myself, like I'm selfish and I'm sad, these are not popular things to say. Giving the listener an opportunity then to either identify, in which case if he sees that in himself, he'll be richer for it because he'll get out of it what I'm trying to tell him, or if he doesn't have the courage to do that or the ability, then he can always say, 'Well, that's how she is.' I feel that the best of me should go into the work. The most illuminating things that I would discover should go into the work. I feel a social responsibility to that.

Wheelchair-bound since 2015, Joni appeared at the 2022 Newport Folk Festival to an ecstatic welcome. It was her first full performance in more than twenty years. An album of the show is in the pipeline, and in 2023, Joni will perform her first headline concert in twenty-three years in Washington.

MICHAEL McDONALD

Singer, songwriter, keyboardist, solo artist and former member of The Doobie Brothers.

ANOTHER MUSICIAN WHO GREW UP WITH AN amateur musician as a father was singer-songwriter and former Doobie Brother Michael McDonald. I hadn't met Michael before our interview but knew and loved his distinctive singing voice. My absolute favourites are 'Taking It to the Streets' and 'What a Fool Believes'.

'My father was a singer. He wasn't really professional, though it seemed to be such a big part of his life. He was an Irish tenor, coming from a first-generation American family. We have a big Irish family, and they're all nuts about music. All our social functions were centred on somebody singing, my dad usually, with a lot of music in the house.

'My father was welcome in every bar in St Louis because he could sing, but he didn't drink. He's probably been to more bars than any drunk you'd ever meet in your life, but he just loved to sing there. I remember the first time he put me up on a bar. I was four years old and I sang some ridiculous song for a four-year-old, like "Love Is a Many-Splendored Thing". Everybody got a big kick out of it and laughed. I'm sure it was horrible, but I remember thinking I'd never done anything up until that point to solicit such a response from people. It made a big impression on me. I always followed my father around. Every Saturday afternoon we spent in bars, meeting different friends – that was his social life. The story he tells me is that one day I pulled on his pants leg and said, "When can I sing?" Then we became a dynamic duo: every place he went, I went with him, if I could and it wasn't too late. I always got to sing a few numbers. It kind of fused itself in my brain somewhere then that [making music] is what I'd do. My social life with my dad was an overriding factor in my life. He was my biggest musical influence at a very early age. I think there's a part of me in the back of my brain that is doing this for my dad, for his attention.

'I think a lot of creative people are emotionally handicapped in some way, usually through experience. Therefore, the creative process is a thing that is developed *because* of those deficiencies, as a way of dealing with the world around them. I've noticed that with a lot of people that urge to be creative, that urge to find that experience over and over again, comes from a feeling of not belonging in this world, always feeling out of place. That kind of forces them to be observers because people who feel that a lot tend to observe other people. I know that's how I was when I was growing up – always comparing everything around you to yourself. I think for people who write, their talent is born out of that constant questioning of themselves versus the environment.

'The real source of inspiration is such an intangible thing, and

I don't know what it is. With song writing, which is probably the focus for me, and even with singing and playing, there's an intangible element to it that I can't describe. When we're really playing and singing well, there's this sum that's greater than all the parts, and nobody knows what it is. With writing songs, it is always a battle with my conscious mind, and yet when it comes down to it, it doesn't have much to do with my conscious mind. But I always put it there until I wear myself out with it, and then I surrender to what's going to come if I just do the footwork, if I just keep going towards it. And then when it comes, I have no idea what it is. It's not necessarily the greatest lyric or the greatest melody. There'll be this one song that actually crystallises; it takes on a life of its own. I wonder what it is that makes a song with relatively mediocre lyrics and a not so inventive melody just have a life of its own – and that's the thing you're always looking for. I have certain tools to work with, but what I'm really looking for is beyond anything I could consciously come up with using those tools. My best thinking is only going to get me so much. The reason I have to drag myself to writing is that I'm all too aware how I dig myself a hole by consciously trying to write a song. When I'm really looking for spontaneity, I can afford less and less to think about it and then write it down. Somehow the minute I start to apply my conscious mind to it, I'm altering it and probably not for the good. I just have to get out of my own way.

'The audience could easily be fifty per cent of the whole musical experience, probably more. Musicians can only respond to themselves so much; in many cases the show has been played so many times that it's only going to be so exciting. The real excitement for them is the rapport with the audience. What the audience feels overrides any element of boredom [from] having just rehearsed and played the same show many times. When you've played the same song for many years, the whole ball of wax is that night: that audience, that venue, and that experience unto itself. If the whole experience was going to be how well you played "What'd I Say" for the fifty-millionth time, you'd walk off the stage!

'It's amazing how astute music is about the feelings of regular people. The media and politics are never in touch with how the people feel and think. With music, people who are totally illiterate can have a talent for musical expression that can be much more profound and much more in touch with what most people want to say or want to know. Often it comes from the most unusual corners of the music industry or from the street level. The most unlikely people have the most interesting things to say.

'Nobody knows why, after a few months of playing together with the band, we break through into another level of communication musically that we could never achieve in a rehearsal. It seems to be honed in live performance; the rehearsal can only produce so much. That rapport in performance is magic; so much of it is done on a non-verbal level. There's a collective creativity energy, and when it's interrupted by personnel changes, it's a shame. I know the band at a certain point would start to take on a musical expression of its own that had nothing to do with me telling everyone what to play. I didn't have to have the greatest drummer in Los Angeles or the hottest players. After about a year, you just know the band is performing at a level that would be hard to describe. You know there's a communication developed that's beyond conscious communication.

'My experiences with drugs and alcohol were – having that

kind of emotional liability as a kid – I used them as a crutch. It only became natural that the crutch permeated every aspect of my life after a while. I couldn't write unless I smoked pot; I couldn't go to the store unless I smoked pot. It was just a huge rationalising process that overtook me. I do think in some respect . . . they saved my sanity, because I was so fearful without being able to admit it to myself, during puberty and high school, so unsure of who the hell I was, who I was supposed to be. I remember that first time I smoked a joint, I just sat back in a chair and felt I was in a big warm blanket. From that point I was always looking for that experience, that feeling of "I'm okay".

'Lately I've been feeling like I actually have something to lose by involving myself in the process and not coming up with something up to my standards. You're always creating this fictitious superstructure around the creative process and putting stipulations on it, time restraints, standard expectations, attaching to it all this conscious garbage. But it is often itself just about the only conscious contact with that inner part of yourself that you make, where you find you have something to say that is surprising to you, whether it's musical or lyrical. It always has the feeling like you've said something, and somebody else says, "That was genius," and you didn't even remember what you said. So, you think, "Oh, well, let me build this situation where I can constantly repeat this." And then all of a sudden, you've built this monster for yourself that has nothing to do with the creative process.

'Creativity is not going to adhere to time restraints; it's not going to meet any specific standards you want to put on it. It's like trying to put those stipulations on a three-year-old child, because in a way it's coming from that part of you.

'When you've worn yourself out with self-criticism until

you can't stand to hear that voice in your head any more, asking you why you can't do this, and all your fears have been exhausted about it, you go into a kind of trance. You finally relax into this endorphin state. You have that feeling you've got nothing to lose. Typically, what I'll do is just mumble into a ninety-minute cassette. I almost try to put myself in that trance state, which means putting down anything that comes through my mind musically or lyrically. More times than not, when I find something I really feel good about, I wasn't even aware of putting it down. I'll take that tape and drive around town listening to ninety minutes of garbage, picking out the gems. I believe that's where I'm going to find the best music I'm going to write – by accident.

'When I create, I give the child permission to speak, to be there. To stand up in front of a room full of people and have a perfectly good excuse to scream at the top of my lungs – which is what the vocal experience is all about. Playing rock 'n' roll music, I feel good inside. That is a big part of who I am. It is one chance in a world full of restraints to actually come out and be that.'

The Doobie Brothers are back on the road together for the first time in twenty-five years for a 50th Anniversary Tour. Five-time Grammy Award-winner Michael has continued to follow a solo career for many years and his most recent studio album was 2017's Wide Open.

STEVE GADD

Session drummer who has played with Aretha Franklin, Chick Corea and Paul Simon.

'MY FAMILY WERE MUSIC APPRECIATORS, BUT MY uncle, who lived with us, was a drummer. He wasn't playing professionally but had played as a kid in high school. I remember coming downstairs and seeing a red parade drum that belonged to my uncle. I was two or three. That was the first time I ever saw a drum, and I'll never forget it. I guess I must have fallen in love with it. They say I always used to bang on things, pick up the silverware and play it on the table or hit on something. So my uncle got me this little round piece of wood and gave me a pair of drumsticks and showed me how to hold them. He had a little round piece of wood and sticks too. At night when everyone was home from work, the whole family would sit in the living room listening to records, and my uncle and I would play along with the music. Sometimes my father would do it; sometimes my brother would play.

'During the day when my parents were working, I'd be with my grandmother and I would listen to music and play along with records for hours. There was always a lot of encouragement. When I was six years old, I started taking lessons. My grandmother used to take me to my drum lessons. My drums were set up in the living room with the record player right behind. My parents let me play whenever I wanted to. They never ever told me not to play. The first thing I'd do in the morning, even before I ate breakfast, was to sit down and play the drums. I'd come home from school for lunch and sit down and play a little bit, and the first thing after school, sit down and play. The people around me paid a lot of attention to what I was doing. I had a natural love of the instrument, but [it was added to by] the encouragement I got from my parents, the happiness they got seeing me do what I was doing while I was playing. They got a lot of enjoyment out of it.

'When I was a young teenager, fourteen or fifteen, my father used to take me to clubs to hear a lot of organ groups, where the groove got so intense. It was in Sunday afternoon matinees where the feeling in the club got beyond age, colour. The music was feeling so good you just couldn't sit still. That feeling made you want to be a part of what was creating it; it was so powerful. To be playing that way would be so much fun, to just be a part of that energy. Plus, I heard a lot of jazz groups, like Dizzy [Gillespie] and Oscar Peterson, Max Roach, Gene Krupa, and I loved them all. I can remember listening to Tony Williams and Elvin Jones, listening to things over and over again. I was so impressed by some of the things they did; they touched me so much. You get something from everyone you hear; you try and take it and use it and pass it on.

'When I first moved to New York, Chick Corea went from an acoustic band to putting an electric band together. It was Stanley Clarke, Chick Corea, Bill Connors playing guitar, Mingo Lewis, who used to play with Santana, playing percussion, and myself. That band was burning. It wasn't like it was coming from me. It was coming from somewhere else, just coming through me. It was effortless.

'In some cases, it's hard for people to know what their gift is. In my case, I started [playing drums] as a child and it just sort of happened. I didn't have to go through that searching.

'I'm a part of something. We're all a part of this thing. If I can live my life and try to get in tune with that, then it's great. The effortlessness that I feel when I'm playing certain music, if I could just take that feeling and live my life on that level, just be a part of that thing and flow with it. I think that the challenge is to try to live that way, to try and just flow with life.'

Steve Gadd had played with an endless number of well-known musicians before our interview in the late eighties, and has continued for many years afterwards, including touring with Eric Clapton from 1996 to 2004. He tours with his band, the Steve Gadd Band, and also joined James Taylor on his 2023 US tour.

JOHN McVIE

*A bassist and founding member of
Fleetwood Mac.*

I FIRST MET JOHN WITH CHRIS WHEN THEY CAME
round to Mick's flat one afternoon for tea in 1968/69. John
was very cool, quietly spoken, with a dry sense of humour and
a moustache that came down past his chin. Then, a couple of
years later, Mick and I, John and Chris, and the rest of Fleetwood
Mac lived together in a large house in Hampshire, where the
sounds of their rehearsals resonated around the house. John
always seemed to me to be very 'West Coast', with his brown
leather waistcoat and records of Don Henley or the Steve Miller
Band drifting out of his and Chris's kitchen.

'There's a presence coming at you. You can't deny that.
You'd have to be dead to miss it. It hooks you in and engulfs
you like a cloud. Everyone sits right in it for a couple of seconds
or an hour. It's like being lifted; it's a physical sensation, and it
doesn't happen one hundred per cent of the time. But when
you're locked in, the band's locked in, I'm locked in with Mick
[Fleetwood] and Chris [McVie], or whomever, and it's just
riding along – that is incredible. It's almost as if you're going

to levitate. When that happens, it makes all the bullshit, all the heartache, all the doubts, all the negative side of being a musician [worth it]. If I could bottle that feeling and sell it. Well, I'd bottle it and give it – I'd love everyone to experience it. It's the most incredible surge, it really is. I've got hot flashes just thinking about it now.

'It's really a oneness with these people, wrapped in with sound – you just float. It might not last for more than a couple of minutes, but when it happens, it's magic. It takes your breath away. It's almost like when you have a déjà vu experience and you don't want it to stop and you're scared that, if you think about it, it will disappear and then, I'm thinking about thinking about it, so don't think about it and it starts trickling. But if it's riding right and you're just riding high, it's just such an incredible feeling and that's worth everything. All the dark side of [the music business], it negates all that completely. There, for me, is a spiritual experience, right there, that's it. I think when people see visions or are filled with the spirit or whatever, maybe they feel like that.

'At the time, it was incredible, being under the influence. I was incredible, I was amazing, I was unique. But the next day, while reading something [written under the influence] or listening [to something recorded while high], it was a bunch of bull.

'All that very special stuff – The Beatles, Stones, Hendrix, The Who – that was such a phenomenon, a lock-in of attitudes: social, spiritual, economic. The wheels just locked right. They pretty much defined the whole generation. We were lucky to be part of that. It doesn't happen today; there's nothing as special today. It's so diverse now; it's becoming a little bit less special; it doesn't have that warmth, that soul. As I'm saying that, I wonder if my dad would have said the same thing in his time about our music!'

RANDY NEWMAN

Singer, songwriter, pianist, soundtrack composer and solo artist.

I SEEM TO REMEMBER INTERVIEWING RANDY IN SOME-
where that resembled a school classroom. I was intrigued to
meet him as I'd loved his song 'You Can Leave Your Hat On'.

'My uncles were musicians, film composers; Uncle Alfred
did pictures like *How Green Is My Valley* and *Wuthering Heights*.
He won nine Academy Awards. Two other uncles did motion
picture music. One used to conduct all the Danny Kaye pictures.
He was musical director. My Uncle Lionel was head of music
for 20th Century Fox for forty-five years. All of them were very
good conductors. My father was a doctor, and he played the
saxophone a little.

'Unfortunately, no one made me practise playing piano. It
was something I was good at and would get praised for at an
early age. I'd play for my grandmother, and she would like it.
She was encouraging but died when I was eleven. My uncles
thought I was sort of good; it wasn't much, but it was enough.

I was seven, and it was always work for me. It was like the family business in some ways.

'Sometimes your subconscious or something . . . it'll just be there, you can see the whole song. It's great, it's like getting a free ride. It happens often with this type of work. Those songs aren't necessarily better or worse, they're just different. You can see all the way to the end from the beginning. It's a real powerful feeling. You can wait for that forever. You've got to somehow make it happen, but I couldn't tell you how.

'I used to take amphetamines to write years ago, and was very frightened not to take them. I figured any kind of edge I can get. As you can tell, it was obviously a traumatic formula. But all in all, it was one of the worst things I ever did; they weren't fun.'

Randy Newman has received twenty-two Academy Award nominations with two wins for his film scores, three Emmys and seven Grammys. He was inducted into the Songwriters Hall of Fame in 2002 and the Rock and Roll Hall of Fame in 2013. He has scored nine Disney/ Pixar films, including all the Toy Story *films and writes songs for TV series. Randy cancelled his 2022 European tour after surgery for a broken neck.*

PART NINE

'Once you know that you can create, then you have no choice. You can't turn it off, it's a one-way tap. Once it's on, it's on. You can try and ignore it but it's far more powerful than you are' —

KEITH RICHARDS

KEITH RICHARDS

*Guitarist, songwriter, singer and founding member
of the Rolling Stones.*

ALTHOUGH I HAVE VAGUE MEMORIES OF BUMPING into Keith Richards at one or two of the clubs we frequented during the sixties, I was actually introduced to him through a drummer I knew called Steve Jordan. Steve was a long-time friend of the Rolling Stones and who I later found out has recently been playing on tour with them since Charlie Watts died. Steve sat with us as I interviewed Keith in a small room backstage. I remember vividly when the time came to transcribe the interview, I had my finger pressed on the rewind button of my cassette player every few seconds in order to catch each gravelly word.

'I first started holding guitars and bashing away on pianos when I was a little kid. My grandfather used to run a dance band, and he turned me on to the playing of music. We were very close to each other. He had seven daughters and lived off the Seven Sisters Road in London, which was pretty ironic.

He had this incredible sense of humour – for one guy to live in a house full of eight women, you've got to have a laugh!

'When I used to visit him, a guitar would be on top of the piano, and I thought that's where the guitar lived. Just a few years ago I found out that he used to put the guitar there especially for my visits. He'd take the guitar out of its case, polish it up, and leave it there. He never asked, "Do you want to play?" He would just let me look at it, and slowly I would ask if I could touch it.

'The drive to create is just something I obey. I hear something and I've got to learn how to play it. Once you know that, then you have no choice. You can't turn it off. This is a one-way tap; once it's on, it's on. You can try and ignore it, but it's far more powerful than you are. It's not a controllable thing; it just keeps coming from inside. You're a slave to it in a way.

'Songs just come to me. I don't sit down and try and write songs. I wake up in the middle of the night, and I've dreamt half of it. I just need to pick up the guitar next to the bed and the tape recorder, push "record" and put it down. I'm not saying I write them all in my dreams – but that's the ideal way. You don't even have to get out of bed!

'Music represents the unconscious feelings of the people, of musicians and their audience. But at the same time, it represents what the record companies think they can maximise their profits on. And so, they'll stuff things down people's throats that they don't really want. A majority of what you hear is formula shit, it's what record companies find easiest and cheapest to produce and get the maximum profit. They like cats who go along with that, and now they've got the possibility with all the toys. They'd love to get rid of musicians entirely, those bothersome things that talk back and want to do it better.

'Music goes through walls – it's like laser beams. The songs are all around us. It's just a matter of whether you're there to receive them. The idea that *I* created this piece of music is kind of pompous and the wrong end of the stick to me. Music is everywhere; all you've got to do is pick it up. It's just like being a receiver.

'As a musician, I just want to make some great records. Unwittingly and unknowingly, it can happen that what you're doing can be interpreted and you're taken to represent everybody – not just authorities or record companies – but the whole mass of the people. You can find yourself being involved without any real intention. In a way, they write the songs for you. "Street Fighting Man" was just a mere comment, but all of that stuff turned us into – which was unbelievable to me – a threat to the British government. You'd think a couple of guitar players are really going to topple the Empire! That's the important thing about music, because it can. That's when you realise it has social and political overtones.

'You can get biblical about it: you have a power, but I don't suppose Joshua took his band and walked around Jericho and blew a few trumpets and the wall actually fell down from that. It was probably some cats inside Jericho who were saying, "Jesus, those guys are playing good! Open the back door and let them in!" That's how I think Jericho's wall crumbled. It's like the Iron Curtain – what happened in Russia is probably an analogy in the same way. The one thing they couldn't stop [was creativity], and it was the one channel that was always open when everything else was "No way".

'Music is very powerful; it's uncontrollable. Some people think you can lessen the power of music by trying to preach with it, but I think that it has its own power. If you want to write a great track and put it to music, that's all right too. But I think the real lasting power of music is on a far more subtle and indefinable level than what people say. It's the total thing.

'I think maybe the audience gets the same feeling that the people who are playing get. They feel connected to each other, and they can lose and forget themselves and realise how much they are connected to other people. All music does is enhance and illustrate the fact that we are all connected; we can't do without each other. People have the need to set people above themselves. The stage is the illustration of that – the demigods. The god thing is an illustration of that very need of a greater power. In lieu of finding out what that greater power is, people set up their own earthly version of it in order to express it. I stand on the stage and I'm thinking, what are you looking at me for, a damn old junkie hacking away at the guitar, what is this? This must be a primal need.'

When not living the quiet life in his cottage in West Wittering or his properties in Connecticut and the Caribbean, Keith continues to tour with the Rolling Stones across America and Europe.

TONY WILLIAMS

A jazz drummer who played with Miles Davis.
A composer who also founded the Tony Williams
Lifetime and the Tony Williams Quintet.

I MET TONY WILLIAMS IN THE LATE EIGHTIES WHILE I was married to drummer Ian Wallace. Ian was a huge admirer of jazz drummers and especially Tony Williams, so when he suggested I interview him, I wasn't sure. I had never been much of a jazz fan but, even so, I accompanied Ian to the little jazz club on Ventura Boulevard. We sat near the front of the room and, once his band started playing, I could not take my eyes off Tony. I was mesmerised. It was not the sort of music I knew or understood, but I just remember feeling as though I was on the ride with him, completely in the moment throughout his whole performance. I was just breathing it in. I had no idea at that time that I was sitting in front of one of the most innovative and influential jazz musicians of the last half-century, someone who was on the cutting edge of jazz-rock fusion. When I interviewed him the following day, I knew I was in the presence of a great musician.

Tell me a little bit about your upbringing.

My parents divorced when I was about ten. I had a sister but she died when she was seven months old so I didn't have any brothers or sisters other than that.

Were either of your parents musical?

My dad played saxophone, but he was more of a hobby musician when I was a kid. He worked for the post office. He liked to play saxophone, but I don't think he ever had the desire or the talent to be a full-time musician, to support a family and make all of his money right through music. So he was just a hobby musician, basically.

Was your mother musical?

No but she liked listening to music. And through her, I grew an appreciation for classical music. She liked the sort of records you could buy in the supermarket, like Tchaikovsky, Rachmaninoff and Wagner, and things like that. So, she would play that around the house and my dad would be playing Count Basie and Gene Ammons and that sort of music. Me and my kid friends were always listening to Frankie Lymon and the Teenagers and The Clovers, groups like that. So, there was a lot of different kinds of music around the house.

How old were you when you became aware of your musical inclinations? When did you first start playing drums?

I was nine when I first started playing the drums. But there are stories and pictures of me as a toddler, I guess, around two or three years old, and I was always performing. My dad would get me to sing little songs. I used to also go out in front of the band and sing and do a little tap dance and things like that.

Would you describe yourself as being an outgoing sort of kid or introverted?

I imagine I was more introverted but I wasn't necessarily shy. I had a lot of friends, so I wasn't a recluse. But I was always comfortable inside. I don't think I was overly introverted.

Did you know what you were going to be when you grew up?

No, not at the time, not when I was really young. I had always thought about being either a draughtsman, or an engineer, or a cartoonist, or an aeroplane pilot, you know, things that kids think about. I didn't really decide that I really wanted to be in music until I was around twelve or thirteen years old.

Do you believe in a greater power?

Yeah.

Does it connect to your creativity?

I believe that, but I don't know how I believe that. I don't know in what way I can explain what it is, whether it's that I was given something or that it has been there and I've been here before, you know; maybe I've been here and the spirit is still learning through time and that these talents are cumulative experience from other times. I'm not sure how it manifests itself. I'm not really that concerned about it, though, it's not something that I need to explain to myself. Whatever it is, I'm happy.

What was it like for you learning to play the drums? Was it something that came very naturally?

Yeah. After about four years of playing, my mom thought it would be good if I took lessons. But they were basically for reading.

When you're playing or writing music, are there times when everything seems to come together – a Peak Experience? What does that feel like?

Sure. It feels good. It comes in different ways. If I'm playing and it happens, like in a performance, it'll happen a few times, and then I just go back, and then it'll come again, it'll be a rush of something. And I'll just do things that really make me happy and smile. Or I'll go for something and then I'll achieve it and that's always a good feeling because I'm always reaching for something. Because that's what I think my mandate is, what my role is, to do that. I'm supposed to be reaching for things, I'm not supposed to just be repeating what I've done. I can repeat things, and I do, but it's no good unless I'm in the process of reaching.

Do you think the audience picks up on those moments?

Not really. But then they are in the sense that I play for people. Part of me plays for an audience. The first time I played a set of drums was in front of an audience, I had never played the drums before. And I asked my dad if I could play with his group, and he said, yeah. We were at this club and at the next set I went and I played for the first time. I sat behind a set of drums in front of an audience. So that's why I'm in music. Because of live performance.

That's part of what I like, and that's what gives me a lot of who I am is my ability to play for an audience. So in that sense, the people who hear what I play are part of it because I try to play really clearly so that what I think I'm playing someone is actually hearing. There is no difference between what I play and what someone hears me play. So, I don't know if they hear the Peak Experience, but I know they hear what I play.

Has your musicality felt sort of mystically inspired, for want of a better word?

After I've done something, I hear it back, certain songs I've written or certain things I've played, I've heard myself on record. But I don't like to think of that. I don't like to presume what it is, because I think I would become more self-conscious. And I would become a caricature.

Yes. Rather than being.

Exactly, rather than being in that moment. I don't like to do that or think about that. I'd rather just, I'm in the business of playing music, writing music, performing music, you know. Just trying to reach for things.

So when you're writing music, does that peak happen at times?

Yeah, it does. I'll come upon an idea and I'll say, 'Wow,' that's a nice idea and that fits with what I'm trying to say in this piece of music.

Have you any idea where the drive to create comes from?

I know part of it comes from a love of what you do. And I know a part of it comes from wanting to express a view of the universe. What you think life in the universe is and about. And a part of it comes from wanting to be connected with life in the universe. And a part of it comes from wanting to be connected with people, to want to communicate with people and to show your own humanity and to show your love for life.

It's quite a drive.

Yeah, I think so. Yeah.

Do you think that everybody has the potential to be creative, or do you think it is a gift?

Everyone has it. I don't think it's necessarily something that people should feel that they have and the next person doesn't. I think everyone has it, it's just that some people have more of an opportunity for it to come out. Or they have the upbringing that lets it come out and it's not squashed. Everyone has it but a lot of people don't develop it, or won't develop it. I think there are other things higher than creativity. I think talent. Everyone has talent. But it takes other things along with talent to really be creative to make it into something. Because a lot of people have talent. I know guys who play the drums and they have a lot of talent, but they don't really play music. You know, or people who can write songs. They write songs, but they don't really write good songs or great songs. People have talent to pick up a brush and paint a picture, but whether it communicates anything to people is something else.

Whether it's got that spirit.

Right. I mean, people can be creative, but it's not necessarily anything that somebody wants to see or hear.

If it touches you.

If it touches people. Right. So, there's a difference between talent, creativity and that other thing that's beyond creativity.

The spirit of it.

Yeah. Yeah. The spirit that really touches people. You know what I mean?

Yeah. It seems that a lot of people can be technically brilliant but they might not have that feel, right?

Right. That flair or that something that takes it beyond talent and being creative. Some people are creative and it's a lot of self-conscious creativity. Like Dali. To me, he was very self-conscious. You know, things he did were very . . .

They lacked the spirit.

To me. Yeah. I mean, he was a great technician. And you could say, 'Wow! This is a nice vision.' But it's rather self-conscious; he did things for effect. To me. But then, you know, that's just my opinion.

Do you have the choice to create or is it something that just happens?

If I'm in the process of doing something, I'm always doing it. So, if I'm writing a song, then it's on my mind and if I sit down and watch TV, while I'm watching TV, I'll be thinking of the song and I might hear something on TV, like a song from a commercial or from a movie. There'll be some kind of music and I'll listen to it and I'll say will that type of thing fit, or that movement, or that kind of motion? And you'll get an idea. I'll be on an aeroplane and thinking, what should I do with this? So that's how it works. Or, I'm not working on a song, I'll be sitting around and the song just comes into my head. I have a couple of micro-recorders, and I would whip one out and sing the idea.

What if you don't? What if you think, 'I'll leave it till later.' Do you lose it?

Sometimes I'll lose it. Most times. So that's why I have the micro-recorders, because it's so easy to think of something and think that it's really good, and then think about it later, like I've woken up in the middle of the night and had a song. 'Wow! that's great, I'll work on it as soon as I get up.' I'll go back to sleep and then I wake up. Oh, it's gone and I don't know where it is!

But I've got into the habit of also singing something to myself and then watching and then visualising the notes on paper. So that helps also. You sing a melody, and you visualise what it would look like written down on paper.

Like a picture.

Yeah. I'm a very visual person, like most men are, so I can visualise a lot of things. When I play the drums, it's a lot of visualisation going on. I visualise where my hands are, where they're going.

At the same time?

Just previous. It's like I visualise something and then I do it. It's like a picture. Because drums are very visual. When you look at a drummer, it's more so than on any other instrument. When you look at a guitar player, he's just standing like that, but a drummer, with his arms, legs and he's doing these things, so I visualise myself when I'm playing.

Are you in touch with the child in you?

Yeah.

What part do drugs and alcohol play with creativity? Do you think they enhance or block it?

I think at some points they can loosen a person up and you can get ideas. But on a regular basis, no, I think they can be really destructive. You can have a drink and get loose and get funnier and get friendlier with people, things like that. In music, you can think of ideas, say, 'Oh, wow, that's a nice idea, I'm going to do that.' But I couldn't write music drunk. I couldn't play drunk. I mean, I have played drunk, not drunk, but I've had like three or four glasses of wine and gone on the stage. And I don't prefer that. I don't really like that. There was a time when I used to smoke grass. It kind of puts you in another headspace and you have these really wonderful inspirations, you know, but a lot of it is self-indulgence. And there's nothing wrong with self-indulgence, if you know where to do it. So, if you're always doing grass, then you lose perspective on where you are. And then grass seems to take away drive, ambition. You become really complacent and self-absorbed.

What are you feeling when you're playing?

I'm feeling music. Music is a feeling, for me. I love the drums, I love the drums as an instrument, I love the physical and metaphysical connection where they both touch each other. And when I put a pair of sticks in my hands and I touch the drums, it's just a wonderful feeling. And things happen. It's like they are my best friend and I'm doing something with my best friend. We're doing this thing together that no one can come between us. No one. Not my mother, my father, my girlfriend, God, nothing can come between us.

Incredible.

There's this thing that happens when I sit at the drums. That is just me. It's just something I do. Someone once told me that if I lived my life like I played the drums, I wouldn't have any problems! [We both laugh.] I keep wondering about that, you know. So, yeah, it's a nice place to be in and it's some place I've been all my life since I started playing the drums. It's something that has given me the opportunity to be the person I am. You know what I mean? Because without that connection to the universe, I probably would be a different person. It's like the stream through my life that has made me want to be a better person. This connection means, when I go out in life, I'm representing that. I'm a representative of that world. And that world is so wonderful. I have a responsibility to be wonderful. So that's the one reason why I never got into drugs. The only things I'm addicted to are cigars, and women (we both laugh) and things like that, rather than drugs and stuff. Sometimes I've done different things and I say to myself the next morning, damn, that person that was that way last night, that's not the person my mother raised. Certain things in life are foreign to this world that I've been given, so I have a responsibility to protect that.

Have you ever thought that there was a purpose or a meaning in your creativity?

I don't know what it is, though, but I think there is a purpose. There's a purpose for this world and for the things that we do. I just don't know what it is. I'll tell you something, this is good.

That's a good question. I was in Paris, and the French always have these political questions in French music magazines and stuff. And they said to me, well, how come jazz musicians don't do political statements? All the rock musicians and folk people, they're always writing these political songs. I said, 'Hey, being a jazz musician is a political statement. I don't have to write a song about Nixon or about the war or about racism. I don't do that. I don't like that for me. That's not what music is to me. Music is above all that. And I'm not going to title a song about the war or about poverty or about this or that. Just me being here is a political statement. And if you can't understand that, then you don't understand what life is about, you don't understand black people, which you probably don't, because you're French. That's what I believe in.'

Yeah, you don't have to spell it out.

I don't have to spell it out. I am political, but I'd rather talk about politics if I'm going to talk about it. I'm not going to put it to music because I don't believe in that. I mean, other people can do that, I'm not saying people shouldn't do it. You know what I'm saying? Because I'm here to do something else. I don't mind listening to Jackson Browne songs about whatever. That's great, that's great stuff.

What I'm saying is that there are other things that people have to do too. Also, I believe that there's a place for everything in this world, in this universe. There's a place for everyone. Let me have my place. And my place is to do what I do best and what I want to do. And that's what I believe about political statements. I believe that me being here is a political statement. In a larger sense. And that being and that picking a role as a jazz musician, for jazz musicians is a political statement because jazz is something and because it comes out of an experience of being black in America. And that is a political statement.'

Tony died on 23 February 1997. He was fifty-one.

BERNIE LARSEN

A veteran musician who has recorded, toured with and produced acts including Jackson Browne, Melissa Etheridge, Rickie Lee Jones, Lucinda Williams and Public Enemy. He spent six years with David Lindley's band El Rayo-X.

I FIRST MET BERNIE, AND THE REST OF THE MUSICIANS IN David Lindley's band, in 1984. They were on tour, travelling around Europe on a coach. I was with Ian, who played drums in the band, and Bernie was his friend. I loved watching Bernie playing his guitar onstage, his eyes closed and his body swaying, as he drifted off, completely immersed in the rhythms of reggae. We have stayed friends ever since – not only my friend, but he's also friends with my daughters and my grandchildren. He has written songs with my granddaughter and encouraged her guitar playing. This interview took place in 1988 at our house in Sherman Oaks.

'I feel that music goes through me. To just let go and play is second nature to me. It happens without much consciousness. To sit down and deliberately write or to create something, it doesn't happen. When I am writing I have a rhythm or a flow, and it's like speaking in tongues. The flow starts happening, and I believe it's connected to a rhythm of life. And it's going on subconsciously. You can relax and not try too hard, and something passes through you. The pre-destiny thing is beyond your control, although you can alter it slightly by going some place else. Life has its own flow, and you get into that rhythm. Eight hours can go by just like that. You start moving as fast as time is going, and words and phrases will come out that relate to how I feel and what's going on around me. But there's no deliberate effort to do it. It's like opening a door and not looking, and when you look back, it's come out.

'When you're playing, you go off into a grey sort of area and then you open your eyes and you're surprised where you are, you're just soaring with that. The writing thing is actual words. There will be phrases, and it's plugged into a motion; you get the gist of the feeling and it's connected to the rhythm, and from that point on you build around it. I will have a genuine emotion or feeling, I'll be empty, and a few lines will come out, and it's totally relative. It even answers questions that I have. Listening back to what I've done, things come out that definitely aren't mine – riffs, lines, melodies and feelings. They're mine – I guess you rent them or something. They come through me, so it's mine, but it sounds like someone else to me.

'It's one thing to experience this stuff, it's another thing to communicate it. I'd have to compare it to making love, very conscious and aware but unconscious and unaware at the same time. You're riding along with it and the momentum of the feeling. It is the *real* me. There will be times you wander from consciousness and then you'll be aware of where you're at, and other times it's downright startling to open my eyes. I will be flying; it's just like soaring. Probably it would be compared to the definition of astral projection; it's definitely up. It's entertaining; it must be like running the big touchdown, and your flow hasn't been stopped. It's a total letting go, because I don't think you can do it consciously. You can be sitting there with nothing much happening and you can hear just a drumbeat, the rhythm thing will start happening, and twenty minutes later you have a song sitting in front of you. And you didn't have that much to do with it.

'To me, it's the movement of life that's not physical. It's like a layer of information that comes through you. After a few incidents [like that] happened to me, I realised somebody else is driving and I'm in the back seat.

'I was never a regular drinker; it nullified my creativity. With coke, I would get so withdrawn; I don't think I ever had a creative moment on cocaine. Now [without drugs] the writing is more consistent. I don't know if the drugs actually blocked that off or if they gave me less stamina. Like life, some days are like walking uphill, and if you do something to your body to make it even harder to deal with the challenges of everyday living, your will to progress is defeated. It's easier to have the understanding that it's not always there, because sometimes it's not there. There's nothing going on and it's fruitless to say, "I'm going to write a song right now." Drugs give some people the carefreeness to let stuff happen; some people think too much about things, and creativity requires a lack of thinking about a lot of things. I know when I took LSD, it changed my life. It literally changed how I thought about mankind and God. It can enlighten you, but the abuse of it is destructive.

'Everybody has the potential to be creative in their own way and in their own time. There are some people who write more complicated things at fifteen than other people would at thirty. But if the person at thirty had the determination and the support, they could achieve that. If you do something every day, one day is going to come along and you're not consciously trying to achieve it, and you're going to let go and get a little trickle of it accidentally. It's a gift that everybody has – it's just there. There is a rhythm to life and anybody can jump on that rhythm and then go with the flow.

'I'm really lucky because I can satisfy myself with a lot of what I write – that's the reward. It's not monetary or approval from other people. I am fulfilled.'

Bernie's work as a composer and writer for film and television include the features Friends with Money *(with Jennifer Aniston, directed by Nicole Holofcener) and* Elsewhere *(starring Anna Kendrick, directed by Nathan Hope), and the 2013–18 CW Network TV series* The Originals. *He has released albums under his own name and that of his reggae group,* Cry on Cue.

RICK VITO

Guitarist, songwriter, singer and solo artist.
Formerly a member of Fleetwood Mac.

I **FIRST MET RICK IN SANTA MONICA WHERE FLEETWOOD**
Mac were rehearsing with their new line-up, which included
Rick and Billy Burnette. It was 1987 and both guitarists had
been recruited to replace Lindsey Buckingham for the *Tango in
the Night* world tour. We did this interview not long after I met
Rick, and have remained friends since then.

'In regards to playing, I could never *not* do it. I don't know
what has made me stick this out through lean years when nothing
much was happening. I think there's a little voice that tells you
if you're special in some way, a little voice that reminds you
not to forget about it. A certain amount of drive comes from
being inspired by other people's work and wanting to achieve
something that you're proud of and that other people will be
respectful of.

'When I was about sixteen or seventeen, I started thinking
that I would play music professionally, not just on weekends in
bars around Philadelphia, near where I lived. But I never made

a firm stand on that until I was twenty, when I heard the early Delaney & Bonnie records. I thought they were really saying something in a rock 'n' roll way that nobody else was at the time. I was determined to introduce myself to these people and, somehow, I got backstage at one of their shows and met them. They were very encouraging, and so the second time they came back, they invited me to play with them onstage, so I sat in with them. It was one of those things that brought the house down; it was amazing. Delaney told me that if I really wanted to get in the business I should move to L.A. From then on, I made up my mind that nothing was going to be more important than that, so I moved to the West Coast.

'A lot of that purity and sweetness of life takes place in your childhood, when everything was innocent and totally creative. Children feel really free, and when I'm playing my best, I feel free.

'I see a lot of technical musicians, and very few of them seem to have that feel that goes along with it. They're able to do technically a lot more than the next guy, but for some reason it doesn't communicate. So, I guess not everyone has that.

'When I was six, I was given a guitar and also had some lessons. There was an identification I can't take credit for. There's just something about looking at the guitar, smelling inside the sound hole. There was a day that I connected how it is that you play chords underneath melodies, and I heard that connection of that whole thing. It's always been such a monumental thing, such a personal thing.

'It is probably one of the few and far between glimpses of paradise that anybody achieves here. When you get that thing going, the energy starts. You don't have to think, where are my fingers going? You've been playing so long that they go not only to that place but something special comes out. You don't create at all; you're an instrument of it, through here somewhere and out there. That is a very peak kind of experience – that's what makes it all worth it.

'I think it comes from playing with others. I haven't had it happen just by myself. The ultimate would be playing with a great band, with an audience that is tuned in with what you're doing. Just the whole place is joined in with the process; it all happens together. I think that's why people go out and hear live music a lot and have favourite artists. It's an exciting thing when that spontaneous thing happens. You never know when it's going to happen. You can't make it happen the same place two nights in a row. It may happen when you least expect it. I wish I could have on tape every single time that it happens, so I could relive [those moments], but you have to let them happen and then let them go, for the most part, into the ether, wherever. That's what keeps bringing you back for more of the same. And that's why musicians are special. It's the special high they get to have. I'm interested in other forms of creative expression: I've acted, I've painted and I've written, and I get satisfaction from all that stuff. But the greatest thing is playing music and letting that happen. If I had to think of never experiencing that feeling again, it's something I'd miss deeply.

'Everyone has the potential to be creative on their own level; I think that's what makes you human. Creativity is different for everybody. There are musicians who I listen to, and then I compare their playing to mine, and mine seems feeble, prehistoric. I don't know if I have the potential to play like them – probably not. But someone else might listen to his playing and think it's prehistoric next to mine, and think mine's wonderful. I'm sure that Eric Clapton went through a lot with regard to that very thing: people saying he's God, and yet he's aware he's just a man, he's reasonably good. But he might listen to someone like, say, Django Reinhardt, and think, "I'll never be able to do that." And maybe Django Reinhardt was miserable because he got ten bucks a night and didn't think he was anything special. So, it's all relative.

'It would be great to say something in a song [that] became popular to make people stop and think about some aspect of the human condition. A musician's responsibility is to say something that has never been said in quite that way before. The whole creative force is what most people probably refer to as God. It's almost incomprehensible; we're just little bits of that, little bits of the whole. It's all energy and communication of energy.'

Since participating in the February 2020 tribute to Peter Green at the London Palladium, Rick is still playing the blues, writing and recording new material for his next solo album, enjoying the ride in his vintage '69 Cadillac, collecting vintage guitars and spending quality time in rural Tennessee with his wife and family.

KOKO TAYLOR

Blues singer and songwriter, sometimes known as 'The Queen of the Blues'. Over the course of her career, she was nominated for eleven Grammy Awards, winning 1985's Best Traditional Blues Album for her appearance on Blues Explosion.

'**I GREW UP LISTENING TO OLDER BLUES SINGERS LIKE** Muddy Waters, Memphis Minnie, Bessie Smith, Howlin' Wolf – people like that – and that's where I got my greatest influence from. Of course, back in those days, singing the blues was really all we knew. Also, gospel. So, during that time I was singing gospel and I was also singing blues. I was not getting paid to sing; I was singing for my own enjoyment, and this was all I knew to do at that time.

'The drive comes from you. You're the one that motivates the drive; it has to be in you. You have to have that spark to say, "I feel good about myself. I feel good about what I'm doing." And that keeps the energy up, that keeps the drive going.

'People can do whatever they put their heart to; they can be creative. But there's a lot of people who don't have confidence and don't believe in themselves. You hear people say, "I wish I could sing," or, "I just can't sing," or, "I just can't write," or, "I can't do this or that." But they really don't know that they can't do it, because they never tried. Sometimes when you think you can't do something and you go ahead and put your mind and heart to it and do it, you end up doing it better than a lot of people. You've got to have plenty of energy to hang in there. I feel really good about what I'm doing and that's what makes it come out right.'

'When I'm singing in front of an audience, I feel like I'm doing something to help someone, making people happy. People walk up and say, "You know that song you did, that really made my day." And that's the whole reason I'm out there in the first place – it's because of my fans. If I stayed home, I'd think to myself, somebody somewhere wants to hear me, wants to hear the blues. There are not a lot of women out there singing the blues – it's mostly men – so it's a must that I've got to hang in there.'

Koko died on 3 June 2009 at the age of eighty.

PART TEN

'Every note of my music is
crying out for freedom' –
FRANK FOSTER

RINGO STARR

Drummer, singer, songwriter, former Beatle and actor. Drummer with his All-Starr Band.

DUE TO MY SISTER PATTIE MEETING GEORGE HARRISON on their film, *A Hard Day's Night*, and later becoming his girlfriend and then wife, I got to know The Beatles. Either we'd all be in one of the exclusive London clubs listening to the latest Motown from America, or spending a few days in Bangor to get initiated into transcendental meditation, and later at Maharishi's ashram in India. Ringo always struck me as thoughtful but with a great sense of humour and the best laugh! For this interview, I met him at his office in London before going back to L.A.

What was your upbringing like?

I'm an only child, spoiled brat, who was very sick and overprotected. My father left when I was three, but I saw him occasionally. I was mainly brought up by my mother and his parents, instead of my mother's parents. So, between them, they looked after me. My mother had to go to work all the time so

I'd go there from school and, when I was older and if ever I was sick, my mother just wrapped me in a blanket and ran me down to my grandmother's.

When did you know you wanted to be a musician?

My grandma played mandolin and my grandfather played banjo. It always sounds like a sob story, but when I was seven, I was very ill with peritonitis and in hospital. They told my mother I'd be dead three times. So that's why I believe in God; you won't die till your time is right. I don't remember, but they told me, during one of my deliriums I said, 'Mouth organ.' It was 1947, just after the war and Liverpool was bombed to bits so my grandfather travelled the streets of Liverpool looking for a harmonica. I believe he found one, but by then I had no interest in it. We always had a piano, which I had no interest [in] either. I used to walk on it as a kid, being spoiled, and I had no desire to play the mandolin or banjo. I was back in hospital again in 1953 when I was thirteen. To keep you busy, you would knit. That would be in an afternoon and I would make things or we'd do some lessons as schooling. But then once every so often they brought instruments in for the kids to play. There were drums, triangles, tambourines, maracas, things like that, mainly percussive instruments. And there was a big easel, and if she pointed to the red dot, I hit the drum and if it was yellow, they hit the triangle. Well, ever since then I would not play in the band unless I had the drum. So that was my first real madness for drums. It was only a snare drum. I used big old cotton bobbins to play on the little cupboard next to my bed where they'd keep the bedpan, I would tap on that. When I came out of hospital, I started making kits out of biscuit tins and putting little bits of metal on them so it sounded like a snare drum. I'd cut pieces of firewood down into sticks. There were lots of parties in our area and everyone had to sing, someone would play harmonica and someone else would play the piano. There was always a guy with a banjo. This was before guitars; you never really saw guitars as a young teenager, people mainly played banjo or piano. I bought this big old bass drum for thirty shillings. I don't know where I got the money from but I used to bore them all shitloads because I wanted to play my drum. It was so loud.

After that, of course, I had to find a job. I worked on the railways and worked on the boats. Then my mum met a guy in a pub who got me a job in a factory and I became an apprentice. I went for the job as an apprentice joiner, but when I arrived, they said there were no vacancies. How would I like to be an engineer? I said, 'Fine.' So I became an apprentice engineer. Our next-door neighbour, Eddie Miles, was one of those amazing guys who if you gave him a trumpet he could play it in five minutes, and he'd play guitar, mouth organ, he could play anything, he could just pick up an instrument and play it. He brought his guitar into the factory and used to play in the dinner breaks. So, we formed what was like a skiffle group. While this was going on, in 1957/58 I met my stepfather, Harry, who had been with us since they married when I was thirteen and he became my dad. One day he went down to Romford, where he comes from, because a relation of his had died and he bought me this drum kit for £12 and took it back on the train. So, then I got together with this Eddie Miles, who later called himself Eddie Clayton, and we became the Eddie Clayton Skiffle Group. Another friend in the factory, called Roy Trafford, played tea-chest bass, so the three of us used to entertain the lads in the basement of the factory. I was seventeen years old and that's where we really started playing. I'd only ever wanted to be a drummer; I had no interest in all the other instruments that were presented to me. From age thirteen I knew I wanted to be a musician. And that's how we started. I was a Teddy boy like everyone else in our area. So, we used to go to all the pictures together, we'd all go to dances together, everybody had to have gangs in case you had to fight another gang. We started playing every freebie in town, there was always talent shows somewhere. We were very good, even though I had no sense of timing at all. You were lucky in those days if you had an instrument; that's how you got in the group – the only thing you needed was the access. We used to play at every club around Liverpool, every pub, every bar, anywhere we could play for free just to get in. One time we played at some dance, we were like an express train, getting faster and faster and I'll always remember these people dancing, trying to keep up with us and shouting, 'Can't you slow down! Can't you slow down!' We couldn't. We just went!

So, we did all that and then we brought in a tea-chest bass player. All the guys were from the factory, so we had a guitar, snare drum and tea-chest bass format. We did 'Maggie May' and those sorts of songs. That was how I first started playing.

The first time we were going to get paid was at the local Labour club in Liverpool. We were doing this gig and we were going to get paid ten shillings each, which went a lot further in 1957, but the MC was so drunk he wouldn't pay us. Well, my mother and all her friends and everybody who was in those clubs all stormed up to the guy and they actually got the money for us and said, 'We're never coming back to this club unless my boys are paid.' My mother had this wonderful friend called Annie McGuire. 'Mrs McGuire,' I had to call her, of course.

And we would be rehearsing in the house, and she was always so supportive. 'I can see your name in lights on the Palladium, son.' She was really encouraging. I also remember the first day the drums came and I set them up in the back room. We lived in a street with terraced houses, so for half a mile around we had complaints from everybody. I only ever went off into the back room once and actually thought, 'Oh, this is what you do to practise.' But the noise from the neighbours was so heavy on my brain that we had to stop. And I think it's from that day on I never rehearsed as a drummer. I can't just sit there and play drums. I have to play with musicians. I was playing with lots of bands and moving from bands. I remember looking at other bands and thinking that's better than the band I'm in. I would get to know them and see if there was any way in. And that's exactly what happened when I was sitting in for The Beatles on the day Pete couldn't turn up. Brian would drive up and ask me to play.

Would you describe yourself as an outgoing kid or are you shy?

I'm a shy person.

Was your mum musical or just your grandparents?

My stepfather was a great singer. When we used to go to these working men's clubs, like the railway club, the Labour club, places like that, they would pay for all these acts. And then Harry would get up and sing, because he had such a dynamite voice. He would do a great Billy Eckstine. He also tried for La Scala, but sixteen years ago he had to have the nodules taken off his throat, but they made a mistake and now he talks like Louis Armstrong. He's got used to it now after all these years but it was really sad to see him because everyone has to sing in our house. If you came to a party you'd have to sing; your auntie, your uncle, everyone would have their song. Elsie would sing 'My Little Drummer Boy' to me and I would sing 'I'm Nobody's Child', and make her cry.

Did you ever feel different from other kids?

The only difference I really felt was I always wanted a big, huge brother, because they were a definite must in our area. We were about eight or nine and we'd have our little scraps, but the next day a humongous brother would just pick you up and throw you against the wall. So, I always had this craving for a huge brother. Maybe that's because I'm an only child.

Did you have any idea what you were going to be when you grew up?

The only instrument I knew was the drums for me. But, in those days, there was 100 per cent work so you could get jobs and you wanted the money; that way you'd buy your Teddy boy suit. If you look back on the fifties in Liverpool, the best-dressed guys were spending all their money on clothes. So you really had to wear good stuff.

Being in the factory skiffle group was a way out of being in one of the gangs. I remember both Roy and me, because we both loved music, listening to Radio Luxembourg in the afternoon. You had to do it – that was like going to church listening to Alan Freeman. And we would hang out in places, like record stores and listen to records. It was a way out of the life we were leading and this gang membership madness. I just wanted to play. I felt it was a better life. It was no great theory that I'd end up as one of The Beatles. If that hadn't have happened, I'd still be playing in Liverpool. When I was twenty, much to the disgust of all the family, I got this job at Butlin's, sixteen quid a week. Are you crazy? This is fortune time here. And I'm doing what I like, playing the rocking Calypso. I'd moved through a lot of bands by then, and now I was with Rory Storm, who was one of the biggest bands in Liverpool. And, as we'd jokingly say, we used to watch The Beatles rehearse while Rory and the Hurricanes were the top band there. I found the diary of when I first played with Rory and we were getting eight shillings one night and twelve shillings and sixpence another night. We were making between £5 and £10 a week playing. That was a fortune! I could buy a car for £75.

When we went to Germany, The Beatles were there. We were famous because we had suits and ties that matched, and when we came it was, like, 'Hey, look out, here come the big guys!' And so that's how I met them. We were all young guys and were all drunk half the time. And I used to request slow songs when The Beatles were playing, like, three or four in the morning. I didn't find out till later, but John told me, 'God, we used to be terrified when you lot came in.' I still had the sideboards, trying to look like a rocker.

Where did the name Ringo come from?

I don't know why I changed my name, and that was Butlin's again. Liverpool was one of those places where you're either called the big M or you're called Mary or you're called the Hammer Man. Everyone has a nickname. So, they started to call me Rings because I began wearing rings when I was seventeen, and for a guy up there, it was a bit weird that he'd have several rings on his fingers. So, because my name is Ritchie anyway, they started calling me, 'Hey, Rings.' Then when we got this gig at Butlin's, we all decided to change our name. So, I decided to move on to Ringo Starr, which is half of my real name and I just added an 'R'. That's how the name changed.

Did you ever have any unexplained or psychic experiences when you were a child, or any significant dreams or recurring dreams?

I used to have a lot of recurring dreams. One was being chased by lions all the time. They never got you and you never really saw it. But it was a lion, and it was usually in my grandmother's house. I had another recurring dream when I was young, that I would dive off cliffs. And the top of it came when I dreamt I was in an aeroplane. I stepped out of the aeroplane and tried to grab the peak of a mountain. I missed, but I enjoyed the whole fall all the way down and into the woods. I do believe in God and I believe in God because of what has happened to me. God is only a word; you can call it energy or whatever you want to call it. I remember being a manic depressive as a teenager, anything would just send me into a gloom, but that's the teenager's privilege. I remember feeling real down one day. We lived in this really small house, the living room was ten by eight, there were four rooms and they were all ten by eight, and I was going through some madness in my brain. I got so depressed that I wouldn't sleep in case I didn't see the street lamps outside our house come on again. I mean, I got so crazy and then, I don't know, something happened to me in the house. It's that old saying, pulling God out of the cupboard? And I remember going through all that and feeling some sort of reassurance of something.

Did it feel like some sort of presence?

Yes. Well, there was no image. I was direct in my thoughts, like, 'Lord, is there anything after death, what else is there?' Whatever I was doing, I was seventeen, but I do remember this almighty feeling of someone or some sort of contact. I had this thought that you only pulled God out of the cupboard when you need it. We just happened to have this little cupboard and maybe was just the direction of my brain, I don't know. But it felt like in that cupboard something was saying, 'Hello.' That was the first memory I have any sort of. I hate to call it religion because I don't believe in religion, but some sort of hello from something, somewhere.

The next question, which obviously answers itself, is do you believe in a greater power?

Yes.

Does it connect to your creativity?

I think the way it connects is it makes you what you are. Doesn't matter what anyone else thinks of me, I have this total belief. So that's what makes me what I am. And the connection comes through, not as a religious thing, but when four guys are playing, and if they've been together long enough so they know each other, there's an almighty feeling when you get it together. When it hits, there's nothing like it. There's really nothing like it and when you're on tour, and it doesn't happen all the time, sometimes just you and the audience connect. As we were, we played every show, and if we'd have farted, they'd have applauded, to most of them it didn't matter. But some nights, besides us being connected – and we weren't connected every night – you just get on and you do the numbers, sometimes it's great and sometimes it's not. We would be the only ones that knew if it was any good or not. But we'd still get the same applause. But some nights the whole place, without the fantasy of guess who they are, you know, because we did have a little problem being monsters. Most people are big, we were monsters. And sometimes you would feel this sort of presence together with the audience and the band. It just did something. It was such a mind-blower.

How did that feel?

It felt better than the other gigs; there was just something you felt inside, a feeling of connection. There was a whole wave of five or ten thousand people coming at you. Of course, at Shea Stadium there was no contact. I'm talking about Hammersmith or places like that where you felt that you and the audience were actually one. We just happened to be playing, they were screaming and dancing and doing what they did. You didn't get it every night, so when you did, you just felt amazing. That thought made me realise why all musicians keep playing. It's cool.

Can you get that feeling playing with just the musicians, or is it something that needs the audience as well?

It's a totally different thing. When you're playing just with the musicians in the studio, you get another closeness. I would know if Paul was going to do something or George was going to raise it up a bit, or if John was going to bring it down. I usually play with my eyes closed so you would know when things like that were happening, but it took a lot of years of playing together, which is what it takes because, first of all, you've got to get to trust each other. I mean, just trust each other in life, never mind as musicians. Then you trust each other as players. And we did the same thing as most groups did when we finally decided, okay, we'll go in the studio. We used to be in there for months on end, and just to get out we'd all say, 'Oh, that's great. Give us a cassette to take home.' And the next morning you'd all go, 'Let's do it again!' Sometimes faking it because you'd want to get out of the studio! But then we'd all look sheepish the next day.

But sometimes it worked out too, because John, with the tape on backwards it was totally unmechanical, and so that's how that came about. Pure chance. The light switch was pretty hard for him sometimes and he put the tape on, saying, 'We're going to do it this way,' and magic would come out of it.

And George went to India and found the sitar. It just added instruments that changed the sound of it, that's all. It was exciting to have these things on.

When you have that connection with the band and the audience, what does that feel like?

Oh, it feels great. It's magic actually, it's pure magic. That everyone who's playing at that time knows where everybody's going. Even, wherever you go, everyone feels that's where we should be going. It's a little strange and there's really no words for it. The emotion you feel when you're playing for hours and it's not working, let's call that the downer, but when it works, when it clicks, there's really nothing like it. There's really nothing like it that I've ever experienced in my life than when the boys are playing together. It's cool.

Did you ever reflect, 'Why me?'

No, not really. Why me? I think it had to be me. This was like some sort of path I was on, and I did try and keep moving into better bands because that was the conscious thing I did. At one point I played a gig in Liverpool, and just by madness, there were three bands on the bill. We used to do an hour each, but broken up into half-hour sections, but once two drummers didn't turn up. So, I just sat there for three hours, every half an hour changing my jacket, playing with the next band, changing my jacket, because everyone wore suits and so I wore six jackets and played in three bands in one night because we all knew the numbers. Everybody knew what everyone was playing. I don't know about the 'Why Me?' situation – it's like, why not? And I am the best rock and roll drummer on earth!

But of course!

That took me a while to get used to. But I am rock steady and I play like that. I play with some sort of beat going on within me. It can be fast or slow, I just feel it. Sometimes it's like holding racehorses back, the rest of the band usually get a bit crazy on a race or a drag. And also, the drummers' bane in life is that, if they all speed up and you don't, they say you're dragging. If you watch any band, if anything goes wrong, they'll go look at the drummer. I always tell Zak, 'They always look at the drummer; just look at them back in the eye, because it's not you.'

Do you believe you're here for a reason?

The reason you're here is you picked it from the start. To be a drummer? To be the father to my children? To marry Barb? Whatever those reasons are, I don't know. Is she here to marry me, or just help me through something? I really have no proof of any of that. I can't help but think there's a reason if I pick this body I'm going through. I can't believe in the humanist where you're born, you die and it's all over. If you look back at the dinosaurs, forty million years and we've been here fifteen thousand as far as we know. Even if we all disappeared tomorrow, the planet would go on and we would be going on somewhere else. I just think a lot of the times we, as the human race, make ourselves out to be so important, and also so silly really, because we were given the Garden of Eden and all we tend to do is fuck it up. And I don't understand why we would do that. I used to have this terrible thing in L.A., because of the smog, and when they tried to bring the converters in for the cars, just to keep the smog down and to keep us all a little healthier, Ford Motors didn't want to do it. So I said, 'What air is Henry Ford breathing?' I could not understand that attitude just because it would put ten dollars on the car. Ten dollars a year isn't bad to breathe better! And everyone in L.A. takes them off anyway because they can drive faster.

Did any of your music ever feel mystically inspired?

Well, the mystic music was George's really. I don't think I wrote any mystic pieces. 'Octopus's Garden' is the most mystical piece I ever wrote and that came about by chance because I was on holiday on the boat, and I ordered fish and chips and the guy brought me a squid. I said, 'That's not fish,' and he says, 'You'll love it, it tastes like chicken,' so I said, 'Give me chicken.'

We were on this boat and the captain was talking to me and he told me octopuses actually build gardens. Well, I didn't know that at the time. They have their little cave and then they go and find all the tin cans, nice bright little rocks, and they do it all around their little house, inside and out. And I wrote it in like fifteen minutes because of this captain.

Do you feel that everyone has the potential to be creative?

I think everybody has the potential. The problem people have is they think they're not creative enough or they compare themselves. I had a very hard time trying to present my songs to Lennon and McCartney, and George did before me when he tried to present his songs. Well, it's a bit off-putting when three guys are lying on the floor hysterical, and I'm trying to play my song. I used to steal. I didn't really steal; I was just not conscious and I would rewrite other songs and think they were mine. So, you've written 'Crazy Arms' again, you know, you've written so and so again, and I would think it was mine. I play three chords on guitar and three chords on piano, though I used to give it to George, who'd make me sound like a genius. But yeah, I had a real hard time and that's what it's like with people now, they feel they can't play because they're not professional, which isn't true. It's like people say, can you give people any advice? As a drummer, could you give little Billy some advice? Well, first of all, get a set of drums. I used to give kids lessons in L.A., and if they didn't get the basic boom-check – that's just plain, straight fours – I would say, 'It's pointless because you don't have the co-ordination to move two arms and two feet, so maybe the piano is better for you.'

What do you think gives you the drive to create?

It's harder for the drummers to talk about it. Well, not all drummers, but I am strictly a drummer who writes odd songs. I've never fronted the group, it's not like Dave Clark. You spoke to Phil Collins? I mean, but he writes a lot, so it's a different thing, though he's a drummer as well. He is also one of the main creative forces. The main creation I gave was the best drumming I could to someone else's songs. So, the writing of the songwriters was the most creative, not the most, but the initial creativity is, 'We got a song now we're going to do the bits.'

Just drumming was my drive. I did one great track on 'Drumming Is My Madness', written by Harry Nilsson. And that's what it is. It's my madness, that's what I do. I love to play.

I honestly think that every child should play an instrument as it brings people so close together anywhere in life, in any little room or a big palace. It brings people together. I remember my musical teaching in school was sitting in a room, bored shitless, listening to classical music on record, and the teacher's taking no interest. He just plays it for forty-five minutes, and then says, the music's over now. I really had no sort of musical education at school, although they played the popular classics.

Who inspired you when you first started playing?

The only record I ever bought was Cozy Cole, 'Topsie' *Part I and II*. The only drum record. I've never been one for listening just to the drummer, I mean, I listened to the drum within a track for stuff, but I've never been one of those people who go and buy all the drum records you can. On Phil Seaman, God rest his soul, he's dead now, but Phil was great. The fastest man on earth who just died, Buddy Rich. Buddy Rich could do more with one hand than I can do with two and two feet. That was never a style I wanted; I always claimed it was like rats running around the kit. I really am a pure rock and roll drummer. That's all I can do. I can't play anything jazzy or fancy. I play rock and roll. That's what I do.

And the best!

And the best!

How do you think drugs and alcohol affect creativity? Do they enhance or block it?

It depends. I usually prefer to work straight. If you're working a long time, sometimes you have a little party, so you have a few drinks. Sometimes that's good, but for me personally, I like to play practically straight. I mean, we've tried to be out of it, and all those bullshit stories that we recorded all this on acid, and we did it on this and that, it isn't true. We used to do all that and then make music. Occasionally, we made music on some substance but 90 per cent of the time it's the wrong word to say straight, because you've actually been all those other places. So, you're not straight really, because you know where the bends are. And so, you use that as well. Overall, I prefer to be practically straight. I like maybe a shot of cognac just to loosen me up because I'm shy.

How many records do you have by a band that are always out of their brains? Nobody has any. Even the Grateful Dead, who were past masters of substances, if you listen to their early music, although they're popular again now, but I think they worked the same way. All the bands I know who actually worked totally coked or on grass or hash or whatever, totally out of it, their careers suddenly disappeared. I mean, a lot of people besides the poor people we've lost altogether and went to heaven. But people who are still around and got caught up in, 'We've got to do it out of our brains,' their careers didn't last long, because in the end, the drug overtakes your actual playing or your singing. I've noticed that with a lot of bands.

What did you think of the sixties?

Flower power. Yes, that was fabulous. There hasn't been a time like that. I was so disappointed, totally miserable when it failed. I thought, God, this is it, all together and all through music. That was great. And everyone was just giving each other flowers, not shooting each other or stabbing.

And the problem, why it failed, is because all the guys who decided to start taking substances decided then to take the hard shit and it fell apart. That's the demon. But that was great. I'm really pleased I went through that. It's hard to explain it to your kids because they can't understand it; they may see Jimi Hendrix and think that's what it was. That was part of it and all the other bands around in those days, but the actual feeling of flying into anywhere in Europe, anywhere in America and everyone was friendly. Now you can't go to New York and just be friendly, even L.A. is not the same. The police cleaned that off as soon as they thought people were having a good time.

There's no straight direction any more.

'How life has changed since our interview! When I came out of rehab at the end of 1988 my sober life gave me renewed energy and the very next year, 1989, I put a band together and started touring – something I never did before and am still doing today in 2023. Grateful to be doing what I love all these years – peace and love, Ringo.'

PHOEBE SNOW

Singer, songwriter and solo artist.

AFTER OUR INTERVIEW, PHOEBE TOOK ME TO THE New York City cathedral where she performed in a tribute to South Africa's Bishop Tutu. She wanted me to see the setting of what she considers one of her most extraordinary moments.

'My feeling is that we are channels, basically, through which the creativity comes. It's not "Phoebe's music". Instead, Phoebe is a vessel that carries around some stuff, and if Phoebe chooses to open the vessel, then it will work. It's coming from this thing that is controlling the whole universe. "Poetry Man" took about five minutes to write. Some people ask me, "What were you thinking when you wrote this?" and I have to tell them I really don't know; it doesn't have anything to do with how my mind rationally works.

'It just comes out. If I think about what I'm going to be doing in a couple of hours or if I remember something somebody said to me yesterday, the flow is really broken and I can feel it. So, I have to hurry back and get into my singing or I feel I'll lose it. I become someone else when I'm up there and yet I'm me.

'The peak is sort of like a rapturous feeling; it's really wonderful. For a long time after my first album was out, I was not very well. I had some medical problems, but I had to slog it out, go on tour, and try to hang in there. The travelling would kill me, but for the hour and a half I was onstage nobody knew I was sick. I might be crawling on my hands and knees backstage, but I'd get out onstage and be transported. I think it comes in varying degrees; there's always a little of it there and sometimes a lot when you've got to almost reel yourself back in.

'Once I was called to come and sing "Amazing Grace" to welcome Bishop Desmond Tutu at the Cathedral of Saint John the Divine, in New York. The occasion was called The Harlem Welcome. There were African dancers, a parade of people playing percussion instruments and wearing wild costumes. There were 5,500 people in the room. I was to perform during the candle-lighting ceremony, where the whole cathedral was lit. The ceiling there is 152 feet high; every bay window has an intricate stained glass. I was supposed to get up on a raised platform and sing. As I got up, they darkened the cathedral and so all you could see was the entire audience holding candles. It took me about a whole verse to get into it; by the second verse I was gone. I was doing it, but it wasn't me doing it; I was nuclear-powered at that point. It was like reflex action. I was so swept up in this thing that by the end of it I forgot who I was, what I was doing. I got lost. I was very disoriented when I finished, and there was Bishop Tutu standing on this pulpit opposite me. The eye contact was intense. I knew I had gotten transported.'

FRANK FOSTER

Played saxophone and clarinet, among other instruments. A composer and arranger who played with the Elvin Jones Quintet and was the band leader of the Count Basie Orchestra.

I INTERVIEWED FRANK OVER THE PHONE, AND although I wasn't able to meet him face to face, I was still able to feel a connection with him through his voice and what he was saying.

'Whenever I perform, especially standing in front of the Count Basie Orchestra, I mentally work a spell on the audience. In other words, I concentrate on the idea of hypnotising the audience, so they get the utmost enjoyment from the music. It's not about picking out a lady in the audience and hypnotising her for romantic reasons or for erotic reasons. It's about hypnotising the whole audience so they get a heightened appreciation of the music and go away feeling inspired and happy and have forgotten their troubles for these couple of hours, not actually understanding why they enjoyed the performance.

'While I'm performing, I will look directly at someone who

is about [at] the mid-point of the auditorium; I can't see their face clearly, but I look directly at them while I'm playing, and I am actually hypnotising that person. I'm aware of some kind of movement, something is vibrating when I look directly at someone, and I imagine this to be some kind of power coming from or through me. It's concentrated on that one point where that individual is, then it vibrates; it spreads from that one point, and it's somewhat the same as a pebble being dropped in a lake. It expands outwards. It expands through the auditorium and spreads to everyone there.

'I think that no matter what type of music, it represents what's happening with the masses. I think the music has done that all through history. Every note of my music is crying out for freedom, is glorifying freedom of the spirit, especially in the area of making life happy or positive for others. That's what music is about. It's not about enslaving anybody; it's all about striving for the most positive conditions. Even the music that is angry sounding, that's anger against oppression and inhumane treatment from one person to another.

'The Peak Experience is really a great feeling. It has to be brought about by certain congruent conditions. For instance, you have to be feeling good and inspired yourself. And then you have to have a microphone in front of you, and a monitor that's working, and an audience that's very receptive, and a group behind you that seems to be particularly on too.

'I've had moments like that, say, with the Elvin Jones Quartet or Quintet, when the inspiration just seems divine, and we could do no wrong. It's all about performance of the group and my own individual performance. I've had moments like that with the Count Basie Orchestra, and I've had moments like that with my own band at certain times in the seventies. And one thing

I've noticed is that it was always when the moon was either waxing towards full or completely full.

'I find that marijuana seems to particularly inspire me to want to create. I've found that some of my most meaningful or deepest ideas have come through inspiration gleaned from marijuana – not that I think it makes me perform better. It makes me feel I'm in touch with forces I'm not usually in touch with when I'm cold sober. I can get out of myself what the Creator has given me to produce whether I'm high or sober.

'I don't think I could do anything behind alcohol; alcohol generally interferes with the motor function. People who get drunk can't perform up to their ability, unless they've been doing it for years and years, like saxophone players who've been drinking all their lives and who can go on all night. Their systems have become sort of immune to the impairment caused by alcohol, although they are going to die from drinking it for so long.

'Everyone has a mission. Everyone is here for a purpose, and not everyone has the same purpose. The person who has the ability to be a carpenter or has the ability to be a builder doesn't necessarily have what I have, and I don't have what they have. Each individual has something, some aptitude or some ability, with which they can serve humankind. I found mine as a musician.

'My music is out to proclaim the glory of God to everybody in the universe and to make everyone happy. Politically, every note is glorifying freedom, to make life positive. I'm trying to play notes that will make that ditch digger want to dig a better ditch. Socially, I think we should all come together and appreciate one another for our differences. Instead of fighting one another, let's love one another.'

Frank Foster died on 26 July 2011 at the age of eighty-two.

STEVE JORDAN

Drummer and bass player who has played with such artists as Keith Richards and Neil Young.

I MET STEVE WHEN I WAS MARRIED TO IAN WALLACE. I would often see his smiling face backstage at concerts and festivals when he was about to play with one of the big bands. He was the one who set up the interview with Keith Richards.

'My parents started giving me records really young. Before I could read, they had given me an extensive record collection. I used to identify them by the label. I heard a lot of Miles Davis: I was very inspired by Tony Williams and Art Blakey. I remember dancing in 1962, when I was six years old, to the original "Twist and Shout" by The Isley Brothers at my aunt and uncle's house. I was always dancing.

'My favourite artists were James Brown and The Beatles. They really are the essence of all the things that I think are important to me musically – everything else is an offshoot from that. The Stones have been very influential, Al Green, as well as Sly and the Family Stone, but that was a little later. The Motown sound: James Jamerson – hearing the sound of that bass – and

Benny Benjamin, the drums on that, it's a part of the way I breathe. Listening to [Donald] "Duck" Dunn and Al Jackson play together – their Memphis sound was very important. Those things inspired me the most.

'When I was little, I banged on everything. I used to get the coffee cans with plastic lids – that was my kit. It sounded good. I got my first drum when I was eight, with the provision that I take lessons at the local music store. The first time I went, the guy sat me behind this great set of Gretsch drums – blue sparkle. I felt just fantastic sitting behind this kit. The guy said, "Do you really want to practise and put the time in? It isn't going to be easy." I said, "Yeah, yeah!" I couldn't wait to get down and play. They didn't give me any sticks or anything, just let me sit behind it and said, "Come back next week." I couldn't wait, every night I was dreaming about the kit. So, the next week I walked in the same room and there was this piece of wood with a slab of rubber on it, and there were no drums in the room at all. It was a practice pad! I was crushed, but I had to start there.

'Some of the greatest things I've ever done – and amazing feelings – have come from things I didn't even know I was doing. And I can't take responsibility for them because that would be completely bogus. I know I didn't do that; it's written down that I did it, but I didn't do that. I have that feeling when I write and when I play. When you write that song and it just comes out automatically, especially if you've been slaving over a song for about a month and it doesn't seem to work, then all of a sudden, a song comes out just like that, and it's the best thing you've ever done. It's the same thing when you play and you've been working on a lick and you just can't seem to get it and then that one time when you go for it in a situation where you wouldn't even try and then you just do it. Like on a recording session when you're a drummer, everybody else can overdub their stuff; if they make a mistake they can punch in their part, but with the drums you can't do that. A lot of the time you might have a tendency to play it safe, so when you go for something that you know you've been practising and that you can't do, and then you do it in a situation where you could blow a whole take that's been going quite well, you know you're not responsible for that.

'There's very little music that's moving anyone. There's a lot of mindless garbage out there, and I think what we were doing on tour with Keith [Richards] was, we were people onstage actually playing, instead of having some machine play tape-recorded background vocals and having everything be the same every night. That's not music – but that's what's happening.

'Besides the voice box, the drum is the first instrument, it's natural – bark and skin – and the first mode of communication to pass messages from village to village, also for music. It's all about timing, rhythm – your heart is a drum – it's all that. If you're really good at drumming, then you're a little closer to what it is that makes it all special: the core. The more I play other instruments, the better drummer I become, and that [also] gets me closer to the core. And the better writer I become, the better drummer. Music is very powerful; it crashes down walls. It's the only universal language there is, and it can knock down barriers quicker than any UN meeting, any NATO meeting. That's why rock 'n' roll has been so powerful. I watched a band from Liverpool change the world. As far as I'm concerned, what else has done that?!

'You zone out during a Peak Experience; a lot of the time

you can actually watch yourself do things, almost like an out-of-body experience. Sometimes you're there but you don't know how you did that. It's all just this thing that happened, and then you go back and you listen to it and you go, "Holy cow, wow!" The classic is when you're doing something and you think, wow, this is incredible, and you look at yourself and try to figure out what the heck you're doing and then you blow it completely.

'Some drugs can make you feel like you're at the top of the world, until you come down and you see what you've done is terrible. Out of frustration, you do drugs when you can't write and you think you need it. You've got to do something, so you hope for a different perspective. On occasion that might work, but usually what happens once you've had one drink, you just want another drink.

'It's a little easier for some people, but everyone has the potential to be creative. All you need is support. One day when I was twelve or thirteen, my mom gave me this little plaque that I still have in my kitchen. It says "Think Big". That changed my life. Everyone needs that to get to where they want to go.

'Some creation, I don't even know where it comes from, it just happens. I just leave myself open and I'll create. Sometimes there's a drive to create that stifles your creation because you want to create so badly that you tense up and nothing happens. If you just stay open and clear, then you create. When you force things, it doesn't happen. When I just let it happen, being open to all the energy, the better writer I become.

'Sometimes you have to be somewhere other than your home to create; sometimes you can't create at all unless you're at home. Sometimes your place needs to look a mess; sometimes you can't do anything unless it's completely clean.'

After he replaced Charlie Watts in the Rolling Stones on the No Filter Tour, Steve has continued to play with the Stones, both live and in the studio. Keith Richards, in his autobiography, says that Watts told him that 'if he ever wanted to work with another drummer, Steve Jordan's your man.'

MIKE RUTHERFORD

Guitarist, bassist, songwriter and singer,
who is a member of Genesis and Mike and
the Mechanics.

'**I'VE GOT NO CONTROL OVER THE CHOICE TO CREATE.**
I'm like a man incontinent. I have a respect for whatever it is that enables me to do it. I try not to abuse it. The biggest high comes when you write something. By not abusing it, I mean I try not to force it; it's too precious. If it won't come, I just leave it and do something else.

'I just sense moments, the feelings that are going on in young kids at certain stages; you hear a song, or you hear a mood or an atmosphere. It's there somewhere, you can feel it. I've always felt the strongest things are subconscious; a heavy lyric or a heavy sound is never as strong as some of those subconscious feelings. I think everyone inside is feeling it, even if not aware of it.

'For a while, I didn't like songs with messages; I didn't feel it was my place to tell people what I thought they ought to do. It wasn't my place to preach, and I didn't like it when people did that. I think it can very often be power misplaced and misused,

341

but I'm changing a little bit. For a Genesis album, I wrote a protest lyric called "Land of Confusion", which shows how I've changed. As I get older, maybe I'm feeling more in a position to comment than I did before. I fight to not analyse it; everything I do is pure gut feeling. I let something inside tell me where I'm going. It's in your stomach, you know, it's just that feeling inside you. I found myself changing the way I write lyrics and being slightly more grown up, but whether I felt older or wiser, I don't know.

'This particular song, "Land of Confusion", was a terribly simple message, which was really, we have a wonderful way of living and what a complete fucking mess we're making of it. It was a very direct lyric, but it was still done subtly. It's more a social comment, but I'm becoming more positive in my writing than I used to be. I think it's all to do with, we grow up, we change, and I like that movement. This creativity thing is affected one hundred per cent by that.

'I know a lot of people feel they owe it to themselves and to the world that, if they're in a position to reach a lot of people, they ought to use it, but I'm very cautious of that. I haven't felt convinced of their genuineness one hundred per cent. The way I work, I do it for myself, it's purely for my satisfaction. And I'm obviously changing as a person because I'm looking at the world more than I used to and making more comments, but it's only because I want to do it. It feels right inside, not that I *ought* to. I can't ever feel I ought to do something and then channel my work in that way.

'During a Peak Experience I'm not quite sure where I am. I'm somewhere else for a while; it's like I come back to earth. Something breaks the moment and I'm back. You don't realise you're gone till something happens and you're back. It's a moment's magic that from time to time touches me, and I don't control it. Like Tinker Bell, it just goes past.

'When I'm playing, though, I never get lost. I never lose myself in the same way. While playing, I get a different high: feedback from the audience. It lifts me somewhere but I always know where I am.

'For myself, drugs have been a destructive force, without bringing any good. That's the main thing – writing and creating have always felt like such a natural thing. It's like you need to cleanse your body to do it. It's the feeling of purity, I think.

'When I write, if I try too hard it's completely hopeless; nothing happens. It's like you have to free yourself up, and if I think about how it happens, the more I analyse it, the more it pushes it away. A perfect example: if I go in one morning to write with the idea that today I'm going to do something wonderful, nothing happens. If I don't try or think about it, with the attitude of "I'll give it ten minutes," it all happens. It's frightening because ideas come so fast. It's a wonderful feeling. You get these moments when you can do no wrong. Everything you play is wonderful.'

Mike continues to tour with Genesis and has written two books. The first, about his solo career, is called Silent Runner *and was published in 2011. In 2014, he published* The Living Years: The First Genesis Memoir.

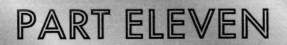

PART ELEVEN

'When writing, that's when you
feel at peace with yourself; it makes you
feel more complete' –

JEFF LYNNE

SARAH WARWICK

A highly talented guitarist, singer and songwriter who has dedicated her last twenty-two years to sharing her skills and encouraging others to find their voice.

I MET SARAH ABOUT TEN YEARS AGO WHEN I JOINED her weekly singing group. I had always been a little self-conscious about my singing voice, but within a few weeks I joined in wholeheartedly with everyone else as we sang harmonies. I later joined her year-long singing/song-writing group, and with Sarah's encouragement and guidance, each one of us ended up writing not only our own song, but recording it in the studio and actually singing it in front of family and friends! The very thought of which would previously have brought me out in a cold sweat!

Tell me about your upbringing, and if either of your parents were musical.

I grew up in a musical family. My beloved father sang in West End musicals as well as singing the latest pop songs live each week on a show called *Top Numbers* on TV. He taught me how to play guitar and we used to play and sing duets together. His brother, my lovely uncle, Norman, had a successful career as an actor and singer in many well-known musicals at the National Theatre as well as other theatres across the country. My brother, Daniel, is also highly musical and a passionate songwriter and singer with his band, Feral Ghost.

From an early age my love of pop music and nature gave me a joy that has always stayed with me.

I started my adult life as a schoolteacher, teaching by day and rehearsing and gigging with bands at the weekend until I decided to take the plunge, give up teaching, and follow my dream of being a pop star. My dreams came to fruition in the nineties when I found my way to becoming a recording artist. During my ten years in the music business, I co-wrote and recorded my own songs as well as singing to millions on TV, radio and on tour. I had five hit records in the UK, Europe and America, mostly under my pseudonym, 'Sarah Washington'. I soon went from feeling unbearably shy onstage to being able to hold an audience of thousands on my own with passion and verve.

What gave you the drive to create?

The driving force behind my passion was the desire to share a love of music and life itself, to uplift others, and bring people together through song. Through performing I was learning to express myself, to be confident, to value the gift I'd been born with, and the opportunity to write uplifting songs. However, trying to please my manager, producer, the record company and the public was a huge challenge! My focus was outward, and whilst I enjoyed so much of all that is involved in having hit records, the stress of trying to 'fit in, write hits and be a shining star' led to exhaustion and serious health challenges.

What changed?

In the summer of 1999, I attended a concert at Alternatives, Piccadilly. An internationally acclaimed musician, singer and sound healer called Chris James introduced me to the healing power of sound. His voice and his songs touched me so deeply and in that moment the trajectory of my life changed. I began training in sound healing, not knowing how much I was in need of healing!

A few months later, on Christmas Eve 1999, I was diagnosed with stage two aggressive breast cancer and was given a thirty per cent chance of survival. This was a shocking discovery, but a small voice inside said, 'This is good. We're going to go on a big healing journey.' So began a new chapter in my life. I listened to my inner voice more than I'd ever done before and I put together a programme of nutrition, homeopathy, sound healing, psychotherapy and many other therapeutic approaches to healing on all levels.

This was a major turning point in my life. Having cancer was like a crash landing back to earth, and to my body's wellbeing. It brought a sense of vulnerability, of humility. I was touched by how much my survival meant to others. I received so much support and love. My heart was truly opened and nourished, and this was the most healing thing of all. Knowing that I was of value. I listened to that still small voice inside more than ever. My awe and appreciation for life was deepened. My longing to connect had become a way of life. I was changed at a cellular level. It was a healing of the heart and it took me on a journey to the very essence of life itself.

Once I had recovered enough, I began to write songs from my heart, for healing, rather than for any record company. It created an awareness of how adversity can lead to deep transformation and connection to the true self, and how it offers a greater sense of purpose. At first, I was nervous to share my songs. But soon I realised others could relate to them, were moved by them and felt the healing too. That was when I decided to help others write their own life songs.

For the last twenty or more years I have been helping others find their singing voice and guiding them in writing the songs that express what is important to them, to enhance creativity and to experience inner peace. Through singing, healing sound, meditation, song writing and other creative practices, such as intuitive painting and creative writing, my work offers deep soul-healing and life-enhancing transformation. I've travelled internationally to facilitate a huge variety of conferences, workshops and trainings, encouraging audiences worldwide to sing together, to experience the power of healing sound, and helping people to develop song-writing skills and create melodies that support the message within their songs.

It is not only a musical gift I feel blessed with, it is also an ability to create what many people call a safe and sacred space, where people can get in touch with their potential. I orchestrate the parts for everyone in the group to sing melodies together in harmony, either the songs I choose from around the world or songs people in the group have written and recorded as they find unknown parts of themselves. The aim of my work is for people to know that singing is their birthright. It is not just for the chosen few; to facilitate a space where people can experience the joy and vitality that comes with singing together. Not only that, everyone has a song inside them. To sing our deepest feelings and life stories can be so joyful and healing. Melody gives our words wings, an opportunity to be witnessed with love as we sing our songs, which is healing in itself.

I love the creative process. Life is creative. The best ideas come in the moment; they come through me, not from me – it's all part of the process.

I always knew I wanted to help others, I wanted to reach more people and share with them the joy of singing. Singing connects us to ourselves, to feeling whole, as it guides people into the zone and beyond the rational. We need this feeling of connection in such a fragmented world. Singing brings light into our world and song writing brings light to our inner world. It gives our spirit wings. My latest recording with producer Peter Coyte is setting Kahlil Gibran's timeless classic, *The Prophet*, to music. His brilliantly poetic fusion of east/west mysticism is brought to life with glorious harmony and spoken word. This truly is a joy to sing. Kahlil's words and the melodies take flight.

PETER FRAMPTON

Singer, songwriter, guitarist, solo artist and formerly a member of British bands The Herd and Humble Pie.

I **CAN'T REMEMBER WHERE I MET UP WITH PETER, BUT I'M** pretty sure he was living in L.A. at that time.

'My father's mother had a piano – with the candlesticks on it and everything – on which she used to play vaudeville music. One day when I was five or six, we went for a visit, and she produced a ukulele. I thought it was marvellous, so she gave it to my father for me to play later on, when my hands were big enough. A couple of years later I ran across the dusty case in our attic and asked my dad what it was. He reminded me of the ukulele, and so I asked him to show me a few chords. My father played guitar in a college dance band before the war, so he knew the basic chords and how to tune it.

'I was about seven and a half when I started playing, and I became obsessive about it at a very early age. When I was eight or nine my grandmother took me up to Shaftesbury Avenue and showed me all of Tin Pan Alley [the musical instrument centre of London]. She also took me to Selmer's [a famous music shop], where I remember seeing [early British rock 'n' roll guitarist] Hank B. Marvin's guitar in a glass case. She encouraged me more than my parents did at the very early stage.

'It was really exciting learning to play. It was something I did very well, very quickly. It came easily, and so I worked long hours at it. It was my hobby, and I was obsessed with being as good as Hank Marvin.

'I have always had a challenge to meet, whether it was to be successful and recognised for my craft or to maintain the success, or just to please myself and grow as a musician, which is the most important thing to me. In my home studio I still go and enjoy myself, and if I play or write something new, it fuels the drive that I have always had to break new ground. There's nothing like coming up with a new piece of music to spur you on to do more.

'Sometimes, it's as if the song is writing itself. The songs that are written in that way are usually the best because they happen quickly and your excitement builds as they do. One of the most prolific times I've had was when I wrote the *Frampton* album. In eight days, I had written the whole thing, including "Show Me the Way" and "Baby I Love Your Way", which were written the same day. I wonder why – and can I have a few more weeks like that? Please!

'In the case of U2, it's such a mood that is created. People have said to me it was more of a moving experience than just a regular show. Knowing how I feel onstage and when I communicate that feeling to the whole audience, it starts to become a sort of emotional feedback. I become totally uninhibited onstage. People in the audience are reacting to my actions and my mood as well as the music. I know that I can control the feeling in the audience.

'I have to feel in a confident mood. If I don't feel good about myself then how on earth am I going to be able to create something that comes from the heart – and that's the key for me. It has to come from the heart.'

Peter was diagnosed with a degenerative muscle disease in 2015 and, in 2019, announced his farewell tour.

JEFF LYNNE

*Singer, songwriter, guitarist, keyboardist, producer
and solo artist. A founding member of The Move,
Electric Light Orchestra and the Traveling Wilburys.*

I HEARD OF JEFF LYNNE WHEN I INTERVIEWED GEORGE
Harrison, who had been playing with him and the rest of
the Traveling Wilburys the night before. My ex-husband Ian
Wallace had known Jeff for some time and so I would often see
him at different gigs where Ian was playing or at our house or
friends' houses for a meal.

'I started out with my friend who had a plastic guitar, and it
had only one string on it, and I said, "Ooh, can I borrow that?" I
borrowed it, and I learned "Guitar Tango" by The Shadows, by
playing on one string. That's how I learned. Then one day, my
dad bought me a second-hand Spanish guitar for two quid, and
then I got some strings. Someone taught me how to tune up,
but they taught me wrong. I didn't know that, so when I used
a book to learn to form chords, it sounded terrible. I thought I
was useless, and then a few weeks later someone told me about
the real tuning. I was about fourteen. I didn't like school very

much, and so when this guitar thing came about, even the one string, I realised I'd found something I'd like to do. And once I got the Spanish guitar, that's all I did – just played it for five or six hours a day. I loved it so much I didn't need anything else at all. I was good at it, fortunately. I could pick it up quickly, so I thought, maybe I'm good at this.

'I got into this electronic stuff several years ago. You end up sitting around the studio waiting for this guy to program all this shit into the computer. You end up saying, "What the hell am I doing this for? I could have played this, and I'd much rather play this." So, I kicked it all out and that's how we did George's (Harrison) album *Cloud Nine*, by just playing everything – real drummers, real guitar players and no sequencers.

'The studio for me is the ultimate place to be. The only time I get near to something coming "through" me is when I'm playing in the studio and get a riff that's really good. It's spotting it that's the hard bit, because there are so many good riffs or so many possibilities. Some are just trash, some you'll get fed up with in half an hour, and some you'll go, "That's the one." And if it comes out, it feels very uplifting and satisfying and it's everything. Then it's like the best bit of your existence. I don't get that feeling anywhere else. It's when you get the right chords and the tune goes just right – it's very rare. There are times when it just hits you and you say, "That's it; I've made a musical statement that I really like."

'I've never even tried cocaine, never wanted it. The first joint I ever had was in 1980. I never got into the drug thing at all. When you create, you've got to be dead straight. I think the most creative part of the day for me is when I first get up and just start working on a keyboard, before [my] brain has had all the crap input. If I ever smoke dope now, I can't play anything. I can only listen back, but as far as performing goes, it just makes it worse.

'When writing, that's when you feel at peace with yourself for a bit, like, "I've done something really good." You feel elated for a while, and it makes you feel more complete.'

Jeff is due to be inducted into the Songwriters Hall of Fame in 2023, a prestigious American institution that seeks to celebrate and honour the contributions and legacies of songwriters of all genres. He is being honoured for songs he wrote, arranged and produced with ELO as well as his work with the Traveling Wilburys.

STEPHEN BISHOP

Singer, songwriter and solo artist.

AFTER SPENDING THE AFTERNOON WITH STEPHEN, I realised that the childlike part of his nature is still very much alive. Stephen seemed to relish devising inventive ways of amusing himself. That day, for example, he showed me his music room, his toys, and then had me listen to his telephone answering machine message. He loved concocting different personalities and imitating the voices of film stars to produce a scenario on his answering machine. He also enjoyed putting together eclectic mix tapes. While I was there, he pulled out numerous photo albums filled with pictures from long ago, as well as everything he had ever written, including his very first song, childhood stories he'd penned, and comic strips he'd drawn. Stephen reminded me of a creative little boy, making up games, skipping from one to the other with such enthusiasm.

'When I was five, my father and mother broke up. My mother was very much into religion; she was an Orthodox Christian Scientist. I was about eight when she remarried.'

Stephen described his stepfather as someone who inadvertently spurred on his creativity.

'He became very strong in the story of my life because I guess he was the catalyst in an inverted way: I was almost *forced* into being creative. He moved our family away from San Diego, where I had tons of friends and where things were always going on and I could walk to anywhere, to an area near the freeway.

'Ironically enough, our new home was right next to Kiddieland, an amusement park where I'd always wanted to stop but had been told by my folks that it was too far out of the way. I was ten and had already been thinking of getting into music, wanting to play an instrument. Before that, I'd never thought of music; my brain cells were on a lounge chair watching *Gilligan's Island*. My stepfather bought me a clarinet, of all things. I started to learn to play it, and in a short time I could play it on my own. But I was very sad. I was forced into creativity because I didn't have any friends and I was very lonely. I would make a sword out of orange crates and have sword fights with a tree – that was the big highlight. I wound up being really resourceful; my loneliness and the situation made me creative.

'I started to make my own little comic books to amuse myself. My name at that point was Earl – I changed it in fifth grade to Stephen – and everybody at school called me Earl the Squirl. So I made Earl the Squirl the character in my comic books. I'd make up his adventures one after the other. Right in front of our house was the freeway off ramp, so next to it I built a shack out of orange crates, with a little roof and a bench. I would sit out there every day after school and wait for somebody to stop and buy my *Earl the Squirl* magazines. As well as playing the clarinet, I began to write little poems. I started being creative at that time, but it came out of loneliness.

I don't think people realise that creativity can be your best friend, because it's a part of you.

'The advent of The Beatles really helped me creatively. They inspired me like no one else. I started playing Beatle melodies on my clarinet. My stepfather didn't dig this; he just hated The Beatles, and he hated rock 'n' roll and long hair. He hated change, it scared him. He wanted me to keep playing the clarinet, but I was on to bigger and better things. Pretty soon I begged my brother, who's nine years older, to get me a guitar, and he did. He got me an electric guitar and made an amplifier out of a stereo. It was exciting creating then because it was such a no-no. It was like having Mamie Van Doren in my closet.

'My stepfather's hatred of it all fuelled my desire, fired my creativity. I'd hear him talking to my mom: "He's playing that damned rock music." I was allowed to watch The Beatles on *Ed Sullivan* only if I cleaned up the yard every day for a year. They represented an energy my stepfather didn't want to look at. He was very discouraging. When I got two Ds in junior high, my mom wouldn't let me play my guitar for six months. That was pretty heavy because I was totally in love with my guitar. I would take it into my bedroom closet, which was quiet, to write songs. I would be in there working on an idea for the verse, really into it, and then all of a sudden, the door would jerk open and there he'd be, "Look at you! You're just banging on that thing, look at you!" I'd be scared because he was very forceful. He would never let up. My creativity was just bubbling; in some ways it was kept down, but in others it was just fuelled by him. Writing songs really became exciting to me; I'd have to hurry up and write a song before he came home from work. This went on for years until I finally started a band, which he was always putting down. I had to keep it undercover.

'When I wrote the song "Separate Lives", I was so into it, so full of emotion from breaking up with someone. It all just came out. That's the best part, when you can hardly wait to write it down. It seems that lately a lot of my songs I've had to work on, I don't express what I really want to say. I try to be clever, and I say all these other things that sound cool. I don't really express as many of my feelings as I used to, which is not very good.

'Creativity is God-given. I believe everybody has the power to be creative and do creative things. Creativity goes in so many different areas, it's not just writing songs or plays or books.

'There are different stages: the fun stage is sitting around and goofing off and coming up with ideas. That's the fun part: no hassle, very relaxed. Then there's the organisation stage, which is also creative, where it's putting all our thoughts together into one cohesive unit and making it work. That's actual work; you've got to sit down and turn off the TV and get into it, which is hard for me. I'm a funster, I love to have fun. I go from one thing to another and say, "What can I do now that gives me fun?" It is fun to write once you're into it, but getting into it is not always fun.'

Stephen's latest album release is 2019's We'll Talk About It Later In The Car, *which he describes as 'a little bit of country, pop and a few tracks that are more broken-hearted love songs'. Over the years, his songs have been recorded by numerous artists and he has written many movie themes. His autobiography,* On and On, *was published in 2022. He has plans to open a music venue within the year, called 'Bish's Hideaway'.*

PETER GREEN

Lead guitarist, singer, songwriter and founding member of Fleetwood Mac.

MET PETER WHEN I WAS GOING OUT WITH MICK (Fleetwood) in 1965. He was a year older than us and a very keen young guitarist. My first impression of him was of a young adult of medium build, with dark, closely cropped hair and mutton-chop sideburns. He was quietly spoken with a strong East End accent. Peter was about to join Peter B's Looners, the band Mick played in with Peter Bardens, and although Peter Green seemed shy on that first meeting, watching him onstage a few days later was like watching a force of nature. He had an intensity that seemed to radiate from his body when he played his guitar.

A couple of years later, Peter put together a band, characteristically not naming it after himself, but instead naming it after Mick and John McVie. He called it Fleetwood Mac. It was a hit!

Peter knew I had been on a retreat in India in 1968 and confided in me that he'd had a spiritual awakening. When I travelled with Fleetwood Mac for part of their 1970 American tour, Peter was high with this new awareness. Somehow, though, this great creativity seemed to gradually overwhelm him. He donned robes, grew a beard and long hair, and looked very much like a biblical figure. A powerful person at the pinnacle of his career, Peter keenly felt the audience's adoration and began to envision himself as a kind of Messiah. He thought that the band should give up their homes and tour around the world like gypsies – at the heart of his artistic prowess he was no longer fulfilled by doing the circuit for fame, money and possessions. Unfortunately, after his dream got squashed by the manager and band members, he left the band and seemed to retreat within himself. This was the first time I had ever seen creativity become a disruptive force.

The following interview was kindly given to me by a music historian, Christopher Hjort, who is currently researching and writing Young Peter: The Story of Peter Green. *Although Christopher never spoke directly to Peter, his interview had been set for spring 2020, then Covid hit and sadly Peter passed away that July. Throughout the previous years, Christopher had been in touch with Peter's brother Michael, who fielded questions large and small to Peter on Christopher's behalf. My thanks to Christopher for answering my questions and giving me the opportunity to include Peter in this book.*

Peter Green lived to be seventy-three years old, but his life and times can be divided roughly in two – from childhood to adolescence and then from manhood until his peaceful but unexpected passing in 2020. Peter rose to fame with Fleetwood Mac in the late 1960s/early 1970s, but he suffered a breakdown which kept him out of the public eye for close to a decade. During the first part of his career, Peter was featured in more than 200 plus interviews, while during the second phase he was interviewed and profiled roughly 150+ times. Peter's breakdown was a recurring topic in almost all the interviews he did from the late 1970s onwards. He was a changed man after the breakdown, but his unselfish, pure and sensitive core remained unchanged.

Were either of his parents musical, and did they encourage him with his creativity?

Peter Allen Greenbaum was born on 29 October 1946, the youngest of four. His family were Jewish and on his mother's side he had Ukrainian ancestors while his father's side were Polish. There was always music around the house, and his parents were musical even if neither his father nor mother excelled at any particular instruments. Peter grew up in a close-knit family where creativity was if not actively encouraged certainly not suppressed, and when he started to play the guitar seriously in his teens his parents backed him enthusiastically.

Peter was shy and quiet as a kid. He was born and spent his childhood in Bethnal Green, east London, and later described that time as unhappy in a tough neighbourhood where he felt out of place, although he was never bullied. This is how he put it in an interview he did in autumn 1969: 'I suppose I was about seven when the other kids started wanting me to go around in one of their gangs at night. But that wasn't me and I told them so: I hated our neighbourhood so much I stopped going out at night.'

The family lived at two addresses in Bethnal Green, before they moved to Putney when Peter was around ten years old (in 1956). This is how Peter described his feelings in the same 1969 interview: 'When my parents told me we were moving to Putney, I felt like running into the street and turning cartwheels.'

Who inspired Peter musically as a child?

Peter's years growing up in Bethnal Green indirectly influenced his interest in music, as he explained how staying in instead of hanging out with kids of his own age kept him glued to the radio and later the television. Peter later said that 'If I hadn't done this, I might not have grown so interested in the entertainment world and my life might have been different.'

Music came easily to Peter. When he was young, he started singing around the house. His brother Michael told me that Peter sang a note-perfect rendition of Laurie London's 1957 hit – Peter would have been eleven years old – 'He's Got the Whole World in His Hands'. At around the same time his oldest brother gave him an acoustic guitar, showed him three chords and from then on, he taught himself to play.

Did Peter have any idea what he wanted to be when he grew up?

Peter had no set dreams of what he wanted to be when he grew up, but after a couple of menial jobs – as a butcher's apprentice and a French polisher – he decided that he wanted to become a professional guitar player when he was eighteen years old. His reasoning was bold and simple: Listening to other guitar players, he thought, 'I can do better than that.' Not for a moment did it strike Peter that his plan would not succeed.

Did Peter have any unexplained or psychic experiences or significant recurring dreams?

There are a couple of instances that have been repeated over time. The first incident took place at the end of 1965, when Peter Green had started to work professionally as a musician with Peter B's Looners (so named after the group's keyboard player Pete Bardens). One night as the four musicians drove home to London, they came upon an apparition they thought was a ghost. As Bardens' father was a television presenter, with a special interest in the paranormal and the occult, he taped the interview with the group. Here it was recorded that Peter Green had in his childhood encountered a case of apparitional haunting.

The other instance is a nightmare Peter had which led him to write 'The Green Manalishi', a song about money and the devil. In a 1993 interview, Peter described this in detail: 'I nearly died one night in my sleep. I don't know if you've ever had the experience; I've had it a couple of times and I'm inclined to think it's an experience that people have. But I was lying in bed, I was dreaming, and this little dog jumped up at me and it scared the shit out of me because this dog had died, and had been dead for a long time. It was a stray dog that I brought to the house and just looked after. And it was strange, kind of spooky, like voodoo. It was a strange little dog. And I was dead and I couldn't move. I couldn't say "I'm dead" – it wasn't available – so I just fought my way back into my body; I thought, "It must come alive," and it did.'

Did Peter believe in a higher power? Did it connect to his creativity?

Peter believed in a higher power. He was brought up in a Jewish household, but was not a particularly religious person when he was young. It was when he entered his early twenties that he became interested in spiritual matters. He 'found God'; briefly embraced Christianity and was fascinated by Buddhism and Eastern religions. His beliefs and concerns affected his lifestyle: he felt guilt about money and wanted to give his earnings away, and he connected this with a sense of creative freedom. If he performed for free, he had no obligations to his audience and this in turn would make him a better player.

In 1970, he stated that 'In my opinion the most admirable and best thing a man can do on this earth is to try and make an effort to be like Him – like God. Peace and love are the two most important qualities. That's the thing – to bring man to God and unite the two.' Once, in 1969, he was asked what he would do if he was God. 'I would make everyone wear a permanent smile, and have everyone being friendly when they meet in the street, and everyone communicating,' and then added, 'Obviously, I'd want peace – but if everyone was communicating and smiling there wouldn't be any arguments.'

When Peter started out as a professional guitar player, he wanted to connect to his audience by playing slowly and, quote, 'feel every note that comes from every part of my body and my heart and into my fingers. I have to really feel it, I make the guitar sing the blues – if you don't have a vocalist then the guitar must sing.' As he explained later, it was not until he shed himself of the business side of music that he truly approached what he described as musical freedom. 'I always play better when there's no weight on me,' he said in an interview from May 1970. 'When I know an audience has paid a certain amount of money and they expect to hear us playing our hits, it is a burden.'

His instrumental composition 'Albatross' was particularly dear to him. When he performed the song in concert, he would often introduce the song as a peace anthem.

What gave Peter the drive to create?

Peter fed off audience reactions which gave him the drive to create and write music. 'Emotion' was a key word for him, and went back to the impact that black blues music had on him. It was also important that his lyrics reflected his own life, and as many of his compositions were heavily blues-based, he explicitly avoided using American towns or situations. As he explained in an interview in early 1968, 'It would be interesting if somebody wrote blues about towns in Britain, like London, Birmingham and particularly Glasgow. There's enough happening there to make a hundred good songs. But I suppose it sounds a bit odd. In the end, it's more natural to write about women, and love. But again, I use personal experience as a basis.'

Outwardly Peter was a happy person but he carried a sadness inside him, which he summed up in a 1969 interview: 'I'm basically a happy person. Since the age of ten I've been happy – perhaps because I was sad before.'

Peter freely admitted his influences and was quick to point to his sources of inspiration. As he repeated in several interviews, the instrumental 'The Supernatural' was based on an idea by his producer, Mike Vernon; 'Black Magic Woman' was indebted to the blues singer-guitarist Otis Rush; 'Albatross' was based on a riff he once heard Eric Clapton play, while 'Oh Well' was inspired by Muddy Waters.

In later years, he could be disparaging about his talent and downplay his own song writing: 'My writing to me is nothing that I'm proud of; it's very sort of basic. Heavy on simplicity.' In another instance, he was asked if he felt unable to express musically what he wanted to do. 'I'm still restricted and I can't learn fast enough to say what I have inside,' he replied. 'That was the problem in the beginning. I couldn't play the things I heard in my head.' Although Peter never articulated it precisely, he hinted that spirituality was behind the creative force. As an example, he credited the song 'Closing My Eyes' as 'a revelation from God'.

Peter said in a 1970 interview, 'I want to play music and give it to people as much as possible and give it free. I feel making music is the best thing I can do. That's what I'm on this earth for.'

Peter died on 25 July 2020 at the age of seventy-three. A concert was organised by Mick Fleetwood in February 2020 at the London Palladium to celebrate the music of Peter Green and honour him as the founding member of Fleetwood Mac.

PART TWELVE

*'If you deserve it and you
work at it, then she visits'* –

HUEY LEWIS

RAVI SHANKAR

World-famous Indian classical sitarist and composer.

I HAD LISTENED TO RECORDS OF RAVI AND HIS TABLE-player, Alla Rakha, ever since I was eighteen, having been introduced to his music while visiting Pattie and George at their home in Surrey. I immediately fell in love with the drone of the sitar and was one of many who watched Ravi and Alla Rakha at the Monterey Pop Festival in 1967. Finally, I got to meet Ravi (a most wonderful man) and his tamboura player, Kamala, as well as an ever-smiling Alla Rakha, in South India. George, Pattie and I joined up with them in Madras for a week, going to their concerts and spending each day with them. Many years later, while interviewing the musicians contained in this book, I felt honoured to meet up with Ravi again at a hotel in Santa Monica, where we began our interview.

What was your upbringing like?

I was born in 1920 in Banaras, one of the oldest, maybe the oldest city in the whole wide world that is still existing. Many cities have been destroyed. My father was not with us at that time, he [had] gone to England and was a lawyer. He was also Chief Minister to the Maharajah in the Northern Rajasthan area. My eldest brother, Dada (Uday Shankar) had left for England to study at the Royal College of Arts. He got a high distinction and became a dancer. When I was ten, he came back to India to form a troupe of dancers and musicians to take back to England, and also to collect my mother and me, two brothers, a cousin and two friends.

Were you the youngest?

Yes, I was the youngest. We moved from Banaras to Paris and Paris became our headquarters. We had a house and that's where all the preparations for the dancers started. I was so awestruck. It was 1930 and I was ten. There was great excitement.

Were either of your parents musical?

Both of them were musical, neither of them professionals so there was not much music and dance in our house, but there was enough. I went to school and all that in Banaras and I didn't have much opportunity to play music, except there was a sitar, harmonium, tabla and a flute in our home that belonged to my second brother. He was like an amateur musician. So, when they were gone, I used to fiddle with those. I was told off for that but I loved to steal into the room and take the sitar and play with it.

It was going to Paris that completely changed my life. I was thrown into this whole atmosphere of dance, music and millions of miles of brocade and costumes being sewn. Costumes of Krishna, Kali, Sheeva, being made for the ballet troupe. They were copying all these costumes from the old temple sculptures in caves. That was a fantastic few years but, of course, my schooling suffered. I did go to a French school for a year and a half but that was more for learning the language. I was having private tuition from my brothers; they were helping me with some English, maths etc., just general stuff. Unfortunately, I don't have any academic qualifications but, on the other hand, I was learning from life, seeing and watching, and I was very, very curious. I still am very curious. So that was great and that was prime time for Paris as a city, as the centre of the art world internationally. I mean, name it, all the great musicians, painters, writers, they were all in Paris. Either they were visiting or staying there. All the American ex-patriots were there. I met Cole Porter, Gertrude Stein, Henry Miller. All of them, and I remember them so well in different salons that I used to visit, and apart from that all the great musicians, opera, and a number of ballet dancers. Pablo Casals lived three houses from ours. He used to come to our house and I used to sit on his lap. I had a fantastic childhood hearing the best of classical music, and when we first came to the States in 1932 with my brother, I was overwhelmed. I had heard a lot of records and I remembered an English jazz bandleader called Jack Hylton. You will know this song (Ravi starts singing 'Sing, Baby, Sing').

Then I came to hear the real thing. I met Cab Calloway, Duke Ellington, Satchmo and Count Basie, and saw all these people performing, and all these great movie people like Eddie Cantor and Marsalis. And then we came to Hollywood. You wouldn't believe it – when I got to Hollywood, I had a fever. I couldn't take it. It was too much. Our troupe became one of the top three troupes at that time. Solomon, our agent, took us to the studios, where we'd see all the stars. I don't know what happened. I was twelve going on thirteen and Maddie

Dresten took such a fancy to me she wanted to adopt me. At first everyone thought she was joking, but she was serious. I wished she would – Hollywood and film stars, to me that was the ultimate. Thankfully she didn't, but I felt very sad.

I was surrounded by all this glitter and glamour and I was learning to dance and I had freedom. I could play the sitar and no one would stop me. But unfortunately, no one taught me properly so what I was doing was just watching and copying and playing to my ears. I was very good at that. I was playing all the pieces and dancing in the background. That's how it was, until 1935. Meanwhile, we used to go to India once in a while for a few months. My mother had stayed only a year and a half as she couldn't take it any more in Paris. She had come back and she was living in Banaras. So, we would visit India, give shows there, maybe have a few weeks' holiday and I would spend time with my mother, whom I loved so much. And then in 1935, my brother wanted to have one of the greatest musicians as a soloist between all the dance items, a fifteen to twenty minutes solo, pure classical. But who? It was my guru, Baba, who joined the group. This was the first time I saw Pablo Gonzalez in all his grace, but I had never seen such a great musician from India as Baba and I was just bowled over. On the one hand he looked very ordinary but there was some inner fire in him which was like a volcano, and he was very temperamental; he would cry in a moment. He was so sentimental he would take off his shirt and give it to a poor man and when he got angry, he would just beat up people, mostly students, not other people. Terrible temper.

Very temperamental, but anyway, he joined the group and, from the moment he did, I became his guide because I could speak French, German and Italian. He was missing his son,

Ali Akbar, who had gone back to India, so he took me as his son and loved me very much. My real father, who was rarely with us, had died about six months before (in 1955). Baba was very sentimental. 'Baba' means 'father' in India and we all called him Baba. When we were standing beside the boat at the Bombay dock, my mother was saying goodbye to us because she was leaving for India. She was so sad to leave me, and perhaps she had a premonition, that she knew she wouldn't see me again. We were all standing near her and she was hugging me and crying, and then all of a sudden, she instinctively took my hand and put it in his hand and said, 'Look, he lost his father just a few months earlier, he has no father, and I don't know whether I will see him any more. Please take care of him. I don't know if I'll be in India for long, please take care of him.' And my God, he broke down, he's such a sentimental person, Baba. He was sobbing and howling and calling my mother said, 'Please don't say that, from today he is my eldest son. I have only one son and from today I have two sons and Robu.' That's my nickname. 'He is my eldest son.' And he really remembered that and always kept this relationship. And if I ever had any love from a father, that was him.

I got this father's love from my guru, my teacher, Allauddin Khan. 'Ustad' is always used before, meaning 'Maestro'. For Hindu musicians, it's called 'Pandit', which means the 'wise one'. I'm known as Pandit Ravi Shankar and he's known as Baba Allauddin Khan.

He stayed for only about ten and a half months. But within that period, he changed the course of my life because I was so spoilt by then. More of a dancer and wearing the best clothes all the time, staying in five-star hotels and I never was as a child. I was grown up in every sense. I was just having a lot of fun singing, writing poetry, painting, everything I did, because I had a lot of talent, everyone would say, that's wonderful. But he was the first one who said to me, 'You are nothing, you can never do anything like this, you are like a butterfly, like a jack of all trades. You have to do one thing properly and I will teach you if you leave everything and come to me.' He said that but nevertheless he loved me so much and he saw whatever talent I had, and things started to change within those ten and a half months. He really taught me all the basics of sitar, a lot of beginners' compositions. Later we improvised but we had to learn a lot of fixed compositions that we call GATs in different Ragas, different cycles. He taught me a lot of songs, some old songs, many of his own songs; he was composing all the time, every day.

He was such a creative person until the end and I learned so much from him. I was also dancing and he was not happy about that, but when he left England he said the same thing, that if you can leave all this and come to me, I will teach you. But it took me almost a year and a half to decide because, at that time, I was becoming even more known as a dancer. I choreographed a solo myself, which was a great success.

Incredible, you must have been so young.

I was really having all this fun, as I said, but the glitter and the glamour of the whole thing was too much for me. But then, eventually, I did leave. The war also helped, 1928, they were absolutely sure it was going to happen and my brother at that time was planning to start an institution for culture. My mother had built a house in Banaras before she died, and from there I went to Maihar, a small town, also a native state where there was a Maharajah who was Baba's student. Baba stayed there and he couldn't believe it when he saw me. Was I the same boy, he thought?

Right, yes, so how old were you now?

I was eighteen. And so, he couldn't believe it, his eyes almost popped out. What have you done? He was always criticising my clothes and he didn't like people to do their hair. So, I had no hair, I was completely shaved! But that was part of play acting. I wanted to please him and I knew this would do it! And it did! When you start acting you get into the part. There is nothing wrong I suppose but at that time I was definitely trying to please him, and he was pleased. That's how it started and I stayed there for almost seven and a half years.

So, you just studied under him.

Yeah, it was the life of a hermit, very difficult, very austere for me because I was in a house next to him, a very old house with creaky windows, creaky doors, lizards, mosquitoes, flies, scorpions, snakes and even wolves in the night and I was scared. It was so uncomfortable, and where is the five-star hotel? And where are the beautiful girls?! I suffered so much. I was really going mad.

He must have been your inspiration.

Yeah. I had him as an example for myself, because he is the one man I have seen in my life that, whatever he said or preached, he lived that way. I have seen many other people preaching a lot but they don't practise it. He did not wear silk or fancy things. He never did. His way of life, his way of living, was comfortable. It was coarse bedsheets, but clean. That's what he believed in, it was a way of life. It was a great strength to see a person like that, and I tried to be like that, but it was tremendous suffering for almost a year. And then it was a spontaneous thing after two and a half, almost three years, that I got married to his daughter. It was very spontaneous, there was no scandal, no love or anything, it was like an offer. In the olden days this happened when someone saw a very meditative student, they wanted to make him part of his family so it happened. Shubho, my son, was born immediately and after that there were a lot of difficulties for me because I was practising and not taking financial help from Baba. He had permitted me to give programmes and also perform on the radio and at different festivals so I was earning a little bit already but it wasn't enough, so I was taking loans from a money lender, which was growing more and more. So, for a few years I had a very hard time while going through the learning.

With my guru's permission, I went to Bombay with my wife and son and there gradually I started giving programmes and little films and little ballets and operas, and lots of concerts. It was really fantastic. Very quickly I became well known. It took me about two to three years, even though I struggled a lot, but still it was a big adventure and I worked hard there. It took me about three to four years to become well known here. And then I got this job in All India Radio in 1949 for five and a half years as Director of Music and also creating a small chamber orchestra, a Vadya (instrument) Vrinda group that I was in charge of. There was a lot of creative experimental work, which I had already done in the films in Bombay, the ballets and the operas. I worked in Bombay and then from Bombay to Delhi.

I don't know how it happened but gradually we were growing apart, my family life, and after a few years we separated but not divorced, just separated. We spent very little time together. My son was learning music, but more of his time was spent painting. His mother, who was a good musician, had taught him sitar for about seven years. He was sixteen or seventeen, but after some time he couldn't take that and by that time I was living in California with Kamala. That was in 1970 and I put him in art school. He finished that but completely left sitar for almost twelve years. It's only three or four years ago he started playing again. Now he appreciates it.

As far as I am concerned, my Delhi period was building me up for further things. While I was there, I had a lot of friends in the foreign embassy. One of the Belgian councillors is a good friend of mine and, through him, we had like a small group either once a week or every two weeks where I would play and sing. We would meet and after some time it became so popular, we were having almost twenty, thirty, forty, fifty people. Then I invited some of my musician friends, some singers or some other instrumentalist who would come and perform. And it became so good. We had been in this country four or five years and we had never appreciated it. I was told I played so beautifully. So, I found out for myself that I could do that. At that time there were no other musicians that had seen me playing.

You broke a barrier.

But then I thought to myself, what am I doing here? Why don't I travel? When I was with my wife, she wouldn't let me go anywhere or do anything, and then, when I broke away from her, I took this risk and that was how I started in 1956. This was the start of another phase and I came to London. In the beginning it was Conway House and small places like that, hardly four hundred people, but gradually it started building up. Then I went to Paris and Germany and Holland and came to the States [in] 1956 and in New York I started in the Kaufman Auditorium on my own. I had just a drummer and then cut my first album in London. The audience was small but each time I played it was larger and by '58 my first programme was in the Royal Festival Hall. Which was almost fully packed. They couldn't believe it, they were such a good audience, and then, of course, after that, I always had a full house. I became well known in the classical circle as an Indian classical musician, with all my records with my talks, my lecture demonstrations and occasional black-and-white TV appearances and a lot of radio.

Then came the next phase, when George became interested. All of a sudden there was an explosion of interest in sitar. Folk groups were very popular in England, and my agent got me to play in venues with them. There I got my first glimpse of all these very special dresses and people smoking marijuana and that was my first little unhappiness, so I told them not to book me in these places, even though they were wonderful people, they were very good, and very appreciative. Then came the big one, coming to America to play at Monterey in '67. That was the beginning of the flower children and love.

That's right. I was there at Monterey and saw you playing.

Do you remember?

I remember. There was a light rain and, as soon as you got onstage, it stopped.

When I watched some of [the] festival, I saw how crazy people were and out of their minds. I saw Otis Redding and Janis Joplin, and Jimi Hendrix breaking his instrument. It was almost a sexual thing, and burning his guitar. I was appalled. I realised they were fantastic musicians but I asked myself, what am I doing here? Then I actually made it a point that I wouldn't play unless they gave me a completely separate slot, nothing before me, nothing after me. The festival went on for two days and I had come three to four days earlier. Then they got this afternoon, if you remember, at one o'clock. What a time! I never perform at one o'clock in the daytime. For the singing it is a strange time, but I agreed. I thought it would be better and at least there was nothing before me. It was drizzling a little. Everything was strange but there was such magic, it was full, full, full, if you remember.

Absolutely, it was the first one of those.

Absolutely, it was the first and I know that almost, I would say, eighty-five per cent were on acid and hashish but still there was something very special; I could give what I wanted and it was very good. But then what happened, my managers had me under contract and they had booked me to play at five to ten different rock festivals. I suffered through many of them as I walked out onstage. I couldn't take it any more because I was seeing them fornicating and masturbating and things like that, like animals. And the worst was, of course, Woodstock. The other day I had an interview with *Life* magazine, regarding Woodstock. I said Monterey was the beginning of the beautiful thing, of that energy, the flower children, hippies and love and the end was Woodstock. Because in Woodstock, when I was singing, it was raining and mud was everywhere. It reminded me of India, travelling outside the city and seeing buffalos lying down. They looked like buffalos in mud, I couldn't recognise anyone! They were all having such fun, they were out of their minds and music was like an incidental, it was like a big picnic party.

We came by helicopter. We couldn't come by surface because it was jam-packed and I don't know what I performed or to whom I performed. So you see many people misunderstand that when I say the thing I am angry about is when they say it was only because of George I got such a big name and fame and I don't say nice words about that period, but I have to be truthful, and George knows, I have explained it to George, it wasn't his fault. He came to me with love and his love is still there, my love is still there but the consequence was the wrong approach, very superficial. They didn't know anything about my music, they knew it through him and they came as if they were going to a pop concert, with the same attitude. You cannot listen to this music with that attitude, it needs the same love, attention and respect as Bach.

Respect, that's what was missing?

Yeah, it's a respectful thing. Even in this country (America), people sit with awe and respect and quiet. So, I used to tell the kids all the time to sit quietly, not to smoke and all that but, it becomes a sticky thing. Gradually, I got out of that and the whole circus of promoters. I broke my contract somehow and I stopped performing in the States, especially for about a year and a half. And then I started again through classical promoters and gradually I came back to the circus. It's like going from a circus and coming back. But now I am very happy because, believe me, I say this all the time, I am repeating this, what, maybe five hundred times, that I find that many of those kids who were there – maybe thirteen, fourteen, eighteen, twenty or whatever – they are still here but without their beards, or long hair, or beads.

Or taking acid.

Or taking acid, and they are so respectful and they are so much more understanding, they are so much more loving and appreciative, so that's what it is today. Today is the best period.

Yeah, I think so. That was a mad, crazy time. Some positive and some negative.

Yeah, it had to be, it was a melting pot, Vietnam, this, that, the whole thing became a rebel of the youth. But you know I am glad I went through that period, but it was very difficult. Maybe if I'd started taking drugs myself it would have been a different story. If I'd cashed in commercially and made it 'Raga Rock', I would have been a king of a Raga Rock group, and maybe become as rich as any of those big pop-rock musicians. But I couldn't do that.

Yeah, it came from a different place.

My principles stopped me from that.

Yes, thank goodness.

So, you know, I'm glad I did it.

Yes, so when you are playing, what does that feel like?

You see it's very difficult to explain but I will try my best. It takes a lot of preparation before. I don't like to talk much with people or anything like that apart from meditating. I do all that and praying, everything which is part of our music history I do before. Starting from having a bath and wearing nice clean clothes, and trying to be as pure outside and trying to make myself as pure inside. That's the whole attitude. And then it's like trying to imagine what I'm going to play because I decide not very much earlier what Raga I'm going to play; it's not like I'm humming it, but I try to feel those Ragas within me. And by the time I go onstage, it's a very strange situation, I am so charged, and then sitting there after tuning everything again, we tune all the sympathetic strings for that particular Raga, it's all in my mind. Now it is very physical and so with the first note I merge into that Raga and that is why it has that magical effect for everybody no matter whether they understand or they don't. Maybe some feel it less, some feel it more, but it does have an effect because what I am bringing out is so much of being with the notes. It is not what note I am using, I am not thinking about what note I am using, because the Raga at that time becomes like a person, it's like making love, in the sense that the whole Raga merges into me and I become one and I try to bring it out. Of course, being a performer, and years of experience, one has to have the other consciousness like being aware of time, duration and not to repeat. It's a training and experience we go through which makes us do it. At least, I have trained myself to do that according to the audience. If I play in India to a small audience with absolute musical understanding, I let myself go in a different way. If it is in India in a big hall, it's a different way, very loving and understanding. Everywhere is different, and at that time, somehow, I feel the vibration, according to that and it just comes out whatever.

And creation or creativity, as you said, they are two ways as far as I am concerned. As an Indian performing artist, our creations are spontaneous because we improvise all the time, we create on the spot, just like I am following Raga. It is a very strange thing, it is partly like a computerised thing. Our training is such that we have been programmed with the Ragas and the ideas by our guru plus years of practice and thinking. There's a format we follow, but what we do is not something pre-conceived, but it comes out of all this programming. It's a very strange thing.

Yes, so you have the structure.

Yes, but that structure is so deeply involved or imbibed that we don't just sort of say, this is 'A', now this is 'B', no, it just sort of comes out. Sometimes in a very long duration, sometimes shorter, which we are also controlling.

Miraculous things sometimes happen while we are doing that (fingers click), something new can come which I have not done before, or I had not been taught before, and when that happens it's a great ecstasy. We try to put it somewhere and use it in the future. It becomes like an addition to the whole thing.

And can you? Can you use it?

Sometimes you can and sometimes it is lost. But most of the time, if it's something outstanding, just a little touch here or there, that's not a big deal, but if it is something really outstanding, then we try to recapture that.

If you have a really outstanding piece, does your tabla-player pick up on it?

Yeah, they can do that, and they can also become lost struggling for a second. When I am writing a piece for an orchestra, or writing a piece for a film, doing any creative work with other people participating, it's completely different. There I have to think of what we're doing as a team, sometimes with a Raga, sometimes without a Raga, just a melody. Sometimes I have colours of jazz, I get some jazz musicians perform on it, even though the music is mine and it's basically Indian. Whatever I do is either folk or classical based. I never try to mix the music. That's one thing I want to be very clear about; whatever I do is based on either classical Raga music or Tambala or rhythmic cycles. Sometimes, even if it is thematic, it does have colours of Ragas in it, so it's basically Indian. But I like to use Western musicians for their interpretations, with their instruments. It brings out the different colours, texture, range, tone and so much volume. So, this is what I exploit more, whether it is Japanese musicians or Russian musicians, jazz, or even electronic I have experimented with. Have you heard *Tana Mana*? *Inside the Kremlin*?

No, I have heard your tapes, the classical Ragas.

No, these are not classical music, these are Private Music Limited, my creative things. One is *Tana Mana*, all synthesiser and electronic along with something else. George has played on one of those. The second record is Ravi Shankar *Inside the Kremlin*, which I did with Russian musicians and choir.

When you are composing, does it ever feel as though the music is coming through you or are you conscious when you are composing?

I use that formula of coming from the head, but that's something which I do very rarely and I don't like it. My first impulse that comes out is always the best. If I try to see if I can do better, I never can. I have tried this many times so I'm resigned to it; it's always the first rush that comes to my mind, which pattern of music or melody, then I can, of course, work on that and make it more elaborate, shape it up, or add something, harmonising, even different instruments, but that's it.

Do you think that everybody has the potential to be creative?

I don't think so. Maybe in a different medium, maybe he could be a better carpenter, or he could be a better watchmaker, or anything else. I'm sure everybody has one talent. That I do believe. But when you said creative, we are talking about music now, well I don't think so. Everybody cannot do everything. There might be a few Leonardo da Vincis, or very talented jacks of all trades, that's a different thing, but we are talking about a gift of being able to create. I think we do have talent of some sort; everyone has, it could be anything. It could be washing clothes, for instance, which he loves to do or can do better than others.

What is your talent? What are you doing now?

What is my talent? Well, I found since I started writing this book I absolutely love doing the interviews. I love talking to people, finding out what they really believe, especially about creativity, and it's something I realise I've always loved doing.

Ravi died on the 11 December 2012 at the grand old age of ninety-two.

PAUL HORN

A jazz flautist, saxophonist, composer, singer and songwriter.

I MET PAUL IN 1968 WHEN WE WENT TO MAHARISHI'S ashram in Rishikesh. It was not long after we left that I heard he'd had a recording made while playing his flute inside the Taj Mahal. We saw a lot of Paul while we were at the ashram, and when I met up with him in L.A. twenty years later, to do this recording, it was like meeting up with an old, wise and gentle friend.

'My mother played piano and recorded music in the twenties. She worked for Irving Berlin's publishing house, as the staff person who played the songwriters' music when they came in. In those days they didn't have tape recorders, so if you were a songwriter and wanted your song to be published by Irving Berlin Music or anyone else, you had to go in and sing the song yourself or bring someone along to sing it. Many times, they didn't have their own accompanist, so my mother would sight-read and sing too, if necessary. She had her own radio show and made records, but she stopped all that when she got married.

'My parents were pretty hip for their generation. They really laid no trips on me and didn't push me in any direction. Their attitude was, whatever I wanted to do was cool and they'd support it. So if I wanted to be a musician, that was fine, even if I wanted to be a jazz musician, which was not looked upon from the majority of the people with too much respect in those days. I started taking piano lessons when I was four. My mother decided not to teach me herself, which was probably a good decision, since we were of like temperament. But she'd be there to support and help me if I didn't understand something with my lesson.

'In playing, what I have transcended is my self-consciousness, my mind drifting on to other things. I'm unaware of myself, I'm totally absorbed in the music, and as I get more absorbed in the music, then more can happen. I turn out to be a channel; my mind doesn't say, "Me, I'm playing good tonight," or, "I'm not playing good." It's not judgemental, it's a happening that's taking place and that's enough, and it's exciting to be caught up in that.

'All music throughout the ages serves two purposes. First, it's a reflection of the state of the world or a particular society of that time. [Second] in the hands of more aware musicians it has gotten past that, and the power of the music can uplift the spirit of man. In the hands of musicians like that, they are not just reflecting the collective unconscious but trying to change it and to push it in a higher direction. I've been to Russia quite a few times now and have seen that music is really a power to bring people together. It is the universal language, and it does have great power to connect people in the world. I think it is one of the most powerful "weapons", if you will, that we have for peace and understanding, and to communicate and begin to connect with each other.

'When I was younger, I didn't know such terms as Peak Experience, but I used to feel really high [at certain times while playing music]. When I started to improvise, I found I could get up and play music, with thoughts coming, and these thoughts could be translated into musical terms. I got an idea of what I could hear in my mind, and my inner ear would somehow find a connection [through] my arms and fingers to my instrument. That excitement is always with me. Any time you improvise it's exciting because you don't *know*; it's always new. Intellectually, by the time you've even thought about it, you're eight beats later.

'The jazz musician will play the melody, and from then on, new melodies are created over the same basic harmonies, and that's jazz; creating a logical, beautiful melody but it's your own. You could play that song night after night and never get bored because it will come out different each time. There's a creative excitement there, an energy. It's a spiritual thing. We learn about "now" – the moment. When you improvise, you're totally in the moment. There's no time to think about it; it has to transcend the intellect; you just have to "be". So, jazz comes as close as you can to the spiritual.

'Having now lived a while and followed the spiritual path, I can see the connection. It forces your mind to really be one-pointed. You have to be focused and, therefore, you're in the now; you're not aware of yourself. It's a transcendental experience in a way. In the true sense of the word "transcendental", there is no mental activity. We're in that place of stillness, which is the "absolute field".

'When I was touring with Donovan, there was just the two of us with 25,000 people out there and you could hear a pin drop – that's power. The power is in the silence, that you got them to the point of being so still. The most powerful music is simple music; so often your intellect gets in the way of the whole thing. As human beings, we complicate things in life. The intuitive part of the brain, if left to be, will usually be very simple. Basic truths in life are so simple we can't talk about them. The power in music, I've learned, is in simplicity. It has nothing to do with technique, complexity – it's beyond that.

'There's a certain kind of magic there, and that magic is what I'm trying to verbalise. The magic is that people can be transformed through sound, simple sound. And also, it's the person that's playing the music who is the channel for the music to come through. Ego will stop the magic. You have to surrender to be a channel, and surrender means to be absorbed in the music, lost in the music, and [to] become one with the music.

'I've had some experience with drugs – not all drugs – and I've never really been heavy into it. Certain drugs with certain people can give experiences that, if you don't get dependent upon it, can be an opening of a door. In the early days, dope was just for jazz musicians. The drug then was simply pot; heroin came later. It seems that most people in show business are shy and that they need something to get past that to get to the music. And if you aren't strong enough spiritually and don't understand how to do that in a natural way, which most people don't, then they have a few drinks or a few tokes, to get past this self-consciousness and get into the music. I'm not saying it's necessary, but I can't block it out and say it's totally no good. There are great dangers in it, and we all know what they are.

'If you get dependent upon it, you can't get past that and the dependency will destroy you. So, it's really a tricky and dangerous ground to walk on, a thin line. If you're strong enough that you can have a taste of it at certain stages of your life and realise it's just a stage and recognise the dangers involved if you keep up with it, and then go on from there, it's all right. But if you go too far with it, then it can block your creativity and destroy you in the process.'

Paul died on 29 June 2014. He was eighty-four.

NANCY WILSON

Singer, songwriter, guitarist and founding member of Heart.

'**B**OTH OF OUR PARENTS WERE MUSICAL. OUR mother was a college-level concert pianist and our dad was a baritone in a barbershop quartet, so we had all sorts of musical influences. We always had a hi-fi, as they called it then, and listened to everything from opera to Ray Charles to Judy Garland to Aretha Franklin. Our parents have been really amazingly encouraging all along. I think it's much more conducive if your parents aren't throwing your records out of the window! [My sister Ann and I] were given piano lessons with teachers, and also our mom would sit down with us a lot, and we'd just pick up things by ear. We always sang as a family and harmonised. It was a fun way to grow up, with music all around.

'There are those magical times when it seems to pour right through you. That's the most incredible feeling I can imagine as far as song writing. You're like the vessel or the instrument itself that somebody's playing – somebody or something. I don't have a specific name for it; there's a lot of names: Buddha, God, inspiration. I really do think that there is a lot of magic in it and a lot of greatness, which being an artistic person brings you a bit closer to it. It can be the same [in playing], but in writing you're probably much more vulnerable because you're wide open and you're trying to push down all the voices that say, "Write a commercial song. Be competitive. You need a song that's more like this, more like someone else." What's hard is to be open enough to just be who you are, without all the other outside expectations. So, if you can find a pretty pure state to write in, that's when it usually happens.

'I like to go out to the ocean. For me, that's always a very religious experience. You go back to that almost like the womb, like going back to being connected to the ocean where it all started. All that power and all that "bigger than you" gives you a neat kind of feeling, and looking at the stars at night. Things like that really help you connect so much faster to that essence of where it all is and where it all comes from and, hopefully, what you can bring from it to the world. So that's a real source. Sometimes it just happens right when I'm at the edge of sleep. A lot of stuff will happen to me and I'll think, "Oh, no! Do I really have to write this down?" But I really do.

'I have a lot of musical dreams. Melodies and songs will happen in a dream, and I'll wake up and try to recreate it. If you can ever catch that, you have the best music you've ever heard, but it's hard to catch. To me, that's probably the most spiritual experience, when you're dreaming and you hear this. For me, it's usually a lot of acoustic instruments with electric guitar, almost orchestra-type music with mandolins and acoustic keyboards.

'I think with playing and singing too – but especially as a guitar player – my philosophy has always been feel as opposed to technique. To me, having all the technique in the world means nothing. I think that's a great thing to know how to do. But it's more important that a musician play through her instrument like a human, in a human sense, the way Eric Clapton and David Gilmour do. Jimi Hendrix was really good at that. He spoke through his guitar; he wasn't just trying to impress you with how much he'd practised.

'You can read a lot of what's happening in the music. You can keep your finger on the pulse of how they feel in the city when you listen to a lot of black music now.

'Usually [when I'm playing] I forget what I look like or who I am. Ann and I would sit and play a lot and just stare blankly into each other's face, and then one of us would say, "Oh, my God, look at your face – your tongue's hanging out!" You kind of lose yourself.

'Onstage it's a little different because the audience is there and the energy level is so heightened. There's so much electricity – not just in the [guitar] cables. Usually what happens to me on those amazing nights is that you really feel truly larger than yourself, like you're 10,000 feet high. You're kind of yourself, but you're also in the audience, so it's like some kind of circular reciprocity – it's all-inclusive. It's one of the best feelings. It can be so thrilling, especially if you feel like you're getting through and touching something deeper in the audience than just the animal instinct.

'I used [drugs and alcohol] for a more direct way of shaking off the outside world and just getting into the more primal world quickly. Ultimately, it doesn't work, because you feel bad all the time. Also, when you're in an altered state, especially with cocaine, you think every idea you have is just the greatest; there's no objectivity. Then when you see it the next day and it's like . . . We ended up by having a joke about it, we just called it "blowatry" – big difference between that and poetry! Cocaine puts you in a heightened state of self-gratification.'

Nancy was inducted into the Rock and Roll Hall of Fame in 2013 as a member of Heart. Her debut solo album, You and Me, *was released in May 2021. She tours with her band, Nancy Wilson's H.*

HUEY LEWIS

Huey Lewis is a singer, songwriter and harmonica player who leads his band, the News.

'**M**Y FATHER WAS AN AMATEUR JAZZ DRUMMER FOR a number of years and flirted with being a professional musician but finally . . . went back to school and became a radiologist. I always listened to music around the house. Dad played in different bands, and he always played music loudly – he was a nut for music. Always jazz, very, very loud, twenty-four hours a day, so I always listened, but since he only played big-band jazz that never had a singer, I gravitated in my early teens to listening to singers. I think it was sort of my way of rebelling.

'My parents split up in '62 or '63, and my mother, who was an artist, started hanging out with the San Francisco beatnik set, so there were a lot of poets over. My house was pretty wild in the creative sense, and when the sixties thing exploded in San Francisco, my mother was well into it. I first went to the Fillmore Auditorium with my mother when I was thirteen years old. She liked the early San Francisco bands – the Grateful

Dead, Jefferson Airplane. I had to rebel somehow, so I always liked blues and R&B music. I got a harmonica from someone and that was it.

'I find it more of a group experience for me. You look around and, all of a sudden, the song is playing and singing itself. It's just like a wave that you ride. It's tremendously exhilarating; it doesn't take any energy and you look around and say, "Yep, this is it!" It happens quite often but not for long periods of time. Almost at every gig that will happen somewhere for a fleeting moment. Some gigs it happens more often than others; and those are the good gigs. The object is to find that thing where you can completely relax and just ride.

'For the artist or songwriter or writer, the object is to get away from society so you can reflect on society. There's a certain tendency to think drink and/or drugs help you do that. It may be correct initially, but the trouble is that it's very unreliable and doesn't work all the time, but half the time maybe. It can be effective; you can have a couple of drinks and maybe get a new perspective on something. The trouble is another time you may have a couple of drinks or a joint or whatever and write a bunch of crap, so it's unreliable initially, and ultimately, it's addictive and never works once it becomes addictive.

'Unless people are encouraged to be creative, they tend to be less creative. Creativity can be trained out of you. You need to be taught to just run with that sort of stuff.

'I don't work best under pressure. For example, I think the real good stuff just comes to you, and those moments are when you have pretty much everything else out of your mind. You're not worried about the day-to-day stuff. A lot of people worry incessantly about the day-to-day stuff and never really try and forget about that. You really have to be empty, or open.

'Artists are meant to put their finger on something society hasn't figured out yet. In a way, artists are meant to be the enemies of society. Society is very structured, and our job is to rattle that cage for better or worse; generally, we're supposed to be sort of "outlawish".'

After many years of playing in bands, making records and appearing on film and television, in April 2018, Huey announced he had been diagnosed with Meniere's disease and was not able to hear well enough to sing. He lives on a ranch in Montana.

ROBERT BURKE WARREN

Bassist, guitarist, singer, songwriter and solo artist who has played with such bands as The Fleshtones and also starred in the West End as Buddy Holly in the musical **Buddy.**

'**M**Y EARLIEST MEMORIES ARE OF MUSIC, MOSTLY THE Beatles. My mother was a big Beatles fan. She was very open-minded, and my father was an amateur musician, a guitar player and singer. In college he played in coffee houses; he was a big Peter, Paul and Mary fan, a folkie. He had taught himself how to play. I can remember him singing and playing. He died when I was seven. Everyone I've met who knew him said he was a natural musician, could just pick out a song.

'I remember when I was really young hearing music in my head, songs. It wasn't until later on that I tried to reach out and put it into another form, to try and communicate it to someone. I started playing bass when I was fourteen. My family encouraged my creativity from the outset. Although when I was seventeen and they saw I was serious about pursuing music as a career, they tried to convince me to put it on the back burner, but they never told me to give it up altogether. Even the other things they encouraged me to do were creative. They said that music was a rough business. My grandfather was a writer for the trade magazine *Variety* and they knew about show business and how it could be. I was a sensitive soul, and they were afraid all my ideals would be smashed – but they haven't been yet.

'When I was around twelve, I used to stay up all night. When everyone else went to sleep and the world shut down, I was able to hear things and commune with things without distraction – just walk around and not have a goal. I'd get on my bicycle and ride through the night on deserted streets; I was very content doing that. I spent an inordinate amount of time alone as a kid, and I got to know myself better. The core of everything is just to know yourself, to know who you are. The only way to do that is to spend time alone and experiment with your environment. I did that a lot.

'I believe there is a transcendent power, and anyone can get to it through the creative act. The outlet is the part of the brain that is more attuned to that which is not temporal. You can open up that receptor within you; you can tap into it through music. The part of the human spirit that music touches is deeper and more connected with that which is transcendent.

'I think music was a more important part of religion than it is now. My main memories from attending Catholic church as a child are of ringing bells and powerful singing. Once my mother took me to Ebenezer Baptist Church in Atlanta, where Martin Luther King Jr had once preached, and I'll never forget it as long as I live. It was an overwhelming sensory experience – the power of the music and the feeling that there was definitely something going on. There was incredible music, people were singing, and there was elation in the air. I firmly believe that music is connected to the spiritual.

'When I was with The Fleshtones, we toured a lot of countries where people didn't speak much English. I remember in Spain, the audience didn't know what the words meant, but they would sing along. It was a real tribal type of thing. They would sing along with just the rhythm of the words; it was the rhythm of the language that got them. They had no idea what they were singing, but it didn't matter. Later it occurred to me that some of my favourite songs are ones where I don't really know what the words mean, but I like the way they make me feel.

'The creative force comes from the collective unconscious, which is the part of everyone that they're not acquainted with on a personal basis. Everyone has a side of their character that will always remain a mystery. That side is more in tune with the collective; it's sort of like a secret club that everyone belongs to, and the initiation into the secret club is the creative act. Everyone yearns for the experience of touching the common ground that they have with everyone else, and the creative act is the only way they can tap into that. When you hear certain music, it moves you, but it doesn't have anything to do with the physical structure of the music. It's *where* it touches you; it unites you with your inner self and thus with everyone else. When people become more in tune with their spiritual selves, music will play a great part in that; you can't have one without the other. I don't think there is any language that can get to the core of things the way music can.

'A while back I was in the studio playing guitar and singing a song I'd just written. It was a song that had come really fast; it had taken five minutes to write. The engineer said later that during the recording the atmosphere became charged with electricity. At the time I could just feel it. It was the most profound peak I'd ever had. There was nothing I had done to prepare for it in any way. I think maybe I subconsciously felt the song was worthy. So many times, you go for the nail and you don't hit it, and this time I felt I had. It was a one-take recording. It was wonderful, just incredible. There's no passage of time, there's no consciousness of anything except what you're singing about. It must have been the combination of having written the song, then singing it and playing it. It was a real breakthrough for me, because before that point, I'd reached a peak only through playing music with other people. It was the first time I'd really tried to pursue singing as a means of getting there.

'When you're a musician, there's a single understated language you speak when you're playing. It's magic. You look and play off each other. It's an incredible feeling, very much like being high.

'Some people think they have to take the same drugs as their favourite musician did, so they can be more like them. If they can't play like their idols, they can at least get the drug addiction right.

'Fear is society's tool to make people be like everybody else. Fear is the biggest obstacle to being creative. People with the drive to create don't have that fear, or they're able to surmount that fear and press on. They've been to the belly of the beast, and instead of being devoured, they come back out.

'Solitude is very important to me. It's your own private ground. I wish I could impose it on myself whenever I want to. When I was a kid, I was never given a concrete rule of what is good and what is evil, so I take it all in and decide for myself. That's become, I think, an unconscious response to everything that goes on around me. I need solitude to do that, and I can't imagine being without it.

'The drive to create is part of me. It's a spark that was fanned to a flame before I could walk. And it will always be there. When I'm playing, it's one of the only times I never feel self-conscious. I feel confident, like this is right, this is who I really am.'

Robert is a writer, performer, teacher and musician, author of the novel Perfectly Broke, *and one-man show 'Redheaded Friend', and editor of* Cash on Cash: Interviews & Encounters with Johnny Cash. *In the 1990s, he performed the lead in the West End musical* Buddy: The Buddy Holly Story. *Prior to that, he was a globe-trotting bass player. He lives in Phoenicia, NY.*

PART THIRTEEN

'If I'm incredibly depressed, I can't write at all, and if I'm really happy, I wouldn't bother to write. I'd go out and do the gardening, so there has to be a kind of middle ground' –

KIRSTY MacCOLL

VERNON REID

*Guitarist and songwriter for the band Living Colour,
as well as a solo artist and producer.*

'**I GREW UP IN AN OPEN ENVIRONMENT, WHERE I WAS**
allowed to have different kinds of thoughts than my
parents. My parents were very strict on one level; on another
level they were very open. I was never told not to read this or
not to read that. I was an avid fan of science fiction and comic
books, and I was allowed to read that. If I had an imaginative
idea, I was never told, "That's stupid." They may have looked
at me funny and said, "That's interesting," but I never felt
like my imagination was stupid. My imagination was allowed
to grow.

'I stopped playing for about six months because my first guitar
was an acoustic, an old Gibson with a very high action and thick
strings. I was skinny, so it was really painful to hold down the
strings. At the end of six months, I said to myself that I'm really
going to hang with this and not let it defeat me. I remember
having that feeling.

'There have been moments when I felt I really latched on to something. I've had those feelings when I've been improvising or playing and I feel like the music is playing me, rather than I'm playing the music. You're in the flow of something and you're not conscious, but you're aware. You're not making decisions on a conscious level; you're guiding it, but it's guiding you at the same time.

'Creativity on demand – I don't know if that's creativity or if that's craftsmanship. To make something happen that's creative, there's a level of craft where you can do that, but that's not really inspired creativity. That's sort of craftsman's creativity.

'There are different levels and types of creativity. Everybody has the potential to be creative, but not everyone puts the time in, and so will be unable to fulfil that potential. That's the unfortunate thing. Some people don't allow themselves to dream beyond just the mundane, even some people who are artists don't allow themselves to dream and just do things. They are afraid of the avant-garde, doing something that will cost them their gig, cost them a regular pay cheque, or make their record fall off the chart. Creativity is not concerned with any of that, it really isn't.

'I can put myself into a state where I can relax, and maybe I'll just wait. That's the thing about creativity; part of it is the waiting. You can exercise creativity, because it is an ability – it's an ability that can be honed and coaxed into happening.'

In 2012, Vernon assembled a jazz-rock fusion supergroup called Spectrum Road. Living Colour broke up in 1995 but reformed in 2000. Since then, they have released three more albums.

BILLY BURNETTE

Singer, songwriter and guitarist.

I MET BILLY THE SAME DAY AS I MET RICK VITO IN 1987.
They were both rehearsing for the Fleetwood Mac upcoming tour after Lindsey Buckingham had left the band. Mick
introduced me to them both, Billy having been a long-time
friend of his.

'My dad, Dorsey, and my Uncle Johnny had a group called
Johnny Burnette and the Rock 'n' Roll Trio. They started off
by writing a lot of the really big Rick Nelson hits. They also had
some success on their own; my dad had a couple of big hits, and
my uncle had five or six in the early sixties.

'I was real young when I started getting into it and singing
professionally. I did my first record, a Christmas song, in 1960,
when I was about seven. I would sing, because I didn't start
playing guitar until I was in my teens. When I was eight years
old, I did a lot of stuff like Dr Seuss records; Herb Alpert used to
produce some of them, so it was fun. I also did some children's
shows. I was about eleven or twelve when I sang with Brenda
Lee, and we toured the world. I loved it. I had it in my mind a

long time before I actually learned to play guitar, that that was what I wanted to do because of the excitement of touring. I can remember being on the road with Brenda and wanting to go out after the gig, but I was too young, so they locked me in my room. At that age I made my mind up that this was what I wanted to do forever.

'My dad was always pushing me. When I wasn't in studying my songs and was out playing baseball, he would tell me to make up my mind which one I wanted to do. I was really young and I wanted to do it, but he gave me that extra little push that I needed at the time.

'I started playing guitar a couple of years after I got back from touring. Guitars were always around the house. It was the next thing for me to do – to pick up a guitar and say, "Dad, show me a few chords." I learned a few, and there were always people coming by and teaching me stuff. I was one of those kids that bugged everybody and asked a lot of questions. Later on, when I was in my twenties, I got to play in my father's band. It was great; he was my best friend.

'With those special songs, you don't even know where they come from. I wrote one that we probably have twenty covers of by now – Ray Charles has done it – called "Do I Ever Cross Your Mind?" It's a song that's special to me, but I feel it was just handed to us one day. I feel like those are gifts. I know from my dad's experience when we were kids, he got out of his sleep and wrote some of his really big hits, like "It's Late". He always told me that the best ones come really quick.

'Once I get that little musical thing in my head, I've got to just give up what I'm doing to rush to a piano or a guitar and see if it's an idea. A phrase or a movie may put me into some feeling I want to write about. Or something somebody says could kick off that thing, which kicks off that other thing that gives the peak altogether.

'The Peak Experience is probably one of the most euphoric feelings I know. It's like a wave that runs through you. When it happens, I've said to myself, "This is incredible. Why can't this last forever and be like this every night?" It doesn't happen every night; it comes around once in a while. I think it's the band and the audience that make that thing happen. When it all gets matched up right, you all lift off. Fleetwood Mac [with whom Billy was then playing] is at the top of the list for getting that stuff happening. I suppose it's the magic they generate themselves.

'Sometimes the songs don't come and you're so desperate and you're trying so hard, and you can't find that "thing" again. So, you go to drugs or booze, try to find it there; then you end up really nuts.

'My dad, Dorsey Burnette, and just about everyone he ran around with would take pills – diet pills, speed, whatever. It does open up that thing where you can go all night creating and writing. I know he wrote a lot of good songs on it, and a lot of people who I know have too, and also without it, so I don't think it really matters. It's just something you get a dependency on where some entertainers feel that they've got to have it, whatever it is – drink, pills, toot – before they go on. It's all in their minds. In my dad's day, they would be on the road and not have any nights off, so that's where a lot of them got started, [being] on the road and you're feeling bad. They used every excuse in the world.

'Before I go on, I like to have a little shot of brandy to loosen me up. I don't like to get out there before I go on, but a little drink is nice to calm me down, because it is a kind of an atmosphere when you play for people. We've seen the abuse and what that's done to you. I think it was a big part of why I lost my dad in 1978. He was forty-six and he had rocked pretty hard in this business, on top of the roller-coaster ride. I think [musicians] need that escape more than people in other professions. You're not really ever secure; when you've hit the big time, you want to keep that going. That roller-coaster effect is what drives people nuts. I started thinking I was doing damage to my body when I was in my early to mid-twenties. I always used to like to take a pill before I went on, because I felt I needed an upper. I knew it was wrong, but it made me feel good. But I finally got over that. And then when my dad died, I felt like, I want to be around a lot longer than my dad.

Billy has written a book filled with his personal memories of those times, and has released a full-length CD to complement the book, titled Crazy Like Me: From Memphis and the Rock 'n' Roll Trio to Fleetwood Mac. *He is about to put out a record that Mick Fleetwood played on, called 'When the Wind Comes Back Around'. His son Beau is doing the video.*

ICE-T

Ice-T is a hip-hop artist and actor.

'**M**Y DRIVE TO CREATE IS REALLY TO HELP MY FRIENDS. I'm not driven like some artists who say they have to make this stuff; I'm really driven by the results. Creating music, or what I do, to me, is not very hard. Rap is nothing hard for me to do because it's my life – it's easy. I didn't realise this is what people wanted to hear until one of my friends told me. I used to try to make stuff that I thought people would want to hear, and they'd say, "No, man, tell them that shit about the neighbourhood." I would think, nobody would want to hear that, that's depressing. And they would say, "People want to hear that; everybody don't live like you, they don't see what you see, you've got to wake people up," and I said, "Cool." So, I did a record called "6 in the Mornin'" and everybody freaked. What I do is very easy for me to do, because all I do is absorb shit during the year and I just speak on it.

'I was always the kind of person who could make it fit, who had ingenuity. Just because somebody told me something couldn't be done, I never accepted it. I had that kind of a creative ability. Not musically creative; that never crossed my mind, because I don't know how to play any instrument, so how was I going to be a musician? I couldn't sing. But poetry was something I had fun with, and I started out making rhymes. Being on the streets, I learned how to rap but not to play music; it was like street slang, and I could fascinate people. The more I fascinated people, the more I could keep people off me. I was in the army when "Rapper's Delight" [one of the first hip-hop singles, by the Sugarhill Gang] came out, and I thought, wow, that's kind of like what I'm doing. I've just got to learn how to do it to music. So, I turned the record over and I started saying my rhymes.

After many acting roles throughout the 1990s and a reality show featuring the home life of Ice and his wife, Coco, Ice began hosting a true-crime documentary, In Ice Cold Blood, *in 2018. He's now famous for his podcasts as well, known as* Ice-T's Daily Game, *which are bite-sized motivational quotes in daily episodes.*

B.B. KING

Blues guitarist, singer and songwriter.

I CAN'T REMEMBER WHO INTRODUCED ME TO B.B. KING. All I can remember was speaking to him on the phone with my trusty cassette player by my side, not wanting to miss a word, and how privileged I felt.

'For some reason I was always crazy about the guitar, and most families in the area had some type of old guitar – that's the one thing families in the area I grew up in could afford. When we went to church, the preacher, who was my uncle's brother-in-law, played the guitar.

'After church the preacher would come to our house, and all the adults would have dinner, and the kids would have to wait until the adults had finished before we could eat. Usually when the preacher would visit, he would lay his guitar on the bed. He always had a nice guitar; the electric guitar was coming in then, and he had a guitar that was amplified with pickups. So when he laid his guitar on the bed and then went in for dinner, I would crawl up on the bed and start playing with that guitar. One time they caught me, and I thought I'd surely get it. But the preacher didn't scold me; he showed me three chords, which I still use today.

'That was my first experience, but I had an aunt who collected records all the time. Some of the artists on the records she had were Blind Lemon Jefferson, one of my favourites, and Lonnie Johnson, another of my favourites. She had many others that included Robert Johnson, but Robert Johnson never did get to me like Lonnie Johnson did. Plus, I had a cousin I was crazy about named Bukka White [a seminal blues player and songwriter]. I was crazy about Bukka, his personality . . . I liked his playing but his personality was beautiful. Then as a teenager I sang gospel and played guitar with several quartets.

'When I sing blues today, I still get some of the spiritual feeling; it's a thin line between blues and gospel, in my opinion, and the roots of all music that I hear, especially in the Western world, seem to fit into the music that I play. So if I border the line of rock, or soul, country, or any other kind of music, I can incorporate it into the blues because there's a place there. [When I play] I seem to get the feeling of being in the village or the area where the character lives that I'm singing about. Sometimes I become intertwined with that person, so I'm really living what's going on. I think that's the best part of being an entertainer, when that happens. Then you don't care what you look like, you don't care what people say about you, they can do all kinds of things to you at that time and you hardly notice because you're so into what you're doing. That is the beautiful, beautiful, part of it and has everything to do with attitude. It's letting yourself be who you are through your playing.

B.B. King died in Las Vegas at the fine old age of eighty-nine on 14 May 2015.

KIRSTY MacCOLL

Singer and songwriter, daughter of folk singer Ewan MacColl. Kirsty recorded several hits in the 1980s and 1990s, including 'There's a Guy Works Down the Chip Shop Swears He's Elvis.'

'AFTER MY PARENTS' DIVORCE, I USED TO SEE MY father on Sundays and visits, and he was fairly encouraging because he was a songwriter and a playwright before that. It wasn't like I was the only one in the family who was creative. It was the norm; everyone in the family was expected to be creative.

'I've written a whole song off the top of my head, which took two hours from start to finish. There was a lot of stuff that had been crammed in there that I hadn't been able to put down for three years [while having children]. After the first song, they seemed to come faster and faster. Sometimes I've written a song, and I've thought that's a bit silly or not really true to life, and then a week later something will happen and it's exactly like I said in the song – that's weird. Often, I've done lyrics and I haven't realised the full meaning of what I've written till a year later.

'I've had dreams where I've written a really good line, and I have to quickly write it down in case I forget it.

'Some people say art and politics shouldn't mix. But politics is everything. It's part of life. The only way you can change things is by changing governments or whatever. I think it's up to people who are creative to make a stand about those things they believe strongly in. But it's very boring if you hit people over the head with a message all the time. You can be subtle about it so people think they thought of it in the first place.

'A lot of creative people have written great things when they've been out of it. I don't think they got more creative because they were taking drugs. They are creative people in the first place, and how they choose to go about it is up to them. There are a lot of people who wouldn't touch drugs with a barge pole but who are still very great artists. If you get to a point where you can't do your work because you're too far gone, it takes eight times longer [to create] than it would when you're straight. People who are really creative are going to be creative up to the point where they black out!

'If I'm incredibly depressed, I can't write at all, and if I'm really happy, I wouldn't bother to write. I'd go out and do the gardening, so there has to be a kind of middle ground.'

Kirsty sadly passed away on 18 December 2000 at the age of forty-one.

ACKNOWLEDGEMENTS

THERE ARE SO MANY PEOPLE I WISH TO THANK FOR their help, support and encouragement. First and foremost, I give my heartfelt thanks and appreciation to all the musicians who graciously agreed to be interviewed for this book. Every interview was unique and I felt honoured to have been invited into their world of creativity, where they shared their thoughts, memories, and their sense of humility towards the creative process. I wish to give a fond farewell to those musicians I interviewed for the book who are no longer with us.

I give warmest thanks to my agent, Matthew Smith, and to my editors Ciara Lloyd and James Hodgkinson, from Bonnier Books, for recognising the importance of the timeless message contained in this book. Thanks go also to audio editor, Charlotte Brown. Their support and enthusiasm for this revised edition has been without equal.

I would like to thank all the photographers who have so generously given photographs to be included in this book, and I'd

ACKNOWLEDGEMENTS

like to acknowledge Holly George Warren who worked with me on our original book, *Musicians in Tune*, released in 1992.

Special thanks to Liz Kalinowska, Sandra Vigon, Aymie Martin, Sally Bradforth for their help and contribution. Last but not least, I give thanks to my husband, David Levitt, who put up with me working all hours!